BMW Files

Selected Road Tests

From the editors of *Motorcyclist*® Magazine

MOTORBOOKS
INTERNATIONAL

This edition first published in 2003 by Motorbooks International, an imprint of MBI Publishing Company, Galtier Plaza, Suite 200, 380 Jackson Street, St. Paul, MN 55101-3885 USA

The information in this book is true and complete to the best of our knowledge. All recommendations are made without any guarantee on the part of the author or Publisher, who also disclaim any liability incurred in connection with the use of this data or specific details.

We recognize that some words, model names and designations, for example, mentioned herein are the property of the trademark holder. We use them for identification purposes only. This is not an official publication.

Motorbooks International titles are also available at discounts in bulk quantity for industrial or sales-promotional use. For details write to Special Sales Manager at Motorbooks International Wholesalers & Distributors, Galtier Plaza, Suite 200, 380 Jackson Street, St. Paul, MN 55101-3885 USA.

ISBN 0-7603-1695-3

On the front cover: The 1995 BMW R1100GS was part of the line of GS bikes favored by world travelers (and wanna-bes) around the globe. *Kevin Wing/Primedia*

On the frontispiece: The R90S, one of the quintessential BMW models. *Larry Griffin/Primedia*

On the title page: The R80RT. *Rich Cox/Primedia*

On the back cover: BMW R100/S. *Bob Osborne/Primedia*

Edited by Greg Field
Designed by Kou Lor

Printed in the United States of America

CONTENTS

INTRODUCTION

Tools of Adventure

Most motorcyclists tend to regard BMW riders as a breed apart. Although riders of other brands tend to believe that they are "rugged individualists," BMW riders most often live the part. They dress differently. They rarely ride in flocks. And they use their distinctive motorcycles as tools of adventure, routinely traveling long distances and finding the roads less traveled.

When *Motorcyclist* Magazine began its relationship with the German machines roughly a half-century ago, they were regarded as the epitome of reliability, comfort, and understatement. The 500 and 600cc twins' low-vibration, stoutly build, and under-stressed engine design—coupled with shaft final drive, then a rarity—made them prized traveling machines. They didn't look, sound, or work like the American or British bikes that dominated American roads in the 1950s and early 1960s, and their reputation as "the quiet motorcycle" further separated them from the raucous majority.

To many motorcyclists, though, BMWs were a bit dowdy—functional rather than fun. The emphasis on solid utilitarianism kept them that way until the 1970s, when the "slash five" series and especially the later R90/S began to rearrange the motorcycling community's image of the marque, both with a change of style and an interest in performance. Next thing we knew, BMW twins were racing—and actually winning—in the Daytona Superbike race, no less.

BMW continued to raise eyebrows and rearrange its motorcycles' image in the early 1980s, when it introduced its own multi-cylinder engines and announced it was going to abandon the opposed twin. Fortunately, the BMW faithful persuaded product planners that the opposed twins were the soul of the BMW line, although this came after BMW rolled out "last edition" twins, which became a sort of camp collectible, like New Coke.

The company kept tweaking our perceptions of what a BMW could be. The GS series and the multi-mode off-roadable twins that brought the company's Paris-to-Dakar winners to the streets had motorcyclists of all persuasions talking and scratching their heads as we arrived in the 1980s. By the end of the decade, the K1, a radically styled sportbike by anyone's standards, broke down any barriers that we might have thought were constraining the company in another direction.

In 1993, BMW revealed its rededication to the opposed twin with the "oilhead" series. The series carried BMW into the third millennium and further expanded the envelope for BMW motorcycles, with bikes like the R1200C Cruiser, another unexpected direction for the motorcycle maker once regarded as the most staid in the world. BMW also put itself at the cutting edge of corporate motorcycle responsibility, with commitments to features like anti-lock braking and reduced emissions.

The editors of *Motorcyclist* magazine have been fortunate to be onhand for BMW's ride from dowdy to debonair and to watch as its motorcycles both transformed to meet changing buyer expectations and changed those expectations themselves. This book assembles many of the road tests we have in our archives, and we hope you have as much fun reading it as we did revisiting our history with BMW.

—The editors of *Motorcyclist*

1

BMW R75/5

Motorcyclist, March 1971

BMW's Biggest Is Considered by Many to be Their Best. We Have to Agree!

As far as we're concerned, we've always felt that BMW motorcycles were just about the ultimate in two-wheel prestige. Members of our staff have ridden them down to the tip of South America, up to Alaska, across Europe, and across the United States in the middle of winter, where temperatures reached way below freezing. In all cases, no matter which model we had, our machines performed faultlessly. Liking the BMW marque as much as we do, it pleased us even more to be able to get our hands on the vastly improved R75/5, for test purposes.

If you know what one of the old BMWs looked like, you'll realize the many changes that have been incorporated in the latest models. This new sporty look seems to catch your eye immediately. The well-formed and much longer gas tank, the narrower fenders, the telescopic forks, and the shorter wheelbase give the new models much more compact and powerful appearance, although there is a substantial savings in weight, rigidity, and stability, as they actually improved. Sidecar mounting lugs have been left off the frame, as sidecars are not really that popular here in the United States. Our test model was beautifully finished in a deep, metallic silver, basic black, polished alloy, and just a tasteful touch of chromium plating.

Outwardly, the engine looks the same as in the earlier models, but many changes were made to the exterior part of the car. The crankshafts are the same in all three models, as is the stroke. The displacement differs only from changes in the diameter of the cylinders. The one-piece crankshaft, with its two counterweights, runs on plain bearings in the aluminum alloy engine housing. In turn, cast-iron sleeves are bonded to the aluminum alloy cylinders and single bolts hold the cylinders and heads to the crankcase. Crankcase ventilation is from a diaphragm valve, and from that point, is piped into the air-filter case, which should make the antismog people very happy.

In the early model, the camshaft was located above the crank, but BMW found that in order to get better lubrication of the cam, they had to move it below the crankshaft.

Camshaft operation is by a spring-tensioned chain. To give you just some sort of an idea of how much thought goes into a BMW, the valves are operated by pushrods made of special steel having the same expansion co-efficient as the cylinders. This means that no matter how cold or how hot your engine, valve clearances always remain constant.

Starting is by the kick method or by the push-button method, whatever turns you on at the time. It is interesting to note that the starter engages with the automotive-type gear by way of an electric magnetic clutch. The starter area of the engine housing also serves as an air chamber to reduce intake noise.

Rated horsepower is a full 57 ponies at 6,400 rpm and maximum torque of 43.3 ft-lb comes in at 5,000 rpm. Compression ratio is 9:1.

If you know anything about a BMW, you'll realize that other than having two wheels, it's almost more an automobile than it is a motorcycle. The clutch and in-line gearbox are a perfect example. The clutch is a single-plate unit operated by a diaphragm spring similar to that found in many sports cars. Gear ratios of the 4-speed box are, 1st: 3.896; 2nd : 2.578; 3rd: 1.875; and 4th: 1.50. In high gear, our test model would roll along at an easy 106 miles an hour, which isn't bad.

Something else interesting is that the driveshaft is completely enclosed within the right swinging arm and sloshes around in an oil bath. With proper maintenance, and no abuse, it should last forever.

BMW, way back in the early 1920's was the first to come up with an acceptable telescopic front fork. For some reason, though, they've stuck with the somewhat heavy and somewhat slow-steering Earles-type front fork for many years, which was introduced in 1956. Now, it seems that the only way you can get the Earles front fork is on special order.

Travel of the front fork is a full 8 inches, and if you don't think that's a lot, compare it to the fork travel on *your* motorcycle. One of the members of the staff, Jim Davis, had the exciting experience of hitting a wet mattress lying in the road, at 60 miles per hour, in driving rain, and as far as he's concerned, there are no better forks. You might or might not agree, but seeing that our staff member is still with us today, he might have a good point.

As we mentioned earlier, rear suspension is by swingarm and looks very much like the swingarm setup found on many other motorcycles. What we liked about the rear suspension on the BMW is that you don't need any tools to adjust the tension of the springs. At the base of each shock absorber, is a lever, hefty enough to get a good grip on. All you have to do is turn it to the position you desire.

Brakes, we all agreed, were excellent. Both units are single leading shoe, internal expanding, and have a diameter of 7.8 inches and a width of 1.2 inches. With large heavy bikes, we've grown to expect dual leading shoes on the front, but for some reason, BMW just doesn't need this. We found that unless we mistreated the brakes badly, we couldn't get them to fade hardly at all. Stopping is sure, straight, and very rarely could we even get the rear wheel to break loose. Both wheels are made of aluminum alloy, and the tire sizes are: front 3.25x19; and rear 4.00x18.

After all our test people had turned in their reports, we found that there were only two gripes that we could come up with, and neither one of these were anything terribly important. The first one involved your left leg, right near the ankle, rubbing against the carburetor intake. It seems that when you're seated in a normal position your ankle should be where the intake is, and the intake should be where your ankle is. As we remember some of the earlier BMWs having this same problem, we guess BMW probably tried to cure this, but seeing it involves moving major components, they probably just forgot about it. Our second gripe was that we felt that the centerstand just didn't do the job. Chances are that even King Kong would have trouble lifting the bike on the stand but this wasn't all. The stand has pads on it that are definitely too small. For use in the dirt, or on a day when the asphalt is soft and gooey, we would prefer the sidestand with its big, large pad.

If you're wondering about those groovy-looking saddlebags, they're made by the Flanders Co., and they're some of the best saddlebags we have ever had the pleasure of using. There was one small problem with them, but we almost hesitate to mention it, as it just wasn't that important. It seems that the saddlebag covers won't open up all the way, because of the seat, and it also seems that the seat won't open up all the way, because of the saddlebags. If you dig the saddlebags as much as we did, you're just going to have to suffer along with this problem.

Following standard automotive practice, the electrical system on the new BMW is exactly the same as on the family car. A 12-volt, three-phase alternator delivers, even at engine idle, enough current to feed the entire electrical system, and keep the battery fully charged. Because BMWs now have electric starters, they are equipped with battery ignition. The breaker cam and automatic spark advance are mounted on the camshaft, and the silicon diode rectifiers will be found in the engine housing. The voltage regulator, starter relay, and ignition coils (one for each cylinder) will be found underneath the gas tank. What's interesting to note, is that the electric starter is fitted with an interlock, which keeps you from accidentally engaging the starter while the engine is running.

BMW R75/5

Engine type:	Two-cylinder, horizontally opposed, overhead valve
Bore x stroke:	82x70.6 mm (3.23x2.78in.)
Displacement:	745 cc
Horsepower @ rpm:	57 @ 6,400 rpm
Compression ratio:	9:1
Carburetion:	Two, Bing 32-mm, vacuum-operated
Maximum torque:	43.3 @ 5,000 rpm
Clutch type:	Dry, single-plate, automotive-type with diaphragm spring

Gear ratios:	
First	3.896
Second	2.578
Third	1.875
Fourth	1.521
Frame:	Double downtube, cradle-type

Suspension:	
Front	Tubular telescopic
Rear	Swinging arm

Tire size:	
Front	3.25x19
Rear	4.00x18

Brake diameter:	
Front	7.8 in. (Double leading shoe)
Rear	7.8 in. (Single leading shoe)
Generator:	Three-phase alternator, with regulator, 12-volt
Ignition:	Battery, centrifugal advance
Weight:	420 lbs.
Wheelbase:	54.6 in.
Length:	82.7 in.
Top Speed:	106 mph
Price:	$1,848. f.o.b. N.Y. & L.A.

ENGINE

Starting	Excellent
Throttle response	Excellent
Vibration	Good
Noise	Excellent

TRANSMISSION

Gear spacing	Excellent
Clutch smoothness	Excellent
Shifting speed	Good

CONTROLS

Handlebar position	Excellent
Ease of operation	Excellent
Location	Excellent

BRAKES

Lever pressure	Excellent
Pedal pressure	Excellent
Fade resistance	Excellent
Directional stability	Excellent
Stopping distance	Excellent

SUSPENSION

Front	Excellent
Rear	Excellent
Ride control	Excellent
Dampening	Excellent

APPEARANCE

Paint	Excellent
Construction and welds	Excellent
Chrome and trim	Excellent

ELECTRICAL

Wiring	Excellent
Headlight	Excellent
Taillight	Excellent
Horn	Excellent

GENERAL

Spark plug accessibility	Excellent
Instrumentation	Excellent
Sidestand	Excellent
Centerstand	Fair
Seat comfort	Excellent
Muffling	Excellent
Tool storage space	Excellent

COMMENTS: Even more quality than before. A quicker engine, the same good brakes, and an all-new look. Top speed of over 105 miles per hour—with reliability! Larger gas tank and no more rusted-out mufflers, thanks to new angle.

The lighting system conforms to all the latest standards and might possibly even be superior to what the standards require. The speedometer light is well lit at night, and even if you don't like the looks of those big turn signal lights, they still at least give you a sporting chance out in traffic. They work, work well, and we'd like to see more motorcycles equipped with them. As for the electric starter, we can say nothing more than it works perfectly and sure life easy during cold weather. The same staff member that zapped the mattress also remembers trying to start a BMW in below freezing temperatures, and chances are he'd still be there if a friendly truck driver hadn't come along with a can of aerosol ether. Oh, if he had only had the electric starter then!

While testing the bike, we talked to quite a few BMW purists who pulled us over to the side of the road and took a look at our test machine. As far as we could tell, they felt the BMW had done them dirty in three major areas, but darned if we could even slightly agree with them. They didn't like the change from Earles forks, they didn't like the larger and differently shaped gas tank, and they didn't like the upswept mufflers. We totally and wholeheartedly have to disagree with them. First the forks: Once you were rolling, and over 30 miles an hour, the Earles front forks were fine. But at slow speeds, most such-equipped BMWs handled like tractors. On top of this, a good bump or hole in the road would shake the complete intestinal tract right out of your wristwatch. The telescopic forks are a welcome change. The bigger gas tank is something else: the tank on our test bike had a 6-gallon capacity. This means that if you're really hooking it on, you can still go more than 250 miles between gas stations. Anyone who snivels about this must not be a true touring rider. Last, but not least, the upswept mufflers,—one of the BMW rider's greatest gripes, has been rusting out in too short of a time. As in the case of an automobile, condensation appears to be the culprit. BMW has seen fit to tip the mufflers where any condensation that builds up between stops, runs out of the muffler and down into the area where the exhaust pipes are at their hottest. What this means to you is that when you crank your engine up in the morning, in just a few moments, any moisture that has collected, will have turned into steam and will have been blown out the exhaust. Even if the exhaust pipes do rust out, which would you rather pay for, an exhaust pipe or a very expensive muffler? Another reason for the upswept muffler is that when you corner hard and fast, nothing drags on the ground. Anyone want to gripe about this?

Motorcycles will come, and motorcycles will go, but chances are, the BMW marque will be with us for many, many more years. When you build a better mousetrap, the world will beat a path to your door, and as far as we're concerned, BMW has built that better mousetrap.

Yes, some changes have been made on the newer models, but as far as we're concerned, every one of them is for the better. The bikes are lighter, go faster, and also look better. Anytime you can improve on something that's already good, you've got a real winner.

2

BMW R90S

BOB GREENE
Photography by Larry Griffin
Motorcyclist, February 1976

Dogmatic Teutonic Quest for Perfection Never Ends, Never More Obvious than in This Supermotorrad from West Germany's Bayerische Motoren Werk

How? How can a 50-year-old engine concept endure—thrive!—in an era of exotica? How can a twin go head-to-head with multis having a *suggested* retail price of 25 percent less? How can one motorcycle corner the creature comfort market? We were about to find out. Taking early command of a 1976 BMW R90/S 900-cc Sport at the first of the week, we would roll 1,100 miles by the ensuing Monday. About 720 of these miles were traveled two-up from Los Angeles north through the historic gold mine country of Tonopah, Nevada and back down through Goldfield and Beatty across Death Valley, with daughter Gayle perched atop a pair of jumbo Krauser saddlebags.

Cool autumn weather suggested heavy riding gear: long johns, Suzuki insulated snowmobile suit and nylon Belstaff outfit, padded Full-Bore boots and foam liners, Harley gloves, Vetter Hippo Mitts, and Bell helmets with face shields to withstand two full days in 35–40-degree weather. But no complaints, the sun was smiling.

Fresh out of the crate, the BMW showed 0 miles at the start of the test, and after a brief 250 miles of citified bedding down, luxuriated in an early second service—timing, valves, and oil change—immediately prior to the northward trek. Everything was spot-on.

Having benefited from a previous acquaintance with a 1974 peasant model 900 Bee Emm, the more spirited Sport at least hadn't fallen into the hands of a freshman. And I was eager to get into the differences between the two, having heard both ways, that the Sport was both superior and inferior to the standard R90/6. Our multishaded gold Sport with red pinstriping was a custom job; no two Sports are alike since each two-tone paint scheme is individually applied and the striping is brushed on rather than taped on. The finish was flawless and drew admiring glances wherever we went, from young and old alike, usually accompanied by a compliment, whistle, or right-on hand signal. Further complementing appearance and utility as a touring mount were optional Krauser bags made exclusively for the Bavarian beauty by one of Germany's largest BMW dealers and accessory manufacturers.

We'd keep an eye peeled for several modifications included in the new Seventy-Sixes. The oil pan, now .4-inch deeper, has the same 2-quart capacity as before but the proportionately lower oil surface stops windage and frothing formerly incurred by the crank and cam cutting through the oil. Superior lubrication and lower engine temperature result. And the pushrods, once steel, are now tubular aluminum for a growth rate more compatible with cylinder expansion, with more constant relationship and quieter running from cold to full operating temperature. Still another change in the attic are self-aligning needle bearing rocker arms which no longer require the previously characteristic BMW readjustment upon each occasion of torquing the head bolts, permitted by positioning the valves at a slightly different angle. At the base of each cylinder, O-rings replace the old aluminum gaskets to eliminate oil weep previously experienced, however slight. Also a part of the revised gasket package is a larger seal behind the timing advance mechanism, along with a cast-iron front cam bearing in place of the earlier aluminum bearing for closer tolerance and cam rotation accuracy. Happily, a reduction in clutch spring pressure, accompanied by a change in handlebar lever pilot point, makes for lighter lever pull and smoother, now completely controllable, engagement, a point of criticism on pre-1976 models. And a simple but clever redesign of the spring-loaded neutral switch detent plunger in the gearbox now actually encourages neutral engagement rather than resisting it. Again, for easier control and greater application of power, the size of the front brake master cylinder, piston, and calipers has been increased. One area in which the front office was obviously quite pleased, however, and felt no change was in order,

Pushrod twin concept is regaining ground by virtues of performance, lightness, and simplicity. Far and away the lightest electric supermotor, the Sport is not to be messed with on the highway.

In the jaws of Death Valley's Wildrose Canyon, passenger Gayle Greene welcomes the chance to bask in the sun.

Death Valley's a fabulous trip in autumn; we hit it in early November, temperature in the low 40s, pausing at Corkscrew Peak, above, to limber up our fine little 35-mm Olympus pocket camera, perfect for bikers.

was the suggested retail price of $3,965 (add $35 for the West Coast), already the most perfected, with the exception of Harley-Davidson, Laverda, and Benelli. To make it more palatable, the warranty has been extended to 6,000 miles or 12 months.

Is it worth it? Gayle and I clicked the Sport into low and headed toward Highway 395 and Bishop, California, to find out. Waddling off the mark, the 180-degree-opposed shuttle motor quickly smoothens as the tach needle approaches four grand and the mirror image crispens. Starting at the base of a 5,000-foot mountain, we were soon to become aware of the high 3.0:1 final drive ratio, as opposed to the standard R90's 3.2 cog, demanding frequent fourth gear and sometimes third to keep the engine on the boil in the hills, between 3,500-4,000 rpm. Executed with skill achieved during previous BMW ownership, gear changes were mostly soft and quiet, often undetectable by the passenger. Out of respect for the engine's low mileage, revs were held to 4,000 for the entire trip, equivalent of an indicated 70 miles per hour, which is felt to be about 5 miles on the happy side. The tripmeter, however, like only the Triumph Trident and Norton twin before it, was right on, simplifying fuel mileage calculations which ranged from an initial 38.6—tight engine, steep mountain—to a later best of 46.58 miles per gallon, and an overall average for the 720-mile weekend round trip of 43.8. Discounting the early mountain leg on the issue of piston tightness—several higher mountain passes ensued—average mileage figured out to be 44.8 miles per gallon, which I feel is more realistic and exceptional for a fresh engine toting a passenger-baggage weight approaching 400 pounds. My previous bourgeois model 900 Bee Emm seldom exceeded that economy in 5,000 miles, riding solo. End of a myth: The Sport, though quicker and more lively than the R90/6, is equally stingy with your Chevron credit card. And the dual slide-type 38-mm Dell'Orto pumper carbs, opposed to the 32-mm Bing vacuum pots on the standard 900, felt to be more out of the way than the Bings, less bulky or better tucked in for leg clearance. Never once did I bang a shin, even though riding double. The Dell'Ortos carburet crisply and unhesitatingly and, when leaning into a heavy load, pull strongly. Engine efficiency, teamed with the 6.3-gallon fuel tank and using an average 44 miles per gallon, gives a paper touring range of 277 miles, at least a reliable 250–to 260 miles, figuring a reluctant few last drops. Following the trip, commuting to work, half freeway and half surface streets, fuel mileage figured out 42.3 miles per gallon, going on Reserve at 235 miles. Topped off at 254.3 miles, the bike took 6 gallons even. Our longest run on the trip without refueling was 170 miles before stepping off for coffee and donuts, but it is reassuring to know that in the middle of the night when whistle-stop stations are dark, you're not going to be stranded or holed up for lack of high octane.

The first leg of our ride ended at Tonopah, Nevada, just after nightfall, in 40-degree temperature. It would be warmer in the morning when the sun

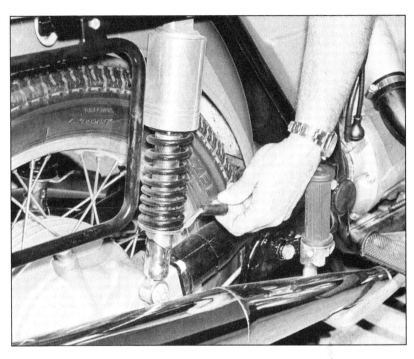

Column right, top to bottom: German-brand Boge shocks, specially valved to accommodate shaft drive tendency to cause chassis rise rather than squat during acceleration. Built-in adjuster encourages proper adjustment.

Only fresh tar from Wildrose spots Sport cases in this candid shot after a long tour—utterly immaculate!

Switches are proper and beautifully detailed.

came out. Oh yeah! There was the sun alright but the thermometer had scrooched down to 35, and I had visions of slow cranking since the Beemer stayed out in the raw weather all night. Surprise, surprise; she fired-off first turn, as though she'd spent the night up in our warm motel room! BMW went to a .6-horsepower starter motor in 1975, replacing the .5-horsepower unit of yore and eliminating all hesitancy. What a difference a 10th makes.

At the outset of the ride, I was curious as to whether the 30-inch-wide Krauser bags and a passenger would have a deteriorating effect on handling. Quite honestly, I forgot they were there, even during the Mojave welcoming ceremony—had to be 60-miles-per-hour-or-better crosswind—and later when negotiating Death Valley's Wildrose Canyon moment-of-truth switchbacks. The Sport held its head high during all of Mother Nature's judo chops. It's no Ducati or Triumph in the corners, but it's not far behind—one of the best. Similarly, the ride, though possibly a thin cut below a Guzzi, is an impressive blend of firm forgiveness, taut enough to be sporting, soft enough to qualify as a prime touring mount. The saddle, while more shallow and aesthetically more pleasing than the standard BMW sofa, is of ideal density and broad enough to provide full support; I prefer it to the stocker, feeling not a hint of soreness after the second day. The tires—Continental or Metzeler, we rode both—hang in there with light load or overload.

Somewhere in the middle of snaking, sandy-cornered, one-mistake-and-kiss-your-fanny-goodbye Wildrose Canyon, as breathtaking as it is, the answers to our opening paragraph resolved themselves. How? The big shafty pulls like a freight train caught in the railroad-classic

Tehachapi Mountain switchbacks, motors turbinelike across Death Valley's silicon skirts at a lazy 4,000 revs and 70 miles per hour, handles and rides majestically, and burbles so quietly at cruise that you can almost hear the electric clock's tick. Succinctly, the reason this half-century-old twin can still command top dollar—about $4,200 out the door—is that it does more things better.

Lightest of all muscle motors at 498 pounds fully gassed, its catlike leanness extracts maximum performance unencumbered by fatty poundage. But lightness is not cheap, qualifying much of the above price. Compared to the heaviest cruisers, the BMW runs riderless, so to speak, or with an equivalent reduction in weight. Or, put another way, the Bee Emm's competition is always riding double. With a top speed of over 120 miles per hour, the BMW, if not the fastest, has a searing top end. And with a breath-sucking box-stock quarter-mile capability of over 102 miles per hour and an e.t. of barely over 13 seconds, it is not an easy mark coming out of the hole. In fact, a production road race version of the BMW just established the new NHRA/AMDRA E/Modified National Record at 118 miles per hour and 11.6 seconds with journalist Cook Neilson up. Shockingly few bikes can best it in a high-gear roll-on; again, so many things so well.

And that crack about creature comforts? Where do we begin? Start with the balancing centerstand that obligingly and automatically lifts the front or rear fork high in the air upon removal of either aluminum safety rim wheel for tire repair; no need to block up the front of a BMW or even require assistance. And the front wheel slides right out forward, without removing fender or brake calipers since the latter are mounted low and behind the fork. The front brakes adjust with an

Brief 250-mile break-in preceded Tonopah run; subsequently *Motorcyclist* rolled a total of 1,500 big ones without slightest hitch. Shortening the throttle throw to 1/4-turn made for quicker throttle chop and synchronized shifts.

Sideload Krauser bags have rain-proof tongue and groove lid and 30-inch spread same as engine for threading traffic and helmet stowage. Excellent bags!

On a clear day you can see Stovepipe Wells.

Even with over half the bottom tread showing, the head has not begun to touch. Cornering clearance on tour is ample for anybody in his right mind.

eccentric, and both wheels utilize the stronger straight-pull spokes rather than the usual flexible bent-tip type. The machine goes up on the centerstand so easily that even the little woman can heist it. Then there's that big hole-burnin' quartz-halogen headlight that casts a shadow of your buddy's bike in his own light beam when the Sport's laser is flicked onto high from behind. A throttle brake is fitted, with a large knurled head that can be dialed on or off using only the thumb while riding, relieving hand muscles of the chore of holding the quarter-turn throttle on hour after hour. Eight inches of fork travel? Why, BMW had it long before the motocrossers. Similarly, rear spring preload is adjustable without tools since a convenient rubber-tipped handle is built right into each five-way shock—5-inch-travel shocks.

The smoothly finished, high-quality toolkit of 24 pieces rests in a lift-out fiberglass deep tray, near-hermetically sealed against dust and spacious enough to hold many spares beneath the locking saddle. An additional storage compartment is included under the glass-skirted tail, along with an air pump. But you won't find a rat's nest of wires there; they're protectively routed through the frame tubing forward to eliminate unsightliness and damage. Remove the rear wheel and notice how easy it is to pull the axle merely by revolving the axle-piercing drawbar over the cammed tip of the left swingarm, which is cleverly contoured to avert needless tugging and speed removal.

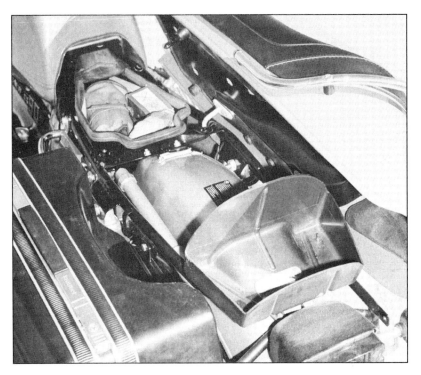

The Sport is super-functional and loaded with novel conveniences, such as the concealed master cylinder beneath the gas tank to eliminate handlebar clutter and the highly ventilated dual brake discs that are perforated to more quickly shed rainwater as well as assist cooling. They work with the greatest of ease and predictability. And I prefer the separate oil reservoirs for engine and gearbox, whereby ideal oil viscosity and compound can be used for each component's needs. Similarly, individual oil supplies are provided for the rear end, driveshaft, and U-joint. How sweet it is not to bother with an exposed rear chain? How many motorbikes do you know of that insist on expensive Timken tapered roller bearings in the swingarm instead of plain bushings? The Germans not only use them here but in the steering head and wheels as well.

Two things especially dazzled me; the habit-forming electric clock, complete with second hand, that makes one wonder why motorcycles were ever built without them, and the emergency-bright segment of the headlight dimmer switch. The switch has an extra detent at the bottom of its throw; bang it down from any

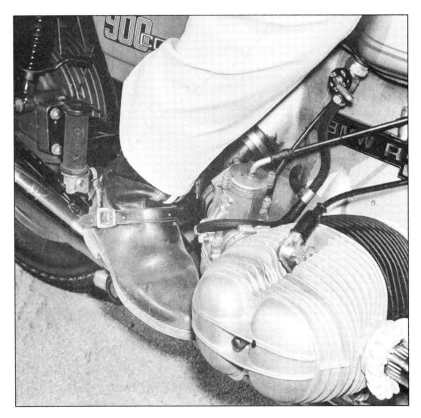

Check the extra storage space under saddle and shin clearance with latest induction angle.

Gayle got a little dramatic at sight of DV sign, recovered immediately at mention of burger and fries.

position, even with ignition and lights off, and you get high beam. Being spring-loaded, the emergency-bright detent automatically returns to low beam upon being released. At questionable intersections repeated intermittent pressure on the button causes a dancing high-low-high-low signal that, though silent, attracts instant attention—less offensive but just as effective as a horn. It can also be used to take a quick peek into an impending dark corner when oncoming cars prevent steady brights. The list is virtually endless—in-gear starter lockout, all four adjustable footpegs, three-way hydraulic steering damper, raked mufflers to clear high curbs, impeccable metal and glasswork, on and on. But our time has come to move on down into the engine room.

The included black-and-white photos show the motor untouched after over 1,100 miles, a tribute to the oil retention of the new seals for 1976. That's dry! Why an opposed twin? Great credibility stems from maximum cylinder head exposure to cooling airstream, and the design provides near-ultimate smoothness from a twin since the 180-degree crank allows perfect balance of reciprocating weight with both pistons simultaneously moving in and out but firing alternately. Steel cylinder liners are centrifugally bonded in hot state to aluminum cylinders by the sophisticated and proven Alfin process for unparalleled bond and heat transfer. The crankshaft, having the same shaft diameter as BMW's 3-liter car, is carried in tri-metal shell bearings, as are the rods, which are fitted with bronze bush small ends. The cam is hung beneath the crank, driven off its nose by an automotive-type, double-row toothed timing chain, beneath the crank to allow higher cylinder placement and better lubrication. Keeping everything slippery is an Eaton-type trochoid oil pump gushing 25 quarts a minute through a replaceable paper cartridge filter. Off the back of the crank is a single-plate dry clutch and 5-speed gearbox with separate case bolted flush to crankcase proper. The hump-backed casting atop the engine houses and hushes a paper air filter and a 240-watt alternator. Of the family of four—R60/6, R75/6, R90/6, and R90/Sport—only the Sport has supplemental breather holes at the back of the housing to assist induction at its anticipated higher rpm. Crankcase breather fumes are directed back through the right-side induction system.

Embarrassingly little constructive criticism can be leveled at the BMW Sport in 1976; they've been fine-combing every test report and have done their homework. Some

BMW R90S

Engine serial: 4990023
Base price: $3,965

ENGINE
Type: Four-stroke OHV opposed twin
Displacement: 898 cc (54.8 cu. in.)
Bore x stroke: 90x70.6 mm
(3.543x2.780 cu. in.)
Claimed horsepower @ rpm: 75 @ 7,200
Torque rating: 55 ft-lb @ 5,500
Compression ratio: 9.5:1
Lubrication type: Full-pressure trochoid pump
Carburetion: Dual Dell'Orto 38-mm slide-type with pump
Air filter: Single paper element
Ignition type: 12-volt Bosch alternator, points, auto advance 25-amp/h battery
Starting: Electric only, 0.6 horsepower

DRIVETRAIN
Primary ratio: Direct drive
Final ratio: Shaft, 3.0:1
Overall ratio: 4.5:1
Gear ratios:
First 4.40;
Second 2.86;
Third 2.07;
Fourth 1.67;
Fifth 1.50
Clutch: Dry single-plate

CHASSIS & SUSPENSION
Frame: Double-loop oval tube
Caster: 61 degrees
Trail: 3? inches
Suspension:
Front Telescopic, 8 inches
Rear Swingarm 5 inches
Brakes:
Front Dual hydraulic disc
10.2-inch diameter
Rear Mechanical drum,
7.9-inch diameter
Tires:
Front 3.25x19 Continental or Metzeler
Rear 4.00x18 Continental or Metzeler
Rim Locks: Front/Rear Safety Rim/Safety Rim

WEIGHTS & CAPACITIES
Weight, wet, unladen: 498 lbs.
Fuel Tank: 6.3 gal.
Oil Capacity: 4.7 pts. incl. filter

test reporters complain of precession and clunking shifts; both exist, but primarily to the non-BMW-oriented rider. Both become less noticeable by the day, as the rider familiarizes himself with the machine, until he has sorted both out. Precession is primarily only noticeable when the engine is accelerated out of gear and quiet shifts become routine when familiarity encourages synchronization of engine speed and shift point. Although the latter may elude some, I find it no problem of consequence. I would like to see a side-stand option or override of the spring-loaded stand that flips up when the bike is moved forward or bumped. And I would recontour the starter button by grinding off the bottom lip to avoid accidental engagement when fingering the turn signal, even though an electric lockout does prevent actuation of the starter when in gear. And a more positive means of determining battery water level, similar to car batteries, would be appreciated; the present system is rather hit and miss. BMW might also look at Ford's double-edged ignition key that hastens insertion.

These piddlin' points aside, is the Sport really superior to the standard 900? And is it worth four Gees? Affirmative on both counts. I prefer the Sport's less plodding gait, more fleet acceleration, taller cruising gear, and lower seating position. And that café fairing does work, up to about titty high. The whole concept sexes me…and I don't think it's just because we're both in our 50s.

3

BMW R75/7

Motorcyclist, May 1977

In a World All Its Own

Think about it; the number of manufacturers producing two-cylinder machines of 650 cc and over—nine at last count—is almost double that of those making fours of any displacement. Think again; the reason isn't because twins are cheaper, not when six of those nine are among, if not the most costly motorcycles. No, the lure of the big four-stroke twin is, rather, its light weight and compactness that encourages superior handling, stronger midrange torque, record economy, and ease of maintenance resulting from fewer components. These are the endearing and enduring attributes of the big twin that have kept it alive and well through the years, against all challengers.

Of those nine marques, four are Italian and two are Japanese, while America, England, and Germany are responsible for one each. Now you can get your cylinders in a soldierly shoulder to shoulder, straight up or leaning rakishly into the wind; fore and aft in a casually wide or shallow V; or as with the lone German, sticking straight out each side like a couple of sore thumbs. Since BMW is the only twin so built, and since they alone have steadfastly held to this concept for over 50 years, it is obvious that the Engineering Department is the heavyweight at BMW. Form follows function, efficiency outranks cosmetics. With All engines being the compromise that they are, we'll get into those pros and cons of the "boxer" engine—so named because of its likeness to two fists going in and out—in our included sidebar treatise on the engine and drivetrain.

Perhaps even more unique than cylinder layout, with the latter-day encroachment of Moto Guzzi, Honda, and Yamaha on the shaft drive theme that BMW pioneered long before these folks got into the bike biz, is the German's featherweight. At 495 pounds gassed, the R75/7 BMW is approximately 35 pounds lighter than a 750 Kawasaki twin and 73 pounds lighter than a Yamaha 750 triple with 4 gallons of fuel. Of course, the BMW holds considerably more than its contemporaries, a whoppin' 6.3 gallons, so it wouldn't be fair to penalize it by comparing weights with the tanks topped off. But even should you do so, the BMW is still by far the lightest of all 750s any way you want to go.

Lightness is always expensive, thus qualifying a considerable measure of the BMW's lofty $3,295. And that's almost $300 less than their chug-a-luggin' 1,000-cc version. Conversely, their bargain basement 600-cc model, possessing all the goodies of its bigger brothers but packing a little less oomph, is a "piddling" $2,995. But Americans are power-hungry, and around 70 percent of BMW sales involve the 1,000-cc twin, 25 percent consuming the 750, and a mere 5 percent going to the 600. Our curiosity was piqued. Accepting the 600 as more of a solo mount for those of modest performance demands and limited budget, we wondered if the 750 was truly all that much less of an adrenaline pumper than the 1,000.

Since the Webco dyno isn't set up to handle a shaft drive machine, the open road would have to be our rolling dynamometer. Things got off to a snappy start when the Beemer cut a 60-mile-per-hour average over our big hill, including a couple of slowdowns for little signs along the road like "Workmen Ahead," "Prepare to Stop," and a few dislocated stones from the previous night's blow. On the far side, on an abandoned roadway, the speedo needle was coaxed to an encouraging 112 with a corresponding 6,700 tach reading—downhill, rider crouched. Redline is 7,400.

Gassing up at a remote desert pump, the urgency of our mountain fling showed up in a still very creditable 35.9 miles per gallon (corrected from a 99 percent accurate tripmeter). That kind of meter reading is rare in testing, being second only to the spot-on accuracy of the British Smiths instrument featured on Triumph and Norton. Up in these same hills we learned that the R75/7 pulls like a long-clawed tiger, causing only a rare dip into fourth gear

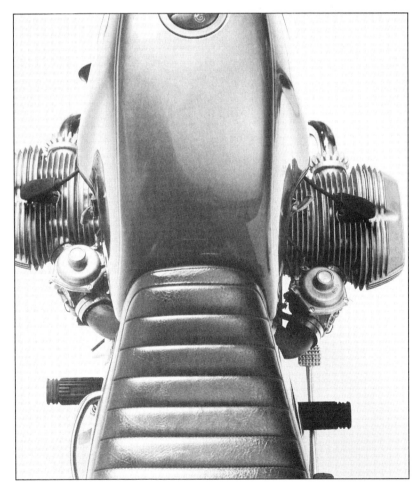

Sexy tank, offset barrels, levers have Teflon bushings; cables, sleeved.

Super-light, 495-pound BMW goes 300 in ISDT trim. Horn is a Fiamm.

to maintain maximum urge pulling the ever-twisting 5,000-foot pass. Since the gearboxes in all slash-seven BMWs are the same, only a slightly lower ring-and-pinion ratio in the rear end was giving the 750 an advantage over its bigger brother 1,000, 3.36:1 compared to the thousand's even 3.0:1. Such a stump-puller is the 750 that good torque is on hand virtually from an idle, being able to stomp along at 15 miles per hour in high fifth gear at 1,000 rpm and move right out without choking or misfiring. Torque is this baby's middle name, becoming impressive above three grand, stronger yet above four. Braking was progressive and sure, never wanting.

Little did we realize the shock we were in for on the ensuing 55-mile section of freeway heading home at a steady and uninterrupted 55 miles per hour (3,200 rpm). Topping off the tank back in Hollywood, the bronze Bavarian took an embarrassing .875 gallon of Premium, meaning that this luxury cruiser had just creamed the majority of smaller so-called economy bikes with a giant 62.36 miles per gallon! That's real, no factory dream-wheel romance, corrected and all. And what it means is that if it is possible to nurse all of that stock tank's 6.3 gallons of gas down the pipe, a solo BMW rider running legal speed could travel 392.868 miles on a single fill-up. By contrast, mixed freeway and city commuting netted 45 miles per gallon corrected. The twin had earned two merit badges; sledgehammer torque and skinflint economy. Did that mean it might be a slug in the get-up-and-go department? Let's roll over to Irwindale Raceway and take its e.t.

Chirping rubber and lofting the front wheel, the R75/7 romped off a best 1/4-mile performance of 13.763 and 94.93 miles per hour, not exactly picking daisies for a tractable, super-quiet tourer of 45 cubic inches. That's only .42-second slower than the R100/7 we tested at the first of the year, the biggest difference being the R100's 3.86-mile-per-hour bulge in terminal speed. Conceivably, a sharp operator on a 750 could get the best of a sleepy R100/7 chauffeur in a drag. Or maybe all the BMW rider has to know is that his 750 is one hell of a lot quicker and faster than the 14.06-second, 91.09-mile-per-hour Honda Gold Winger in the quarter.

Maneuverability and control at all speeds must be termed excellent, feeling secure and manageable, town or turnpike.

Tool set and monogrammed towel live in lift-out box. No wiring rat's nest.

Even rearmost cylinder has this shin clearance. Pedal is work of art.

Adjustable shocks incorporate handle. Pinion cog has straddle-mount.

Straight-pull spokes anchor in reinforced hub, single disc, offset axle.

Steering geometry is neutral in a bank, with no trace of the quiver that would occasionally (though admittedly rarely) descend upon former BMWs in a slow corner or downhill packing double under light throttle. Thicker-wall frame tubing, an extra horizontal crossbrace between the two front downtubes, and increased swingarm gusseting have chased the last of the gremlins from this still super-light frame. It's a commendable accomplishment considering that the bike has picked up only 13 pounds in the last five years and probably no more than half of that is a result of frame modification. Playing a major role in its sure-footedness were the Continental tires at each end, RB2 front and K112 rear. These Conti "SuperTwins" contribute second-stage handling to the BMW, assuring noticeable confidence from the first turn on. They're a turn-on all right. Tire balance and trueness are guaranteed by Conti's extraordinary and time-consuming practice of mounting and spinning the tires twice before they leave the factory. After mounting and being spun-checked for high-speed balance, they are dismounted and remounted on another fixture to determine run-out. Additionally, they stick wet or dry, and they endured over 2,000 miles of testing here with negligible wear. Tough skins. Carrying the "H" rating, Conti Twins are built for sustained speeds of 130 miles per hour, a little overkill on the 105–112 -mile-per-hour R75/7 that nevertheless makes a body feel better at full chat. And chassis hardware is high enough off the deck that only the bravest of the brave need be apprehensive about dragging a rocker cover.

With 7.9 inches of travel front and 4.9 inches rear, the BMW handles most irregularities with an ease best described as posh/firm. But as deep as it is, stepped impacts such as driveway entrances are terminated a bit more harshly than might be expected. The final inch or so of movement, especially at the front, goes home more abruptly than it might. A by-product of valving and spring rate, one gets the impression that although 95 percent of the suspension's functions are fulfilled most satisfactorily, especially on the open road, BMW still has that last mile to go in this area. Though longer travel than the Italians, for example, they still don't have quite the latter's sensitivity and progression.

What the BMW fork also does better than most is take the weight of a fairing without going down on its knees. The German wire is up to this task but should it go away with use, S&W stands ready with a slightly more Spartan set of front coils that we have found to endure. For it was at this point in the test, a little over halfway at the 1,200-mile mark, that we dressed the R75/7 with a Wixom frame-mount fairing, jumbo Bates saddlebags and ride-off centerstand, and S&W air shocks. We also rode up to see Reg Pridmore's neat-as-a-pin BMW shop in Goleta, California (just above Santa Barbara), for it is a custom performance haven for tavern-to-tavern and touring aficionados alike. Our impressions of these travellin' goods and Reg's speed emporium are scattered about somewhere. Hope you like the added touch. The timing was right on since immediately afterward California's months' long drought was momentarily terminated when the skies opened up.

Long-legged Beemer still offers rubber gaiters, locomotive quartz light.

Having warped the R75/7 over the road to the tune of over 2,000 miles in a month, we had developed more than a casual relationship, reinforced by one member of the staff's personal experience with a privately owned 900 BMW twin over the past three years. We learned that the two worst features of the BMW are its battery layout and fly-away sidestand. Although easy to get to—the 12-volt Varta battery resides directly under the lift-out tool tray—service and removal are crude at best. Each of the six plastic filler caps must be pried out with a screwdriver, permitting chunks of broken plastic and dirt to fall into the cells. And construction of the level tubes is such that it is most difficult to

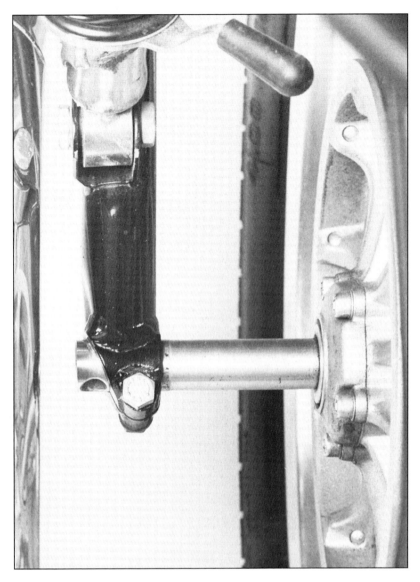

Here's that 24-second rear wheel. Note hole in axle, cammed arm tip.

determine proper water level. Cables are held to terminal posts by nuts and bolts that are prone to corrosion and erosion. Finally, you have to be a lifetime member of Bill Pearl's Gym to be able to muscle the thing past frame encroachments, after undoing two frame retaining bolts and two battery pan bolts. We'll buy the tight fit and removal routine but strongly recommend a change to the gang-type automotive filler caps where three caps each are incorporated in a pair of single easy-lift-out blocks. Also the level-depth tubes should similarly be automotive style, where a definite depression in the water becomes obvious when the level is proper. Finally, screw-type cable retainers, ala Yamaha, would be a definite improvement. Battery life has been a bit of a problem on pre-1977 models but the new 28-amp unit, assisted by a lower-geared starter ratio, promises to have cured that problem.

The spring-up sidestand never caused us a fall-down-and-go-boom problem because we never used it. The stand itself is okay but the instant weight is taken off, it springs up. If a toddler bumped it, he'd get flattened. We didn't like the tricky thing, and it appears that the majority of BMW owners agree with us. We suggest that it be modified to a more conventional design and operation.

And gear shifting requires more of a knack going from third to second than most. The other gears come easily, though generally not as silently as its contemporaries until the operator has familiarized himself with the proper drill. For crisp shifts, engine idle speed when hot should be no more than 700 rpm, and the clutch lever should be grasped up close to its pivot point. Drivetrain lash is virtually nil because of the all-gear hookup from clutch to wheel.

Weighting the scale heavily on the plus side are no less than 36 unique features or BMW firsts. Here are just a few: the all-day saddle that needs no aftermarket replacement; the quartz-halogen headlight that burns holes in the night and is without counterpart in motorcycling; straight-pull spokes front and rear that can't straighten out and loosen; rider-adjustable throttle cruise control that eliminates hand and arm cramps on tour; adjustable footpegs; perforated front brake disc for water purging; Magura offset clutch and brake levers; Spring-loaded headlight warning flasher; real hand striping;

concealed frame-mount front master cylinder; petcocks visible from the saddle while sitting straight up; progressive rear springs; and a multitude of other refinements unparalleled in class. What they all add up to is the fact that, for the purist at least, the BMW *is* well worth the money, particularly as a touring mount.

Getting back to our original concern about how the R75/7 stacks up against other models within the BMW line, we have come to the conclusion that, sales figures aside, the 750 is the most practical of the three, having ample power to push a full-size frame-mount fairing and jumbo bags in any circumstance, solo or two-up. The 750's outstanding fuel economy and noticeably smoother engine over the 1,000 make selection of the bigger motor a questionable luxury for most riders directly proportional to the o.d. of their wallet.

Bates Kingsize Bags

Like the chicken and egg bit, sometimes we have to stop and ponder which came first, the motorcycle or Bates. This premier accessory manufacturer has been around longer than most of us can remember, back at least 25 years to their fine custom leather saddles for off-road scoots. Now deep into the whole spectrum of bike goodies, from clothes and gloves to saddlebags and fairings, their quality is always above reproach. Take their saddlebags.

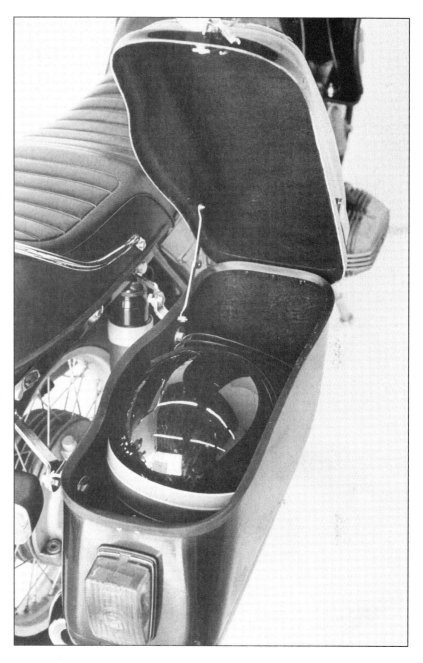

We did, bolting them onto this month's BMW instead of the usual factory-touted Krausers. Installation time: one hour, during which period a Bates ride-off centerstand somehow also sneaked aboard. But it looked trick, it was chromed, so what the heck. The Kingsize bags of laminated fiberglass were, as we expected from Bates, impeccably finished and glass-smooth, spacious enough to hold the largest helmet.

But since the bag tops cannot be removed because of their hinged anti-loss feature, they must stand off from the motorcycle 2 1/2 inches or so. This clearance is also necessary, again because of the hinged feature, for the tops to be able to swing up past the saddle and passenger grab rail. As a result, overall spread of the bags from side to side is exactly 3 feet, wider than a fairing, making them critical to maneuver in traffic or other tight places.

Although the BMW already has the easiest-operating production centerstand available, the Bates ride-off centerstand is nevertheless an extremely functional and worthy product. Easily lowered into position by most riders from a *seated* position, it retracts automatically when the bike is put in gear and *ridden* off, making for a fast getaway. All that can be said against it, at least on the BMW, is that it occasions a slight reduction in cornering clearance, scraping the tip of each foot when banked smartly. Very substantial, it affords a steadying 20-inch-wide footing, wider than any standard stand. The feet are threaded onto the legs proper with a large locknut, to provide just-right adjustment for any model. Priced at $49.50, Bates' ride-off stand is a justified addition to heavy machines in particular because of its easy operation, wide stance, and instant getaway.

The Wixom Frame-Mount Fairing

At a glance, most frame-mount fairings look pretty much alike, thereby nurturing the impression that they all work alike. Looking back, we plead at least partial guilt to this line of thinking as we bolted the Wixom frame-mount to this month's BMW. Curvaceous in almost every plane, the fairing reflected first-class workmanship and materials and took easily to the buxom Bavarian. It was only necessary to trim 1/8 inch from each of the fork's turn signal stalks once the side lamps were removed to permit the forks to swing from stop to stop.

Initial impressions of overly voluptuous styling soon gave way to zealous appreciation of the tunnel work that had obviously dictated the form of the slippery exterior. For we could detect not the slightest degeneration in handling or chassis feedback; the impression being that stability was actually enhanced, if anything.

And the drumming and wind flutter occasionally arising in some fairings was nonexistent in the Wixom, which might as well have been integral with the chassis. With an overall spread of 33 inches, it is 2 inches or more narrower than some and positioned more to the rear, closer to the rider to move the airflow boundary farther away from his body. Only a slight tug at the outermost edges of the arms and tip of the helmet showed that protection was as near perfect as practical. The lower draft level hits about midshin, exposing only the bottom half of full-length boots.

Although we've seen some fairings that were aesthetically "cleaner" as they say in aerodynamic jargon, we found that our visual appreciation was strictly in the eye of the layman, for we've never experienced a fairing that pierced the air with less ado, with more solidarity or absence of buffeting. True, those with more frontal overhang and wider bays do offer marginally more storage space in the side panels and up around the headlight, but if it comes down to a sacrifice in slight interior space vs. a bulbous exterior, we are inclined to opt for the former tighter concept. For the Wixom feels dead-right in the air and provides a maximum of protection with a minimum of bulk. We also felt good about its base price of $230 plus $35 for mounts and hardware ($45 for the Honda Gold Wing).

Installation takes a little over an hour and no special tools are required. Final conviction came with the second high-speed run, after the fairing had been installed and the bike still registered the same top speed—112 miles per hour—as it had unfaired. Even more surprising was a 6 percent *increase* in fuel economy with the Wixom fairing and Bates bags! At a steady 55 miles per hour, the BMW now got 66.16 miles per gallon corrected. At this rate it had a potential 416.8-mile range!

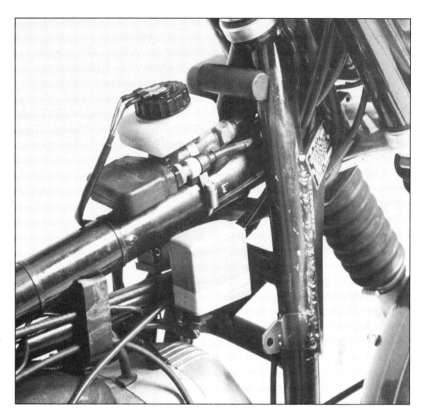

Massive tank conceals master cylinder. Note double downtube gussets.

BMW R100/S

BRAD ZIMMERMAN
Photography by Bob Osborne
Motorcyclist, November 1977

Touring Oregon (Plus 4,000 Miles of Side Trips) on One of BMW's Best

In retrospect, you really couldn't call it a tour. A "blitz" would be more like it. When my tour kit consists of: one motorcycle; one rider; limited luggage; and a straight, ultra-fast Interstate—it becomes a blitz. A 900-mile day is average. An 1,100-mile-day is good, and hitting the 1,200-mile mark is excellent.

This particular trip started out long before a leg was thrown over the seat. We were receiving a BMW, a new R100/S to test. My only previous experience with a "BeeMer" was in the 1,000-cc tour test a few months ago. At that time I got aboard the R100/7, and although it was nice, I wasn't overly impressed.

Then the information trickled in about the R100/S. It had more horsepower, a higher torque curve, and the final clincher—higher overall gearing, identical to the gearing found inside the ultimate R100/RS. That made the decision.

The fighting among the staffers over the BMW was amazing. Everyone wanted to do the test, each with a different idea. All arguments were thrown out in our staff meeting, each having valid reasons. I waited until last, knowing full well that everyone was pretty saddle-sore from the recent 750-cc tour test and most didn't want to take a tour on a bike minus a fairing. My idea, that of going through California, leisurely touring around Oregon, and then shooting through Washington up to the Canadian border, was brought up. I backed it with the fact that the overall cost would be low, considering that I could leech off friends in the Portland and Tacoma areas, plus had an offer from my old buddy Oz, who volunteered to take photos and run me through the high points of Oregon and Washington.

Just like Perry Mason, I won my case. I had two days to prepare. Preparation, in my case, consists of stopping by AAA and grabbing a map, making sure I have clean socks, and making sure the bike is in tiptop running condition.

Saturday was D (departure) Day. At four in the morning, the choke was pushed down, petcocks opened, and the starter motor engaged, bringing the two 500-cc pistons into left-to-right motion. A few seconds of warm-up, one last check of the lights, and the driveway was vacated.

Interstate 5 was the main route this time, more for saving total riding time than for scenic beauty. If you've never had the pleasure, I-5 is boring, enough so that if you were to release a herd of stampeding buffalo loose heading in either direction, they would all be in a semicoma within 5 miles. But it's fast, direct, and undemanding on brain or bike.

The first problem occurred less than 100 miles out. For some reason, the high-beam part of the quartz-halogen headlight decided to retire, leaving me with only a low-beam setting, still brighter than most high beams on the Japanese models.

Getting through the Grapevine area, a twist of freeway ranging through the mountains north of L.A., on low beam, was interesting. Fortunately, the Grapevine is a truck driver's raceway, and if I didn't go at least 75 miles per hour, I would be mowed down; thus the lighting problem wasn't really critical.

In the gigantic San Joaquin Valley, I found a riding position that proved to be the hot setup for the remainder of the trip. With the rear footpegs folded down, my legs were supported by the balls of my feet. A small tank bag took the pressure off my chest, as I could then lay down on the motorcycle, and tuck behind the small fairing on the S model. (In this position, you could easily travel well over 100 miles an hour, decrease the wind buffeting problem, and ride relaxed.) The only drawback I had was that I couldn't see out of the mirrors, necessitating a head turnaround every few miles to check for law enforcement accompaniment.

The BMW is awesome at high speeds. It's the most stable motorcycle I've ever been on; 75 miles per hour feels more akin to 40 miles per hour, and traveling at a

This Sitka Spruce, measuring 12 feet, 6 inches in diameter and over 420 years old, is just an indication of Oregon's biggest resource—wood products.

steady cruising speed of 90 to 95 miles per hour didn't feel in the least bit uncomfortable; as a matter of fact, it became the norm for the California portion of the trip.

Midstate, just south of Patterson, there is a large cattle-holding pen, where perhaps over 1,000 head are held for shipping, as they have been for years. It seems that regardless of when I leave home, I always seem to hit the holding pen around 6:00 to 6:30 a.m., perfectly timed to enjoy the aroma of many years' worth of cow manure, the smell of penned animals, and wet hay. This usually benefits me in two ways: First, if I'm drowsy, this rude nostril awakening does the job better than NoDoz, and second, it usually ruins my appetite for breakfast, thus the upcoming McDonald's doesn't do much business in Egg McMuffins.

While my speed held in the above 80-mile-per-hour bracket, the temperature soared, leveling out at 116 degrees well before 10 in the morning and staying there until after dinner. Riding in heat like this, you begin to curse the horizontal cylinders for their heat, praise upcoming roadside taverns for their cold beer, and finally forsake safety for survival, gradually eliminating more clothing until you find yourself in only tennis shorts, shoes, and a helmet. Damn what the Arabs say about keeping bundled up in the heat. They rode camels, not BMWs on hot asphalt interstates.

The extreme high heat necessitated numerous stops, often at gas stations for a quick shower using the radiator water hose, and an eventual slowdown in progress. The first night, I only made it to Medford, Oregon, after flying through the exciting twisty road through the Mount Shasta and Grants Pass areas.

A word of warning when you're going through these and other heavily wooded areas. The Mario Andrettis of the multiwheel set, especially the logging truck drivers are extremely fast; I clocked one at 87 miles per hour on level ground. These drivers get paid by the log load, thus are always in a hurry. The local police tend to look the other way when a logging truck comes WFO down a mountain road. You'd better be sure you're keeping an eye on the mirrors. The loggers will give you one toot of the horn, then pass either on the right or the left regardless of the fact that there may or may not be a passing lane. Logging truckers figure that if it's flat dirt, it's just as good as asphalt for passing purposes.

After the overnight in Medford, it was just a quick jaunt to Portland to load up with film, grab the Oz and his cameras, and start exploring Tillamook County.

Out of Portland, we headed through winding Highway 6, which skirts around the Trask Mountain area, and gives the rider the impression that around the next corner, he'll be greeted by "BP-Shell" banners, a corner flagman, and a grand-stand teeming with spectators. It's that kind of road—obviously designed by a bulldozer with racing in mind.

Once through Tillamook, our first stop was the Cape Meares State Park to check out the lighthouse, which according to original plans, shouldn't be there. You see, Oregon had wanted a lighthouse built in the area, but wires were crossed somewhere, and it was erected at Cape

It's a small fairing, more for looks than function, but will break the wind well if you crouch down behind the glass. The headlight is the most powerful we've found.

Tucking down behind the small fairing you'll find the usual speedo and tach, accompanied by a clock, voltage meter, and sanitary European-type switches and controls.

The seat and rear section are hinged on the R100/S, providing access to the toolkit cavity and small above-fender storage area.

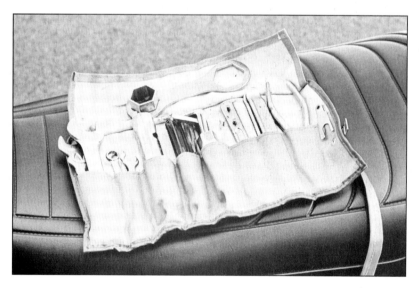

BMW boasts the best toolkit of any street machine. Not shown is the tire patch kit and tire pump that resides below the seat on the upper frame rails.

Meares instead of Cape Lookout. So much for extensive planning.

From there it was northward again, riding up Highway 101 along the coast, taking in such sights as the Tillamook cheese factory, the last functioning steam locomotive (retired in 1964) that worked the logging trails, and up through Manzanita, Rockaway, Cape Falcon, and Arch Cape, all previously Indian land, now owned by real-estate moguls.

Our next stop was Cannon Beach, named when an old cannon, washed up from a wrecked Spanish galleon made its way to land. On Cannon Beach, you can take your motorized vehicle (car, bike, camper, whatever) right down onto the beach, drive up and down, check out the "haystack and needles" a strange rock

In Astoria you'll find the Astor Tower, with Oregon's history painted in a circular pattern up the tower. It's also the site of the world's first cable television operation.

The town of Tillamook, famous for its cheese, isn't a biggie. This shop owner was gracious enough to let us use the only car wash in town—the hose behind his shop. Notice how the BMW stands out in any crowd!

formation just off the coast, and, of course, applaud the jogging women in swimsuits working up and down the beach, much to a photographer's delight.

Further north is Seaside, a small town overflowing with neat little shops, such as a candle factory, homemade ice cream shop, a cookie store, Dutch shoe store, and the required number of antique (recently called so after being referred to for years as "old furniture" before the money value was realized) stores.

Finally the northernmost point of Oregon was reached. The town of Astoria, named after Englishman John Jacob Astor, was started in 1811, and it was named as a tribute to the man who started the trading companies in that area. The Lewis and Clark expedition passed through, working its way down the bordering Columbia River. They set up camp in Astoria for a few months, taking a breather before heading eastward again.

In Astoria, you'll find perched atop the largest hill, the Astor Tower, a mammoth column that has the entire history of Oregon scribed in a circular pattern. At the base of the column is the grave of Chief Comcomly, complete with his traditional burial canoe, an honor relegated him due to his assistance of the Lewis and Clark expedition, and his suggestions to the Astor family in setting up their "trading post" (now would be called a department store).

From Astoria we traveled south back towards Portland along Highway 202, zigzagging the Klaskanine River and running through the Clatsop State Forest, passing appropriately named towns such as Knalla, Clatsop Crest, Clatskanie, Mist, Pittsburg (somehow out of place), Timber, and my favorite, Scappoose.

The following day we headed out of Portland once again, this time heading in a southeast direction towards one of Oregon's largest ski resorts—Mount Hood.

Once more, the names of towns got the imagination running, trying to figure out their origins. Places like Rhododendron, Zigzag, Bull Run, Eagle Creek and Gov't Camp are all on your list before getting to the Mount Hood summit.

During the summer, even when only the small ice glaciers are left, Mount Hood is bustling with tourists. The new lodge is being built, mountain climbing groups leave early each morning (despite the fact that it's easier to hike to the summit in winter with snowshoes), and skiers go up to check on the progress of the ever-increasing number of ski lifts.

On a clear day, which is usual for Oregon, you can stand at the top of Mount Hood, and see mountain peaks in the outlying areas of Vancouver, Canada; Seattle, Washington; and Redding, California. From just one vantage point, by merely rotating yourself 360 degrees, you can take in three states, plus Canada.

From Hood, it's north again, to the border between Washington and Oregon, the great Columbia River, which is the route that Lewis and Clark finally ended up on when traveling through the thick forests, making their voyage practically impossible.

Along the Columbia, you'll find very little industry, and for the most part, the river is identical to the old days

The large-capacity gas tank holds over 5 gallons (good for 200-plus-mile trips before refueling). Footpegs are very comfortable, gear shift is mounted properly, and the new carbs feed the horizontal cylinders nicely. Black valve covers are also found on the R100/RS model.

Road-wise Metzeler tires take corners with ease, while the offset axle forks and good disc pads insure straight and quick stops. Due to the drilling (both for water displacement and cooling), the brakes send out a mechanical whine when pucks increase pressure on the discs.

A rubber cover protects the shift linkage.

before so-called civilization moved in. The only blemish is the Cascade Locks, needed for running Portland's power plant and moving ships through the ever-changing altitude of the river.

On the southern side of the river lie the most beautiful waterfalls in the Northwest. Bridal Veil Falls, a two-stage waterfall, cascades some 200 feet to the river. Horsetail Falls, which partially breaks in half through its descent, is backlit in the late afternoon hours, showing the sun's rays through like a daily rainbow.

Finally, it is the granddaddy of them all, the largest waterfall in the West, Multnomah Falls, reaching a height close to 400 feet, plummeting water down at over 100 miles an hour to a shimmering pool below.

You have to hunt to find these places in Oregon, but these, and others like them, are in good supply and easy to reach

Cable lock under seat is standard.

Note the clock at upper right of dash.

with a local map and some info from a native. The BMW also enjoyed the trip immensely. Through the coastal route, it went through tight corners marked at 35 miles per hour, almost effortlessly at 80. After a while any sign with a curved arrow and a posted suggested speed meant turning the throttle further open, upshifting and leaning through corners, often changing lanes—not because you had to—but because you could.

Through the Mount Hood area, many of the corners were posted at 15 miles per hour, some of them uphill, in off-camber fashion. We never really got the BMW to scrape bottom, unless you counted the centerstand, which quickly lost most of its paint.

During the descent from Hood, the excellent brakes came into play. The front dual disc setup, drilled for water dissipation, made the most beautiful sound when the pads were squeezed. So pretty, that I went out of my way to go a little too fast so I could hit the front brake lever a little too hard, rewarding me with a sound similar to a small motor. Neat.

The BMW has superb handling, outstanding brakes, and once you get used to very positive shifting and a resulting loud clunking noise, good gearbox action. The only thing I had to watch out for in Oregon was the abundant wildlife—deer in the early morning and late afternoons and the all-day road-crossing procession of chipmunks and squirrels.

The R100/S and I reluctantly got back on I-5 for a shot up towards Tacoma, Washington and settled down once again to a smooth, high-speed run. The scenery

This sign seemed to exemplify our feelings about riding a thoroughbred like the BMW down the interstate at the legal 55 miles per hour. The bike was more comfortable in the 80–90 range and was happy to run well over 100 miles per hour.

fortunately was better than in California; the further north you get, the more abundant are trees and greenery. Once, after gassing up, we again hit a cruising speed of 85 miles per hour. We were quickly (and quite suddenly) passed by two yellow Porsche Turbo Carreras—traveling a lot faster than we were. A quick twist of the throttle and we were in tow—running along at 100 miles per hour all the way into Tacoma, where the twin $28,000 cars bid us goodbye, really hit the gas, quickly disappearing ahead.

A tip for the touring rider in Oregon—watch out for the logging trucks! In this photo we were traveling along at 80, and were overtaken by the truck.

As this (and our cover) shows, we got plenty of giggles at Cannon Beach, Oregon, doing non-advised power slides down the beach.

Resting in Tacoma was the agenda for the day, plus a search for a new headlight bulb, eventually found at Federal Way Kawasaki/BMW/Yamaha a few miles north.

The trip back down to smoggy Southern California was not as enjoyable as the ride up. Another early morning departure, it was a straight 18-hour drive back home, once again going quickly but without the enthusiasm of the northbound trip. All the while the BMW ran fantastically, used only a quart of oil in its 4,000-mile trip—and never missed a beat.

During that ride back, I had a lot of time to think about the machine. This was the first big experience I've had with a BMW. I was greatly impressed. It's a no-nonsense motorcycle. There isn't anything on it that shouldn't be there; yet it's missing nothing to make it work perfectly. It goes very fast, the engine barely turning

In the background is Mount Hood, favorite ski resort of Portland natives, and one of the largest mountain peaks in the West.

• The mass scramble for first and second dibs on the BMW has finally subsided and quite frankly I can't figure out the reasons for all the pushing and shoving. I took several quick rides totaling about a hundred miles, and though I haven't spent much time aboard BMWs, I'll stand strongly behind my first impressions. I mean, gee whiz, BMs are supposed to be neat and everything, but really, how can they charge nearly $4,300 for a machine that rattles your teeth, shakes the mirrors into a frenzy, and produces numbness in your hands every time the tach needle drops below 3,000 rpm? Who are they trying to kid? And the Magura grips? They're harder than old cement.

The bike has a definite personality, but it surely isn't its ability to transport a working person back and forth comfortably. Between all the twisting and lurching caused by engine and drive shaft design, and the loud gearbox clunking when shifting through the gears, it's not on my list of desirable commuting bikes, especially when I could buy three other machines for the price of one BMW.

The BMW does, however, have a place in this world and that's out on the open road where it can glide over long distances effortlessly. Take it away from the hassles of city traffic and it becomes a different machine—like a Dr. Jekyll and Mr. Hyde. Even though the speedo is slightly optimistic (it indicates 60 miles per hour while officially traveling 54 miles per hour), you'll find yourself over the speed limit constantly. It's the type of bike that's best to take out on weekends—when there's time and running room to properly exercise your expensive toy.

—Rich Cox

• The cost of a BMW is the key to understanding it. True, the German mark is the strongest currency in the world and it takes extra U.S. dollars to net the same profit on a BMW bought here as one bought in Germany. True, the R100/S comes with a clock and hand pinstriping and other extras not found on competing brands. True, the tradition of German engineering and precision craftsmanship merits extra cost. But how can you account for a BMW costing $4,295 when its technological and performance equivalent, a Honda GL1000, cost $2,938? Volume can't justify a $1,357 discrepancy in price. Neither can international monetary exchange or varying costs of raw materials.

Prestige is the difference, and much of this is self-generating by the high cost itself. Back in 1973 when BMW released the first R90/S, everyone thought its $3,500 price tag was folly. It was a daring move, but it was based on the psychological tendency of the human mind to equate the most expensive with the best. BMWs were suddenly dripping with prestige because they cost so much. The public's fascination with wealth and expressions thereof culminate for motorcycling in the BMW 1,000s, and that, as much as speed, comfort, smoothness, or any functional superiority which might exist, accounts for brisk sales. Buyers are pleased with their ability to afford a BMW. BMW is pleased with profits, which are not entirely undeserved.

—Dale Boller

• The BMW folks never cease to amaze me with their "antiquated" engine design that first appeared in the 1923 BMW motorcycles. There have been many changes and improvements, but these have been accomplished in the traditional Teutonic fashion: make haste slowly, perhaps, but make it correctly. The BMW design never seems to get older...it just gets better through refinement.

Having spent many, many miles in the saddles of BMWs over the past calendar year, I tended to have some preconceived notions about what to expect. The 1,000-mile tour test we did in the January issue of this year included a BMW R100/7, which wasn't sporting enough for me. But the R100/S is everything the famous R90/S was and more. A standing start quarter-mile in 12.48 seconds at 102.32 miles per hour isn't at all slow, and when ridden moderately the S will deliver 50 miles per gallon. Add the flawless paint, controls that control, brakes that stop, and an excellent suspension in spite of its softness, and you've got a machine that I can defend if someone questions its rather expensive price.

—Jody Nicholas

over, it shifts well once you learn its habits, the stopping power is awesome, and despite the fact that it's got that tiny little fairing, it's the most comfortable stock motorcycle I've ever ridden. You've probably read the praises of the BMW in other road tests. After putting so many miles on it, I've got to admit that most likely all the praises are well founded. From its excellent loud horn to its built-in tire pump, it's a completely professional machine.

BMW R100/S

Suggested retail price:	$4,295

ENGINE
Type:	Horizontally opposed OHV twin
Bore x stroke:	90x70.6 mm (3.54x2.78 in.)
Piston displacement:	980 cc (59.8 cu. in.)
Compression ratio:	9.5:1
Carburetion:	Two Bing 40-mm CV-type V94
Air filtration:	Dry paper
Ignition:	Battery and coil
Brake horsepower @ rpm:	No claim
Torque @ rpm:	No claim
Lubrication:	Trochoidal pump, wet sump
Electrical power:	280-watt alternator
Battery"	Varta 12-volt, 28 amp

DRIVETRAIN
Primary transmission:	None
Clutch:	Single-plate, dry
Secondary transmission:	Shaft and hypoid gear
Gear ratios, overall:	
First	12.80
Second	8.32
Third	6.08
Fourth	4.86
Fifth	4.37

CHASSIS & SUSPENSION
Suspension:	
Front	Telescopic fork, 8-in. travel
Rear	Swingarm, 5-in. travel

Tire	
Front	3.25H19 Continental RB2
Rear	4.00H18 Continental K112
Brake:	
Front	Double disc, 10.25x1.33 in. (260x34 mm)
Rear	Drum, 7.9x1.16 in. (200x29.5 mm)
Brake swept area:	193.63 sq. in.
Rake/trail:	28.5 degrees/3.62 in. (93 mm)
Wheelbase:	57.5 in. (146.1 cm)
Seat height:	32.5 in. (82.6 cm)
Handlebar width:	27.5 in. (69.9 cm)
Ground clearance:	6.7 in. (17.0 cm)
Instruments:	Speedometer, tachometer, brake, neutral, oil, generator, turn signal warning lights, hi-beam indicator Stands Side and center
Tire retention device(s):	Retaining notches

WEIGHTS & CAPACITIES
Fuel capacity:	6.3 gal. (24 liters)
Oil capacity:	2.1 qts. (2.0 L)
Weight, wet, unladen:	514 lbs.

PERFORMANCE
Standing start quarter-mile:	12.48 sec. 102.32 mph
Average fuel consumption:	44.14 mpg (corrected)

	BMW R100/S	KAWASAKI KZ100	HONDA GL-1000
Price	$4,295	$2,575	$2,938
Weight	514 lbs.	589 lbs.	669 lbs.
Cruising Range	278 miles	230 miles	194 miles
Quarter-Mile Time	12.48 at 102.32 mph	12.72 at 101.58 mph*	14.06 at 91.09 mph*

*With fairing

Thus, I encounter one of the dilemmas of this job. After riding the BMW, I want one. I can easily justify the relatively high cost by remembering what it was like to ride the machine. It's worth the money, you surely get what you pay for, which is another dilemma. If you decide to buy a BMW, don't ever let a friend ride it. You'll put him in a bad situation, when he experiences what the Bavarian Motor Works people have to offer. Then he's got to go through all the hassle of selling his current mount to buy a BMW—which is exactly what will probably happen. I found out that the more experience you have with motorcycles, the more you know about them, and the more different bikes you have an opportunity to ride, the more thoroughly you'll appreciate and respect the BMW line. I never would have admitted it before, but Bob Greene was right—it's the ultimate machine—for just about anything.

BMW R80/7

Motorcyclist, June 1978

5

BMWs have always been the alternative. It was true when British motorcycles dominated the market, and it's even more true today when Japanese iron has driven every brand but BMW and Harley-Davidson into relative obscurity. Of the 25 different Japanese models available above 500 cc, none resembles a BMW even slightly, either technically, in tradition, feel, looks, reputation, or image. Because of this wide gap, the BMW is a radical alternative, but one which must have considerable appeal to sustain healthy annual sales at prices that are often double those of other bikes in the same class.

The new R80/7, punched out 2 mm from last year's 750 to 797 cc, probably typifies BMW more than any other of their five models. It has everything the owners defend and the detractors criticize. If you have grown up on Japanese motorcycles, which are very much the same in layout, feel, controls, etc., the BMW will seem foreign and unnatural.

Exactly how is the R80/7 different from mainstream motorcycling? Distinctive appearance is most obvious. The Japanese don't make pancake twins. BMW has stuck with this design since 1923 for many reasons: (1) it facilitates shaft drive; (2) it allows the use of an automotive-type single-plate clutch which has proven to last almost indefinitely; (3) the opposed cylinders cancel primary engine vibrations; (4) no engine layout has better cooling; (5) accessibility of valve mechanisms and electrics for routine maintenance is unsurpassed; and (6) the design seems to result in a fully gassed machine 40–50 pounds lighter than Japanese fours, and that's with at least 2 gallons more tank capacity, or another 12 pounds.

The disadvantages are several as well: (1) many people think cylinders boldly jutting sideways are ugly; (2) in vigorous mountain-road cornering the valve covers can be made to bump the road surface; (3) in hot weather the heat pouring off the cylinders can overheat the rider's feet (BMW riders do not get cold feet in winter, however); (4) the cylinders are especially vulnerable in a crash if safety bars are not fitted; and (5) when winging the throttle at a standstill, an uncancelled torque reaction tilts the motorcycle to the right.

Aside from looks, which is purely personal, the flat-twin's advantages are considered by most to offset these shortcomings.

Japanese bikes do not feature leading axle forks. BMW uses them to extract extra travel—7.9 inches—the most on the street. BMW has stood alone for years in suspension theory: make it soft, compliant, and provide a lot of travel. Softly sprung Boge shocks have 4.9 inches of travel in back. The goal is comfort—comfort of the type that allows uninterrupted hours in the saddle. No one denies that a combination of seating position, seat, engine smoothness, and the BMW theory of suspension achieves this goal. But the disadvantages of such soft suspension are highly visible as well: (1) the front end dives harshly during hard braking; (2) the suspension compresses during fast cornering to reduce ground clearance; (3) soft shocks can promote wobbles in high-speed sweepers; (4) indelicate shifting or jerky throttle action can make the bike rock on its springs; and (5) cushy as it is on the open road and as well as it handles potholes, the R80/7 still pummels and hops on freeway seams. This unique suspension, alone in motorcycling, is one of the strongest contributors to the BMW's alternative character. Of the above criticisms, the only one which truly affects most BMW riders, is the last.

A blindfolded person placed upon a BMW would instantly know he wasn't sitting on a Japanese motorcycle. The difference is subtle, but unquestionable. Narrower bars with less rise tilt the body slightly forward to better buck the wind and add to the rider's endurance. The long-touted German seat does not reach its pinnacle on the R80/7. We feel the BMW S-model seat, the Moto Guzzi seat, and Yamaha's XS Eleven saddle are all more comfortable, but this merely reflects the difference between a grade of A and A+.

Our same blindfolded rider would be lost with the BMW's controls. In redesigning the hand switches two years ago, the factory could have conformed to the Japanese turn signal, beam, and horn location, but BMW doesn't care how they do it in Japan. On the R80/7 the right thumb, not the left, activates the turn signals with a vertical flipper switch. This is OK, except it's too easy to turn on one signal while turning off the other, especially with a gloved thumb. The audible beeper, which cleverly doesn't beep with

We marked a crate at random and that became our test bike. Then we witnessed its routine preparation. BMW wanted to prove we weren't getting a prototype or ringer. Test began with 1 mile on the odometer and finished 3 weeks later with 1,157.

the gearbox in neutral or the clutch disengaged so as not to be annoying while the rider waits to turn, is way too loud when it does beep. People in fully closed cars and pedestrians half-a-block away abruptly turn to see what's going on. Another vertically operating flipper switch on the left employs your thumb to activate high beam. Unfortunately this flipper blocks quick access to the horn button above it; we often bumped the beam switch en route to the horn. Once pushed, however, the button blows the loudest and best horn in motorcycling.

No other components on the BMW illustrate its differentness better than the handlebar switches. They also hold the key to coping with many of the bike's distinctive characteristics: acclimation. Within 1,000 miles the rider slowly becomes accustomed to the BMW way of doing

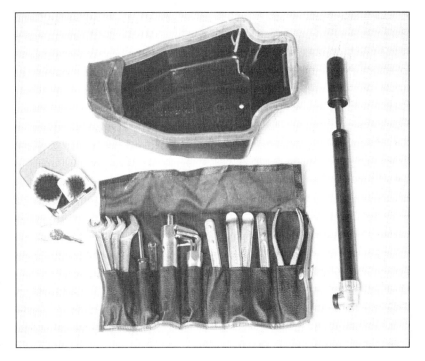

Always superior BMW toolkit even comes with a feeler gauge for tune-ups.

Removable rubber dash panel streamlines appearance around bar mounts.

things and the BMW version of motorcycling. Soon he isn't comparing it to what he's used to, he's judging it on its own merits, which will continue to be strong enough to win over a steady percentage of riders. As you ride a BMW it becomes clear that many of the things people consider wrong are merely different. Switching the turn signals on and off with your right hand instead of your left becomes second nature after the acclimation period. You no longer notice the engine's torque reaction or front-end dive while braking. What you continually notice and appreciate is the BMW's long list of strong points, many of them exclusives.

For instance, this is one of the few machines with a quartz headlight, complete with a flasher button and a specially designed lens to spread the beam in the manner of European sports cars. If you want to reposition the light, just reach forward and push or pull on the headlight body–it moves precisely and stays put. The shock springs preload is adjustable in an instant without tools, a handy feature when passengers hop on and off frequently. Somehow the tank is syled to hold an incredible 6.3 gallons without looking like a jerry jug. The gas cap, for and seat locks are all secured by the same clever folding key. The German-built speedometer and electronic tach feature perfectly uniform illumination and flutterfree needles, although the speedo reads about 4 mph fast. No tires are better than the fabulous Conti Twins which came stock on our R80/7. An unprecedented warranty or 12 months with *unlimited* mileage reflects the factory's confidence in durability and reliability. Natural rubber innertubes rather than synthetic rubber ones have far greater resistance to the tearing that causes blowouts. Few rear brakes are better. No other street bike has straight-pull spokes–the strongest type–front and rear on both sides of the hubs. The engineers are so concerned with reliability that the engine, gearbox, drive-shaft and ring-and-pinion chamber all have their own oil, so it can be exactly the type that works best with those components.

We noticed many of BMW's old problems no longer exist on the R80/7. Previously grabby clutches used to be tough on passengers and new riders; this one releases smoothly and gradually. Our shins didn't seem to interfere with the carburetors hardly at all anymore. Shifting was more precise, though still clunky. The engine's torque reaction also seemed to be less, due partially to different flywheel weight. The 80 runs smoother than the big 1000s, especially below 3000 rpm. Starting is practically instantaneous hot or cold and carburetion on this model cannot be faulted–the engine always settles into a stall-free idle and picks up instantly with the first degree of throttle rotation. These refinements definitely reflect BMW's reaction to constantly improving Japanese machinery. If BMW still had only British twins and Harleys to worry about, their bikes might not have evolved so fast. Still the Japaneese have yet to influence *how* BMWs evolve, much to the delight of their owners.

There were a few items we simply didn't like. The sidestand props the bike safely with ideal positioning only and it drags too easily in left-handers. Through fitted with non-reflective glass, the instrument lenses still blind your eyes when the sun hits them just right; convex lenses such as those on the GS1000 Suzuki all but eliminate this problem. The hand grips are too short and too hard; squarish grips with rounded corners are due next year. The fork tops-out rather easily, but this is said to be normal and harmless. Within 500 miles the pipes blued severely, but this only effects cosmetics since bluring does not signify lean carburetion or overheating. A passenger's feet too easily bump the rider's feet as he moves them to reach the controls or change position.

Perhaps our main complaint about the whole motorcycle centered around the front brakes. To us it didn't seem strong enough. BMW purposely designs the break to it won't lock because they feel the strongest stopping power occurs just before lock-up. They also

feel a brake the locks is dangerous to new riders. BMW told us their extremely hard puck material takes 1000 miles to break-in, but even after that figure the brake wasn't strong enough for us. It also dragged, even after careful adjustment by a technician at the distributor. BMW mounts their floating caliper with a single live puck on an eccentric axle to facilitate wheel removal, a system not as conducive to eliminating drag as dual retractable pucks. On the plus side, however, we found that the holes in the stainless-steel disc reduced weight, added to styling, and contributed to better braking in rain by giving water a place to go as the pads squeezed it away. Mounting the brake fluid reservoir under the tank is also good because it isolates the unit from damage in a crash and frees it from tampering by the public.

Riding the R80/7 reveals further, more important differences than the ones evident on the specification chart. A distinctive, but quiet exhaust note is punctuated by intake drone during hard acceleration and the combination sounds powerful and pleasing. BMW virtually invented the quiet motorcycle long before Federal noise regulations, and this was a great selling point to many touring riders. Pushrods and valve clearances of .004–.006 generate a ticking noise in the cylinder head, but it's an efficient sounding tick that isn't irritating or disconcerting. At 80 miles per hour the sound is only a clean, tight, crisp hum from the engine—resulting in a sense of security and safety. There's something about German engineering and BMW's reputation that's calming while you fly along the road.

Conversely BMWs have never been known for their high-speed mountain-road prowess. You don't assault a set of switchbacks and pretend you're at Daytona. Ridden briskly instead of breakneck, the R80/7 will do just fine with its neutral steering and superb tires. In the city the machine is agile because of its light weight, and easy to ride because neutral isn't elusive and the clutch releases smoothly. Clunky shifts can be avoided with a little practice. BMW riders are the type who would pride themselves at developing the finesse and technique to shift with Dynaflow smoothness.

Suggested retail price:	$3,850
Warranty:	One-year unlimited mileage
Number of U.S. dealers:	475
Cost of shop manual:	Included

ENGINE

Type:	Four-stroke OHV opposed twin
Displacement:	797.5 cc
Bore x stroke:	84.8x70.6 mm
Compression:	9.2:1
Carburetion:	Two, 32-mm Bing
Ignition:	Battery with points
Lubrication:	Engine 2.2 qts.; gearbox 1 qt.
Lighting output:	280 watts @ 5,500 rpm
Battery:	Varta 12-volt, 23 AH

DRIVETRAIN

Primary transmission:	Does not apply
Clutch:	Single-plate dry
Secondary transmission:	Shaft 11/37 3.36:1

CHASSIS

Fork:	BMW 7.9-inch travel
Shocks:	Boge 4.9-inch travel
Front tire:	3.25-19 H Continental

Rear tire:	4.00-18 H Continental
Rake/trail:	30 degrees/3.6 in. (91 mm)
Wheelbase:	58.5 in. (1,486 mm)
Seat height:	32 in. (813 mm)
Ground clearance:	5.3 in. (135 mm)
Fuel capacity:	6.3 gal. (23.8 L)
Wet weight:	484 lbs. (220 kg)
GVWR:	881 lbs. (400 kg)
Colors:	Blue, burnt orange, metallic black
Instruments:	VDO tach and speedo with odometer and tripmeter

PERFORMANCE

Quarter-mile:	13.68 sec. @ 96.66 mph
Average fuel consumption:	39.88
Touring range:	240 miles
RPM @ 60 mph:	3,850 rpm
Speed in gears @ redline:	
First:	38.07
Second:	58.56
Third:	81.08
Fourth:	101.59
Fifth:	113.02
Speedometer error:	30 mph, actual 31.79
	60 mph, actual 56.49

	BMW R80/7	YAMAHA XS750E	SUZUKI GS750
Price	$3,850	$2,298	$2,299
Weight	484 lbs.	557 lbs.	539 lbs.
Quarter-Mile Time	13.68 at 96.66 mph	12.94 at 102.56 mph	12.70 at 101.12 mph
Mileage	39.88 mpg	45 mpg	41 mpg

To want a BMW a person must have the sophistication to recognize what this motorcycle offers and understand himself well enough to be sure this is what he wants. People don't buy them spontaneously because of their high price.

The BMW is a counter-culture motorcycle. Because it is so different, and so personal, *Motorcyclist* can't say, "This is the greatest thing since Raquel Welch, go out and buy one today." We can only say that the R80/7 is an excellent example of the BMW experience. Some *Motorcyclist* staffers aren't overly impressed with this experience. Others have down payments ready. There are more of the latter than the former.

6

BMW 650 R65

Motorcyclist, July 1979

A Reworked Middleweight with a Fresh Personality

Believe the voice of rumor, and you'll bank that the BMW R65 will be the only BMW flat twin in the future. It is whispered with increasing frequency that the big Beemers, the 800 and the 1000, are headed for the history books. They will be replaced by some new configuration, perhaps a vertical triple. When that happens, the tradition of the horizontally opposed BMW twin will be carried forth by the 650 (and the 450, which isn't sold here).

But even if the rumors are wrong about the bigger twins, the 650 is still the BMW of the future. It has shed many of the traditional BMW approaches and components, inherited the best of five decades of constant honing, and taken a slightly different stance than any previous BMW. As a result, the R65 is the most refreshing and, we believe, the best BMW ever.

We suspect that the demonstrated willingness of the R65's designers to break with customary BMW practice will enrage a portion of the BMW faithful, which counts among its number some of the most hidebound enthusiasts in motorcycling. But changes in tastes, technology, and the competition demand that BMW go forward or be buried in the opposition's dust.

For the traditionalist this new BMW middleweight still retains the same basic layout and look of past Bavarian twins. It also uses many of the same pieces as its bigger siblings including crankcases, gearbox, some electrics, and other minor items. The bike has its own frame without the oval section downtubes and with less gusseting and bracing than the bigger BeeEms, but it still has a bolt-on rear subframe.

Most of the changes made on the 1979 R80s and R100s are also incorporated in the 650. These include O-rings in the cylinder base area for better sealing, a single-row timing chain with an automatic tensioner, new handlebar switches, new grips, a shock absorber in the drive shaft, and an Oldham coupler to drive the ignition's breaker point cam and isolate it from camshaft flex. The new ignition arrangement should also be quicker to time.

The changes made in creating the R65 seem small, but they add up to a significant deviation in personality. Instead of the perennial 70.6-mm stroke of other BMWs, the 650's is just 61.5 mm. BMW has managed to turn this into a 2-inch reduction in engine width and an improvement in cornering clearance. With the engine narrowing has come an equally important change: the carbs have been tucked in closer to the cases and away from the rider's shins. This has eliminated most of the problems some of us experience with the carbs on the bigger BMWs, even though the carbs themselves are the 32-mm CVs used on the R80.

The marque's traditional dry, single-plate-type clutch is used in the R65, but the 650's clutch is 20 mm smaller in diameter. This clutch is perhaps a little more progressive in its engagement than the bigger bikes' units, but more important is the difference in weight. The combined weight of the clutch and flywheel are approximately 3 pounds lighter than in the bigger BMWs, and the change is terrific. Heavy flywheels have long been a fixture in BMWs, and were originally employed to help deal with the weight of a sidecar. On solo bikes the heavy flywheels have served mostly to complicate shifting, since BMW engines have always had enough low-speed power to provide smooth getaways without a massive flywheel. The R65 revs quicker, makes smooth shifts with less exact synchronization of engine and road speed, and probably accelerates a tad faster than it would if burdened with the traditional BMW monster flywheel. We prefer it this way.

Of course, a few pounds of flywheel one way or the other don't make a huge difference in performance. The BMW 650 won't be known for its speed. A simple twin with two pushrod-operated valves in each cylinder head usually won't perform like a multi. That's why the 450 isn't being imported, it's far too slow to be successful in this country. The R65 will be out-accelerated by many other middleweights including the Honda CX500, Honda CB650, Kawasaki 650, and Suzuki GS550. The BMW's top speed is about 100 miles per hour.

The R65 does rev a little freer than the bigger BMWs (redline is at 7,600-7,800 rpm instead of 7,100-7,300 rpm on the R80) and the power is concentrated at higher rpm. The 650 seems to wake up slightly at 4,500 rpm, but there's still plenty of response when you flick the throttles open at 1,800 rpm. Much of our testing was done while riding two-up, and we sometimes had to downshift if we wanted to accelerate on long uphills with a passenger. Lazy passes were possible in fifth gear, but we normally used third or fourth for getting by slower traffic.

Throttle response was as good as we expect from BMWs—excellent. We experienced no hesitation, surging, or detonation. Our fuel mileage, however, wasn't as frugal as the 50-mile-per-gallon R100RT involved in last month's comparison. Because much of this test was done while packing double and while romping through the mountains, we wouldn't expect the average mileage to be as good as the 1000's was, but even while cruising comfortably, the 650, which doesn't have the 1000's torque, is running at a larger throttle opening and using more gas. For this reason, the 650's average of 42.3 wasn't as good as the 1000's.

Although neutral-finding sometimes took a few seconds, the R65's gearbox was otherwise flawless. The 650 has the same linkage—and the same smooth, quiet shifting—as the newer big-bike models. There's also very little drivetrain lash.

Chassis performance is what really distinguished the 650 from the bigger BMWs. The R65 is lighter, quicker, tauter, and steadier. Through a careful fat-purging program,

BMW has carved almost 40 pounds off the R80 in making the R65. Some of the areas are obvious, like the smaller, lighter engine. The chassis is also smaller. The wheels are 3 inches closer together due largely to a shortened swingarm, which still rides on tapered roller bearings. The 18-inch front wheel (instead of the customary 19-inch) has also shortened overall length and reduced weight. Other changes have helped bring down weight: a smaller battery, no passenger grab rail, different (but still quartz) headlight with new mounts, a smaller (5.7 gallons instead of almost 6.4) and sleeker fuel tank with only one petcock, a simpler front brake system, and reduced suspension travel.

This last change is especially significant, and may alienate those BMW owners who have enjoyed pointing out their machines' motocross-like fork travel. The leading axle forks of the bigger bikes are replaced with a center axle fork with 6.8 inches of travel instead of nearly 8 inches on the bigger bikes. The R65's fork has much more preload than the leading axle fork. This allows use of all the travel without the usual mushy feel and severe nosedive during braking. The rear shocks are the same as on the bigger bikes but because of the shorter swingarm, wheel travel is reduced about a quarter of an inch.

Set up this way, the BMW 650 is much more nimble, responsive, and fun through corners than the larger Beemers. We spent about 1,500 miles with the Western Adventures tour galloping through the hills, mountains, and canyons of Arizona and Utah where the R65's sporting personality really emerged. The tauter front fork provides a more responsive, stable feel than the soft long-travel fork on the bigger bikes. With the stiffer suspension, short wheelbase, and narrower engine, there's more banking clearance. Even though the R65 is only about 10 pounds lighter than Honda's CX500 shafty, the difference seems much greater because the BMW's center of gravity is so much lower. Shorter riders and beginners told us that the German bike seemed much less formidable when they were manhandling it at a stop. This lightness is transformed into nimble, responsive handling in corners. The R65 can be flicked into a corner very easily, even if you're on the brakes, and midcorner corrections can be made quickly and easily with a minimum of effort. You can charge the BMW through a tight, back-and-forth ess bend without a pause when you change direction, and all the while everything feels tight, steady, and accurate.

The bike retains that steadiness over bumps and at high speeds, where there was no hint of a wobble. Unlike the larger BMWs with their soft suspensions, the R65 rises and falls very little when the throttle setting is changed, and this helps make it more manageable than the big BMWs in corners.

Instead of using a cable to actuate the front brake's master cylinder under the gas tank as on other current BMWs, the R65 uses a conventional arrangement, with the master cylinder mounted on the handlebar at the lever. This makes the master cylinder more vulnerable to crashes and vandals, but it also eliminates the small amount of mushiness associated with the cable. This front brake has a more powerful, positive feel than the other BMW front brakes, but still isn't super-strong. A kit to install a second front disc (standard equipment in Europe) is available. Added braking power, less machine weight, and reduced nosedive make the R65 the best, most controllable stopper in the BMW line. The front brake lost some of its power in the wet but the rear drum was unaffected.

The rear brake and the shaft drive mechanism are both on the right side of the wheel, which greatly simplifies rear wheel removal—just pull the axle. The mufflers have been carefully bent to clear the axle.

BMW R65

		CHASSIS	
Suggested retail price:	$3,445	Fork:	BMW 36 mm, 6.8-inch travel
Warranty:	12 months, unlimited miles	Shocks:	Boge, 4.8-inch wheel travel
Number of U.S. dealers:	475	Front tire:	3.25-18 Metzeler Rille
Cost of shop manual:	$53.90	Rear tire:	4.00-18 Metzeler C66 TS
		Rake/trail:	28 degrees/N.A.
ENGINE		Wheelbase:	54.8 in. (1,391mm)
Type:	Four-stroke, horizontally opposed twin	Seat height:	32.4 in. (823 mm)
Displacement:	649.6 cc	Ground clearance:	6.4 in. (162 mm)
Bore x stroke:	82x61.5 mm	Fuel capacity:	5.7 gal. (21.5 L)
Compression:	9.2:1	Wet weight:	475 lbs. (215 kg)
Carburetion:	Two, 32-mm Bing CV	GVWR:	881 lbs. (399kg)
Ignition:	Battery with points	Colors:	Silver beige, metallic red, bronco
Lubrication:	Wet sump	Instruments:	Speedo, tach, tripmeter resettable to
Lighting output:	280 watts		zero
Battery:	12-volt, 16 AH		
DRIVETRAIN		**PERFORMANCE**	
Primary transmission:	Helical gear, 1.5:1	Fuel consumption:	35 to 48 mpg, 42.3 mpg average
Clutch:	Single-plate, dry	Average touring range:	241 miles
Final drive:	Shaft, 3.44:1		

	1979 BMW R65	1978 HONDA CX500	1979 HONDA CB650
Price	$3,445	$1,898	$2,448
Weight	474 lbs.	483 lbs.	476 lbs.
Quarter-Mile Time	14.31 at 92.24 mph	13.90 at 91.93 mph	13.37 at 95.64 mph
Average Fuel Consumption	42.3 mpg	49.0 mpg	44.3 mpg

Because the R65 really leans on its sidestand, the stand was much more useable than the one on the R100RT tested last month. As with all BMWs, the 650's sidestand snaps up when the bike isn't leaning on it, but the rider must retract the centerstand. Both stands are hard to deploy unless you get off the bike, and this was sometimes a minor problem. The R65 is easier than most bikes to lift on its centerstand.

A Bosch horn replaces the ultraloud Fiamm horns used on other current BMWs. The 650 shares the same piercing turn signal beeper, which only beeps when you're in gear and rolling. This bike has slightly bigger instruments than other Beemers, with the usual warning lights grouped attractively in the face of the electric tachometer. There's also an over-rev warning light next to the redline area and this light glows when the tach needle reaches redline. BMW is proud of their anti-glare instrument glass, but we notice more glare on BMW instruments than on most others. The R65 has the same excellent toolkit as other BMWs, and the plastic side panels on the 650 snap into place instead of relying on the rubber band method.

The R65's seat is shorter than the saddles of the bigger Bavarian twins so a passenger isn't quite comfortable. The rider's portion of the saddle got just a little stiff after a couple of hundred miles. It wasn't quite as good as some BMW seats we've lived on, but it was nothing like the hard R100RT seat reviewed last month either. The leaned-forward riding position suited us perfectly in all situations, and we stayed pretty comfortable and alert on long rides.

We didn't really miss the extra softness and travel of the bigger BMWs' suspension. When you're sitting on the bikes, they both have enough compression travel left to soak up big bumps, and the R65's extra preload made very little difference over small bumps, but other middleweights have more compliant rides.

The only area where the R65 disappointed us was vibration. Below 3,000 rpm (50 miles per hour in fifth gear), the bike had a high-magnitude, low-frequency shake noticeable primarily through the handlebar, especially during acceleration. Between 3,000 and 4,000 rpm, the 650 was pretty smooth, although vibration wasn't completely absent at that speed either. Above 4,000 rpm (70 miles per hour in fifth) there's a strong, higher-frequency buzz, which is at its most annoying in the non-folding foot-pegs. We found that vibration was only a fatigue factor when you were riding continuously at the speeds where the bike buzzes. The passenger never had any complaints about vibration.

The R65 is different than other BMWs; its character is much more sporting. Riders looking for a place to hang a fairing and saddlebags will do better elsewhere. The weight of major accessories will obscure the R65's strong suit—handling—and emphasize its weakness—power. Riders looking for a simple, probably reliable sport-tourer with the emphasis on sport, couldn't do better.

Last month's test of the RT left us pessimistic about BMW's future. The R65 has restored our faith. Although burdened with a price between $700 and $1,200 more than comparable machines, the R65 is a complete, polished effort. More importantly, a unique combination of features—middleweight displacement, shaft final drive, and ultrasporting handling—have carved the BMW 650 its own niche. No other bike combines all three of those qualities for any price.

7

BY RICH COX
Photography by Pat Brollier
Motorcyclist, November 1980

KRAUSER MKM 1000

At $14,000, this BMW-Based 1000 Is One of Europe's Richest Delicacies

As a performance enthusiast with distinguished taste, have you ever envisioned what form of exotica you'd be straddling right now if you'd been blessed with infinite wealth? I surely have. In some of my wildest dreams I've seen myself proudly propped atop the most extravagant two-wheelers the world has to offer. And for one extraordinary day this past month, those images evolved into heart-stopping reality, and I was bodily whisked into the exorbitant and uncompromising world of the filthy rich. The afternoon I spent zipping through L.A.'s surrounding canyons astride Krauser's new MKM1000 was an unforgettable, mind-blowing experience. The feeling of excellence this bike projects and the way it can seduce the wavy pavement is simply incredible. As each corner flashed by, faster and faster and the lean angles got sharper and sharper, I could sense my enthusiasm and pride being pumped to the gushing point. When the day finally ended and I hung up my perspiration-soaked leathers, there was no doubt in my mind that I had once and for all experienced the ultimate all-time sensual limits that motorcycling had to offer.

Take a look, a long hard look at the MKM1000. At this time it is the only one in existence here in the United States. Chances are you'll never see one again, but that isn't to say it's unobtainable or a pure fantasy either. On the contrary, there will be 100 of these beauties made, and with the selling price set at $14,000, there will undoubtedly be plenty to go around.

The MKM is not, as you might be thinking, a limited production machine from the BMW factory. It's solely a product of the Krauser Motorcycle Luggage Company. Krauser, if you didn't already know, is the world's largest manufacturer of detachable luggage. Most of their sales are concentrated in Europe, but with the opening of a new U.S. headquarters based in Seattle, Washington, they're hoping to expand Krauser awareness in this country.

So you're asking: Why is a luggage company building a hybrid GP street machine, or better yet, where have they acquired the technical background to even do so? Well, you'll have to admit the MKM makes for one flashy advertising gimmick. But more than anything, the project stems from the loves and desires of Mike Krauser, president of Krauser International. Krauser, who himself has been a world-class competitor, is still entranced with the sport and is currently sponsoring such greats as Freddie Spencer, 250 GP champion Anton Mang, and the current GP sidecar champions.

Five years ago Mr. Krauser set out to design a road machine that would redefine the limits of motorcycling. With the help of two West German engineers who have raced extensively on the European long-distance circuit, the three-man team searched intensively into alternative methods of motorcycle design and manufacture at Krauser's West German testing facility. The result is an entirely new frame concept, which Krauser calls the "tubular grid." Hand-built of high-quality alloy, each frame is constructed using 52 straight and 4 curved tubular pieces, and is joined at 150 separate welding points. Encompassing the engine like a gigantic birdcage, the frame structure is extremely light (Krauser claims it weighs only 25.3 pounds), strong, and highly rigid—all contributing factors which allow the MKM to track more solidly through a series of twisties than any other BMW I've ever ridden. Naturally, a certain degree of its prowess must be attributed to the fact that the bike's weight has been trimmed down to a bare minimum. Weighing in at 496 pounds—and that's with a full 5.5-gallon fuel load—the MKM undercuts such sporting bikes as the Ducati Super Sport and the Moto Guzzi Le Mans, and runs almost dead even with the ultra-exotic Bimota Suzuki 1000 SB3, which we tested earlier this year.

Mike Krauser has always felt that as street machines, BMWs still afford the greatest quality, simplicity, durability, and worldwide service available. Consequently, he based his design around that familiar marque and incorporated as many of the stock components as possible. All of the running gear—the engine, brakes, wheel assemblies, and drivetrain—are standard BMW production-line items. But he *has* blended in a few modifications of his own to increase the MKM's handling qualities. For example: to facilitate cornering clearance, the bone-stock R100RS engine is set 25 mm higher in the chassis than standard 1,000-cc models, which makes it virtually impossible to grind off the valve covers during all-out cornering. The once-stock swingarm has been widened, but not necessarily strengthened, to fit the frame. In the front brake department you won't find the 1980-styled remote reservoir master cylinder; it's been replaced with one from the R65 model—without the remote unit—which does indeed supply more positive braking without all the sponginess at the lever.

Other modifications include lengthening the wheelbase to 60 inches (the production big bores waver around 58 inches), setting the steering head angle a bit steeper at 28 degrees, increasing front wheel trail to 3.94 inches, and reducing the travel of the stock BMW forks to 6.3 inches—the stockers travel almost 8 inches. BMW connoisseurs would find the MKM's general ride and handling properties quite familiar. But as a result of the beefed-up chassis and carefully engineered geometry, the bike is much steadier in its movements, as if it has been honed to a razor-sharp edge. Pitch her down hard through a series of choppy S-turns and the MKM shows no significant signs of wallowing or sloppiness, just a constant hunger for higher speeds. And considering the MKM's freight train–size length, it makes directional changes incredibly quick, with the steering accuracy of a monorail on tracks! When Krauser went tire hunting, he obviously knew his rubber too because the new Metzeler V-rated tires he's mounted offer excellent control and all the cornering traction any "sane" person could possibly want. And, with a $14,000 investment on the line, we seriously doubt whether anyone will be crazy enough to search for the MKM's limits.

A good deal of my initial infatuation with the MKM was created by its bold, GP-styled bodywork; there's nothing like a long, slippery-looking full-faired bike to pump the old ego and jerk the heads off every fellow motorcyclist within sight. Appearance-wise, you'll have to admit that Mr. Krauser did a beautiful job of creating the aerodynamically proven fiberglass monocoque body shell and fairing combination, the latter of which is basically an RS fairing modified into a Formula One design. The standard RS front turn signals have been nicely molded into the fairing and the cockpit contains the usual BMW instrumentation, including the familiar voltmeter and quartz clock clicking away on the fairing dashboard. Generally, I'm not too enthused with fully glassed machines because they're usually just a hassle: the glass is always cracking, nothing fits right, the vibration is terrible, and the seating arrangement is always uncomfortable. But I was, for the most part, really impressed with the MKM's glass layout—it's really engineered with care. Krauser does all their own fiberglass work in-house and the quality is excellent. The reinforced glass fairing pieces are all solidly secured on cushion mounts and during riding there's hardly a trace of vibration inside the cockpit. The fairing, which consists of a lower belly pan and center section, is pieced together rather intricately with 10 dzus fasteners, but it can quickly be removed entirely in roughly 15 minutes, or in sections, for accessibility. During this process the standard BMW quartz headlight remains intact with the bike, only the instrument wiring needs to be unplugged. The body shell and plastic rear fender can also be lifted off in one piece quite easily with the removal of four nuts located under the seat. Krauser informed us that a passenger seat is available upon request and they'll even paint the machine to order. And, in the event the Krauser showpiece falls off the mantle into the fireplace, parts are available.

In addition to selling the house, car, and disowning the wife and kids, you'll have to make one more small sacrifice to own the MKM: your body. As you might expect from a racetrack-to-street motorcycle, the MKM leaves a little to be desired in the comfort department. Depending on your body structure and the way you ride—sitting forward or way rearward—you may or may not feel at home on the MKM. In order for me to comfortably

KRAUSER MKM 1000

Suggested retail price:	$14,000
Warranty:	None
ENGINE	
Type:	Four-stroke, OHV flat twin
Displacement:	980 cc
Bore x stroke:	94x70.6
Compression:	8.2:1
Carburetion:	Two, 40-mm Bing constant-velocity
Ignition:	Battery with points
Lubrication:	Wet sump
Lighting output:	280 watts
Battery:	12-volt, 28 AH
DRIVETRAIN	
Primary transmission:	Helical gear, 1.5:1
Clutch:	Single-plate, dry
Final drive:	Shaft and bevel gear, 2.91.1
CHASSIS	
Fork:	36-mm BMW, modified to 6.3-in. travel
Shocks:	Boge, 4.9-in. wheel travel
Front tire	3.50V19 Metzeler Perfect ME77
Rear tire	130/80V18 Metzeler C88A Touring Speed
Rake/trail:	28 degrees/3.94 in. (100 mm)
Wheelbase:	60.0 in. (1,524 mm)
Seat height:	32.0 in. (813 mm)
Ground clearance:	6.25 in. (159 mm)
Fuel capacity:	5.5 gal. (21 L)
Wet weight:	496 lbs. (225 kg)
Colors:	Specified by buyer
Instruments:	Speedometer, odometer, tachometer, resettable tripmeter, voltmeter, and quartz clock

reach the bars, I was forced to slide up tightly against the tank—and then my knees were playing dodge ball with the fairing. And the seat certainly doesn't offer much more than an hour's worth of bun protection. But nevertheless, I wasn't that uncomfortable, and I'd definitely rather spend an afternoon aboard the MKM than either the Suzuki Bimota SB3 or Vetter's new Mystery Ship, both of which I've ridden.

In closing, let's just keep the old fantasy flaming and assume you *do* have the kind of money that's required to purchase the MKM. Keeping in mind that the bike has absolutely no warranty implied, and that that's a dead-stock 60-horsepower motor beneath all that glasswork, is it really worth the ungodly price of $14,000? Well, if you're the type of person who can afford five-digit play toys, you probably aren't concerned over denominative worth. Does it *work* like a $14,000 motorcycle should? That's the real bottom line for heavy hitters. The answer is definitely YES! You've all heard the expression "I feel like a million bucks." Well, if I could have cashed in those feelings I had after that memorable afternoon ride, that MKM would definitely be sitting in my garage right this minute!

8

INSIDE BMW

By C.D. Bohon
Photography by C.D. Bohon & Dick Lague
Motorcyclist, February 1981

The Bavarians Have Great Plans—And a Few Worries

Does BMW have a future in motorcycling? And does anybody care? The answer to both questions is yes, although as short as two years ago, it certainly didn't seem so, at least in the United States. At that time even poor, struggling Triumph was selling more motorcycles in America than BMW, and many enthusiasts considered Bee Ems to be expensive, outdated, and overrated. Like Harley-Davidson and Triumph, BMW appeared to have backed itself into a corner by selling refined versions of an ancient twin-cylinder design that appealed only to a small group of badge loyalists; loyalists who might be disaffected if the company undertook a major redesign effort and produced something modern, something "Japanese." It looked like BMW, with rumors of thousands of unsold bikes gathering dust in warehouses, might be the first of the three legendary companies to fold, despite various tantalizing glimpses of "modular motorcycles" and the like unveiled from time to time by the German company.

After a visit to BMW's Munich R&D center and the Berlin factory, we feel confident BMW will be building motorcycles for many decades to come—and desirable motorcycles at that. One of the major problems BMW had selling their machines in the United States was caused by a less-than-satisfactory commitment to handle the marque by the company's old U.S. distributor, Butler & Smith. Many people we talked to alleged Butler was not interested in stocking parts for and servicing the machines it sold, and raised retail prices higher than they reasonably should have been. As of October of last year, BMW of North America, which has been importing BMW automobiles since 1975, became the sole importer of BMW motorcycles into America. That means from now on Munich will have its fingers directly on the pulse of the U.S. market, and should be able to offer far better service than BMW owners have been used to.

BMW recognizes the limits of the flat-twin design and has plans for an entirely new motorcycle, which should debut around 1984, but the company is increasingly convinced that, with proper development, the boxer can become—in fact, they believe,

Improved fairing and load-leveler shocks are new on the 1981 RS. And who says the BMW is an "old man's" machine? It's an Alpsblitzer for sure. Berlin's Hansjoachim Lobert poses beside an assembly-line-fresh R65. Note the R65's gas tank–mounted toolbox.

already is—one of the finest motorcycle engine designs available. They feel simplicity and light weight are paramount virtues in a motorcycle, and are not to be sacrificed merely for the sake of a gain in horsepower and reduced quarter-mile times. So, although they are making a major investment in plant expansion to produce the all-new BMWs, the old plant facilities will not be switched over to building the new series, but will continue to turn out updated versions of the six-decades-old boxer twin.

An idea of BMW thinking on how the traditional horizontally opposed motor will be developed for the Eighties—and Nineties—can be gleaned from the "Futuro" machine shown at the recent Cologne show. The Futuro, a strikingly modernistic machine, was an outside design by Frankfurt Autoveredler b&b, commissioned by BMW to make the most advanced motorcycle possible, keeping only the flat-twin and driveshaft layout of traditional BMWs. With technical assistance from the Battelle Institute and the ominous-sounding German Technical Surveillance Association, FA b&b looked at what the motorcycle is, what it is supposed to do, and how it can be made to do it better. They decided that a commitment to join the "horsepower race" was counterproductive—a conclusion we have heard voiced by such diverse companies as Triumph, Harley-Davidson, and Yamaha over the last year or two. Frankfurt Autoveredler decided that superior performance should be achieved by reducing weight and optimizing aerodynamics. Previously the research group had worked on Porsche modifications, advanced vehicle electronics, and the Mercedes CW311 sports car prototype. But this was their first attempt at designing a motorcycle.

What they came up with was a wind tunnel–tested complete fairing enclosing not only the front, but also the rear of the motorcycle, with internal luggage compartments. The center of gravity was lowered substantially and the frontal area of both the bike and rider streamlined significantly. Powering the machine was a familiar 800-cc flat-twin motor, turbocharger-equipped, tuned to turn out 75 horsepower, a figure admittedly modest, according to FA b&b. Why bother with a turbocharger when dealing with such small output? To provide greater torque at low and medium rpm, according to the researchers. Boost is controlled by a microprocessor, which continuously monitors the running temperature of the engine. Bosch LH Jetronic electronic fuel injection with hot-wire air metering serves to ensure smooth engine running and maximum fuel economy. That power plant, coupled with a dry weight of only 396 pounds gives the machine a top speed of 130 miles per hour and very good "sprint" and midrange acceleration, according to the Futuro designers.

The super-low weight figure was achieved by making the frame and swingarm of aluminum, and performance was enhanced with aerodynamically favorable solid disc wheels and center-mounted cantilever-style rear monoshock spring strut, which has a titanium spring. The fairing is made of carbon-fiber.

Other goodies on the Futuro include a reaction-type steering system that takes up driving and braking torque, eliminating a couple of typical BMW reactions that can range on current machines from annoying to disconcerting, depending on how enthusiastically you are riding. Two homokinetic universal couplings ensure smooth driveshaft operation. The disc brakes have sintered metal friction surfaces for good wet-weather braking and are coupled, Guzzi-style.

It is highly doubtful the Futuro will ever be manufactured by BMW, but it does give us an idea of their thinking for the future. Simplicity, quality, modest

No Japanese-style uniforms are worn by workers at the BMW factory in Berlin, only a taxi-ride away from the Soviet's infamous wall, beyond which are no BMWs.

horsepower, and super-light weight: those should be the hallmarks of all BMWs ever built and should, BMW management hopes, result in a fine-performing, distinctive motorcycle highly desirable to the affluent biker looking for an alternative to the machines the Japanese produce.

We were surprised to learn how BMW's concern for light weight came to be. While chatting with the engineer instrumental in developing the R80 G/S enduro bike recently unveiled, we discovered he had long been a Triumph fan and had owned several of the machines. BMWs used to be known years ago as the Harley-Davidsons of Europe, heavy, solid machines more at home bolted to a sidecar than blitzing the Alps. This despite the fact that back in the Thirties they had raced some superb GP machines. That image

The assembly line is as modern as those in the Far East. A worker may stop the line himself, if he encounters a problem that will need a bit of time to fix.

began to change in the early Sixties. Said our engineer, "In 1963 my boss told us we should start developing new motorcycle models. I was a fan of British bikes and felt we should try to make a BMW that would be a better sports bike than the Triumph. I had bought one of the first Bonnevilles, then the finest motorcycle available, and incorporated the philosophy of its design into our first new project—the 600-cc cross-country bike that won a gold medal at the ISDT.

"We were not satisfied with this machine; it was far too heavy for a cross-country bike. But we found the frame was very good for a road machine. This became the grandfather of the /5 models. We had the ISDT prototype developed by the end of winter 1963–1964, won the ISDT in 1964, and began work on the /5 in 1966. We marketed it at the end of 1969. That gives you an idea of our lead-time for new models, and may tell you when we will introduce what we are working on now.

"The idea for the /5 Series—which was far more sporting than anything we had built before—came about because I became disenchanted with Triumph," the engineer continued. "My first bike was a BSA B31, then I got a Tiger 100, then my '62 Bonneville. The thing which dampened my enthusiasm was that I had the same troubles with my Bonnie as with the Tiger 100, which was eight years older than the T120. How could anybody continue to manufacture a defective machine for so long and not correct the faults? It took me a year to fix the Bonneville so it ran the way it should have in the first place. After this I was convinced BMW should build a German "Bonneville." I suggested the idea at a meeting, the concept of a light and sporting BMW, and management was pleased. This was no easy decision for them to make, for BMWs had always been designed to accept sidecars, and it was impossible to design a light bike that could also handle a sidecar.

"Two years ago, after those troubles that almost killed us, we got new management who are very interested in new models. The first result of that is the G/S. BMW has competed in off-road sports for over 50 years and yet we have never built such a bike before—a replica. I couldn't understand that. In my opinion it was high time to commit our sports experience to our standard production. I urged our new management to do it. And they concurred. Now the G/S is available and demand is far greater than I expected. We also have the Futuro, some of the features of which will shortly show up on BMW production machines. There will be new models. And you will enjoy them."

We talked with the recently acquired new management personnel about BMW's future and the market niche it sees for itself in an era of absolute dominance by the Japanese tyrannosaurs. How can a small, engineeringly conservative outfit continue to sell motorcycles which are far more expensive than the competition and which, frankly, are no longer so vastly more reliable or of higher quality

We encountered a number of Asian gentlemen putting Bavaria's finest together. This man appears to have made his way to Berlin from the wilds of South Vietnam.

than other makes? It would be a rare fool who would describe, for example, a Kawasaki KZ1000 as unreliable; in fact, a KZ1000 owner might feel justified in referring to the BMW as unreliable compared to his mount. That contention could be argued far into the night over innumerable steins of beer and cups of sake. BMW is aware of the problem, although they feel it is one more of image than reality.

"The BMW is a motorcycle designed to run forever," said one top BMW staffer. "To be ridden hard and still run forever. We do not build motorcycles to be traded in every two years on a new model. You should only have to buy one BMW. If there have been complaints about troubles with BMW servicing in your country, it was not the fault of the motorcycle or the factory that built it, but of poor after-service attention by our former distributor. That will not happen in the future. Our most important foreign market is the United States. We are planning a major push for market expansion there, and we will do it with the very finest motorcycles available on the world market. Here in Germany the best-selling single motorcycle type is our own R45. The next most popular bike is

BMW's future may look a lot like this: an outside design study dubbed the Futuro, unveiled last fall at the Cologne motorcycle show. The body-enclosing fairing is a low drag coefficient wind cheater, the frame is as solid as the Siegfried line, and the turbocharged 800-cc motor delivers fine fuel economy and lots of low and midrange grunt.

Honda's CB900, then Yamaha's XT500. Now, as you know, our motorcycles cost more than the Japanese, yet we manage to outsell them here, where we control our marketing and service. Now that we have the same situation in the States, we don't see why we cannot challenge the Japanese for sales superiority in targeted displacement classes."

But, we asked, isn't that wildly optimistic? "Price is the main problem in the U.S. We believe we have a potential market of well over 10,000 machines a year.... BMW pricing is the same all over the world," the BMW manager said, "but the Japanese adjust their market price by country. For example, the CB750K lists in the USA (as of fall 1980) for about $2,975. In Germany they sell it for 8,000 DM (about $4,400). Now the R65 sells for $7,290 DM ($4,000) in Germany and $4,250 in the States, a reasonable increase in price considering we ship the bike to the USA and incur costs. Yet the Japanese ship the CB750 to both the USA and Germany. There can't be such a huge cost increase in shipping it to Germany as opposed to shipping it to America. After all, you crate the bike and load it on a ship no matter where you send it. No, the Japanese are clearly adjusting price by market, slashing prices where they can get away with it to maintain sales, raising the price in other countries where competition is not so fierce. We can't do that, and our sales effort in America will clearly be hindered by this sort of cutthroat price policy of the Japanese.

"But," the Munich executive went on, "we have one advantage over the Japanese: BMW survives in the USA because it is *not* made in Japan. Even if the Japanese were to start manufacturing a horizontal twin of their own, it would not hurt us." You don't think then, we interjected, that the new Yamaha V-twin will hurt Harley-Davidson? Clearly they aimed deadcenter at the Harley customer. And we have heard rumors one of the other Japanese companies may soon market a midsize flat twin of its own design.

The executive paused and looked thoughtful. "Really? A flat twin? Is that Suzuki? We've heard such talk before.... I don't think it would hurt us.... Perhaps with the younger buyers. But, no, I don't think Yamaha can hurt Harley-Davidson, although we will watch what happens with keen interest. You see, if what you say is true, and the Yamaha V-twin reinforces our belief in the viability of our traditional engine concept.... the horsepower race is ending. The world oil situation, if nothing else, will force it to end soon, no matter what. Simple motorcycles are selling well now, so we may not need...."

May not need what? May not need an entirely new motorcycle engine design? "We are seriously considering what to do about that now. You know, our car division had plans not so long ago to build a V-12 engine, manufacture the finest-performing sports sedan in the world, utterly overwhelm Mercedes and Jaguar. But fuel economy became more important suddenly, and there will never be a BMW 12-cylinder car."

What you are trying to tell us, we guessed, is that all these rumors about in-line twins and threes, a V-4 and the like, may be true or partly true, yet you may manufacture none of them, nor in fact, *any* new motorcycles at all?

"We must be very careful. The forte of BMW has been the special engine concept, which gives good low-speed torque. And fuel economy. We also have a name for chassis/running gear excellence, suspension superiority. We were the paragons... We would like to set an example of excellence once again. But I cannot be more specific. It may well be we will stick to the boxer. The sensible motorcycle. You see, the BMW is an ideal harmony of shaft, motor, suspension—all things together. You can only achieve this by having manufactured such a machine for long years, gotten so you know it completely, have perfected it right down to the last detail. If we were to come out with a totally new design, would we be able to maintain this same standard, a standard our customers expect as granted?"

Just above, a factory hand checks a Beemer fresh off the line to make sure it meets emissions specifications.

Berlin's Managing Director, Dr. Wolfgang Aurich.

At Munich, R&D engineer Rudiger Gutsche told us how the /5 series and the new R80 G/S evolved.

You mean, you are afraid any new design you build might have bugs in it which your traditional customers would rebel at?

"It's possible. It's a risk. We of course have confidence in our engineers and our manufacturing ability. We are investing large sums of money in expanded production facilities. You may be pleasantly surprised to see what we do. Don't forget, we are associated with a company that produces the finest motorcars in the world. We can call on all our parent company's expertise in design, engineering, wind tunnel testing, automated manufacturing, whatever we need. We are definitely not a Harley-Davidson, definitely not a Triumph. You may think because we are a survivor and our current product has evolved from one of the earliest motorcycle designs (BMW first marketed a flat twin in 1923) and is, in fact, a recognized classic, that we may have the same troubles as these two companies. But we do not. We are BMW, and that makes us different."

We paid a visit to the BMW factory in West Berlin to see just where the legend for Beemer quality originated and to see just how well those fabled German craftsmen really do work. A surprise we should have expected, of course, was the fact most of the workers at the plant are not German at all. Most are Turks, with a number of Vietnamese and Koreans filling the ranks, too. But BMW brass are quick to point out all management positions are filled by Germans.

The BMW factory itself is housed in ancient buildings, constructed in the closing years of the last century, when the Prussian government had them built to house an arms factory. Siemens bought the place in 1928 and began turning out aircraft engines there.

Their company was also called BMW—Brandenburgische Motoren Werke. In 1939, the "real" BMW—Bayerische Motoren Werke—bought out Siemens and took over the production of aircraft engines for the Nazi war machine. It might be appropriate to point out here, if you're not already aware of it, that the BMW insignia, a quartered circle, is supposed to represent a spinning aircraft propeller. Over the next half dozen years BMW engines came crashing down out of the skies everywhere from Malta to Moscow, Glasgow to Gaza, as the aircraft they powered became popular targets for drafted anti-aircraftsmen from a dozen nations.

The factory was dismantled in 1945 right after the war ended, but by summer of that year it was back in business turning out sickles and scythes. Four years later motorcycle parts production began, as the factory became a subsupplier of the main BMW plant at Munich. Over the next two decades motorcycle production was gradually shifted completely to Berlin. In 1969, 400 employees were turning out 30 motorcycles a day. In 1972 the 50,000th BMW motorcycle was manufactured at the Berlin factory. Within three more years the 100,000th had been built, as production climbed and climbed again. In 1978 the 200,000th BMW motorcycle was turned out.

When we showed up outside the gates two years later, the factory was turning out about 150 motorcycles a day, the maximum the facilities would permit. Two shifts of 25 workers turn out the engines and one shift of 35 assembles the completed bike. The factory supervisor told us 700 machines a day would be an ideal figure, but they just didn't have the capacity as yet to do it.

At the right, a technician quality-checks the same bike on a roller, running it through the gears and rpm, testing lights, horn, etc., to make sure it performs just as a BMW should. Total time on the rollers: about 90 seconds.

We remarked on the general air of cleanliness and efficiency of the plant, and the quietness—Berlin was the quietest factory we've visited, excepting the Meriden Triumph plant, which was all but shut down—and asked about the quality and newness of the manufacturing facilities. The plant manager responded, "We are using the same equipment to produce our bike as are the Japanese, but our production is small because our facilities are limited. This is one of the major reasons our machines are more expensive than the Japanese. They have an economy of scale we cannot match.

"But we are planning a reorganization within three years that should see us able to rationalize about 10 percent of our employees as we reorganize our model plan. We will need more automation, of course, but right now we must have floor space. We'll be buying a lot of new machine tooling to fill that space, to build our new models. The new engine can't be built on the old engine assembly-line carriage."

New engine? How will the new engine differ from the current motor, production-wise, we asked, eyes all wide and innocent.

The top air box goes on European BMWs. It's plastic. The box below it with all the garbage goes on U.S. BMWs. It's aluminum.

"Well," said our factory tour guide, "The boxer engine was developed in the Sixties and is expensive to build. It is made from one casting—very expensive. The new motor will be made from two castings; we are trying to make it an industrial design. It will have some synthetic materials in it, but we have been experiencing difficulties working with these new materials. We changed engine castings and it took three months for our supplier to reach our standards.

"The new frame…" he continued, "Our present frame is very complicated, and has to be almost entirely hand-welded. If you start with a new frame, you can design it to fit automatic welding equipment, and reduce costs greatly. In 1978 we rationalized the welding system of our present frame and saved 30 percent—in time, the time it took to make, which works out to a significant cost reduction."

As we strolled through the plant, we were surprised to see the shift end and the workers head for home. Our watch said only 2:30. Our guide responded to our puzzled query with a laugh and the explanation that most factories in Germany, including BMW's, run from 6:00 in the morning to 2:30 in the afternoon, with a one-half-hour lunch break. Seemed like a fairly decent shift to us. We couldn't help being surprised to learn that all parts for the motorcycle must be sent up to the assembly line via elevator, as the line is on the second floor of the old building. The speed and capacity of the elevator limits output severely. As we rode down the elevator after seeing the last of the bikes for that day's shift come off the assembly line—one every three-and-a-half minutes—we learned that the 1,600 BMW Berlin employees, including 120 quality-control inspectors, take about 20 hours to build one motorcycle, for which they get paid, if they are untrained beginners, $12 to $13 an hour. This figure goes up with experience. In addition, workers get a healthy year-end bonus and 30 working days paid vacation each year. We asked where the employment office was, ready to fill out a job application, but then hesitated. If everything is so wonderful here, how come you can't find enough German workers to man the assembly lines? "Ah," our guide answered, "Berlin is an island, you see, surrounded by the Soviet occupiers. Turnover among German assemblers is about 80 percent a year. Young people don't want to live here. It is a problem. Berlin is growing old. The young people leave and no one wants to move here. Only foreigners come prepared to stay. Now 49 percent of our personnel are foreign, mostly blue collar. Much of our white collar force is actually Austrian."

Does that imply, we asked, that in the future BMW will be forced to move production facilities from Berlin, just to keep its employees? "No, certainly not. We are committed to Berlin. Our future is here. Over the last three years our capital investment here has been 150,000,000 marks (equal to about $80,000,000) and over the next five years we plan to

Before shipment each Beemer is sprayed to resist corrosion.

invest double that amount in buildings and machinery to produce our new models. We plan to renew everything, renew the total structure. Frankly, two or three years ago we were thinking of abandoning making motorcycles entirely, but now we will not. With the trend to touring bikes and simple motors we feel we have a bright future."

After our visit, and the cordial hospitality of our German hosts, we can't help but feel our guide was right, that the next few years will see the finest BMW motorcycles ever produced, machines that will really give the Japanese a run for their money.

Bound for Japan.

9

BMW R65 LS

The State of the Art in Germany

Photography by Bill Jennaro
Motorcyclist, June 1982

The cop followed us home. Right into the driveway. Uh-oh. Must have missed a stop sign someplace. He rolled down his window. "Say, who makes that anyway?" BMW. It's an R65LS. "Yeah? Never seen a bike quite like that. How much does it cost?" About four grand. His face fell. "Well, it sure is a nice-looking bike."

And so it went. Guys in Porsches, other bikers, even a pedestrian or two: they all wanted to know what it was and how much it cost. BMW's latest offering has all the curiosity quotient of Suzuki's Katana, even though it is far more understated, both in styling and performance.

What makes the attention-demanding motorcycle look different from previous Bavarian boxers is the small cockpit spoiler/fairing. According to BMW, it reduces front-wheel lift by one-third at highway speeds, making the bike much more stable. The cockpit contains an electric tachometer as well as speedometer with tripmeter and a full complement of idiot lights. The handlebar is low, European sport style. An electric heater to keep the grips warm is available as an option. The 5.8-gallon gas tank looks smaller than it is and blends gracefully into the mildly stepped seat, which is surprisingly comfortable for a German item. The seat ends in a stylish fiberglass housing with integral passenger grab rails. The housing contains the Beemer's legendarily complete toolkit and is large enough for the kit to bounce around in; it thumps annoyingly if you don't stuff a couple of shop rags in to keep it still. Our motorcycle was painted a bright red, which contrasts nicely with the white wheels and black exhausts. The bike is also available in silver-gray.

The frame and motor of the LS are identical with those on the standard R65, but the final drive ratio has been changed from 3.56:1 to 3.44:1 to provide a little higher top speed. That change shows BMW is still not dialed in to what American riders need in a motorcycle. You may be able to blitz the autobahns of the fatherland as fast as you want, and a bit higher speed-potential may be a definite advantage, but over here, the way the

LS is geared only means it vibrates right at the speeds you'll be riding at most often: 40 to 60 miles per hour. The bike doesn't vibrate all the time, but right in the 2,900-to-3,100-rpm band the handlebar develops a shudder which shifts to the footpegs at 3,800 to 4,000 rpm. The footpeg shaking is not so bad, but since the handlebar is little more than a stub to rest your hands on and all your weight bears down on it at moderate speeds, the vibration there is annoying.

The LS can boast of a more useful change from the standard R65: its wheels. The company wanted to combine the flexibility of a conventional spoked wheel with the rigidity and freedom from maintenance of the cast wheel. To do that they developed a patented composite-alloy design, the rim section of which is made of hardened aluminum, cast positively around the softer, star-shaped pressure-cast hub. These wheels reduce unsprung weight by about 4 pounds on what is already a very light motorcycle.

At 452 pounds wet, the LS undercuts the XJ650 by 22 pounds, the GS650E by 27 pounds, and the CB650 Nighthawk by 39 pounds. That light weight, combined with the bike's low center of gravity, neutral steering, and overall excellent handling, make the motorcycle a delight to slip through the mountains on. Don't let those two cylinders sticking out on the sides fool you; the motorcycle has plenty of ground clearance—and the tires to let you use it all. There's a 3.25x18 Continental up front and a 4.00x18 Conti in the rear.

The nose cone on the LS, while distinctive and attractive, is purely for function. It creates downforce on the front wheel, keeping it firmly in contact with the road at speed.

Together with the low-rpm pulling power of the motor, these assets combine to produce a machine that our hottest throttle jockeys say they could take through a twisty section of road as fast as, and with less work than, any number of high-horsepower, high-tech Japanese motorcycles. This, despite the fact that the throttle takes a double handful to open fully and the horsepower, at a claimed 50, is 12 to 23 horses down on the power the various similar-displacement fours claim.

Stubby bars and integral cockpit give the LS a purposeful look from the seat.

The motor which produces that modest power is of a design synonymous with BMW motorcycles since 1923: a horizontally opposed OHV with two-valve head. It was derived from the R80/7 motor back in 1979 by chopping the stroke from 70.6 mm to 61.5 mm, a change, which cut overall engine width by 2.3 inches. It shares crankcases, gearbox, and most of the electrics with its bigger brothers, and is the first BMW motor to incorporate the smaller clutch and a 40-percent-lighter flywheel that all the boxers now have. As a result, it revs quickly and shifts smoothly. The clutch is a dry, single-plate unit with diaphragm springs. It has a very light pull, but abrupt engagement. The transmission is a five-speeder, not, unfortunately, close ratio. The step from second to third is particularly wide—or at least seems to be when you are downshifting from third to second in a tight corner. The resulting chirp of the tire can be disconcerting. Final drive is, of course, by shaft.

When it was first introduced, the engine had iron cylinder liners. These have been replaced by an electronically impregnated nickel-silicone coating, which improves heat dissipation and cuts weight a tad. For 1982, the intake and exhaust valves were widened by 2.0 mm to bump horsepower up from last year's 45. Carburetion is by 32-mm constant-velocity Bings. Ignition is handled by a Bosch electronic unit.

To meet the Fed's clean air standards, the LS is equipped with the BMW-designed Pulse-Air system. Small vents just past the exhaust valves squirt jets of air into the egressing fumes, allowing burning to continue into the header pipe, making the final exhaust cleaner. The vents suck air from the air box. A reed valve stops the exhaust from forcing its way into the system.

The frame is a double downtube steel item with bolted-on rear. Suspension is handled by a nonadjustable BMW center axle fork with 6.9 inches of travel and Boge dampers with dual-rate springs. The shocks have three-way adjustable spring preload, easily adjusted with Bee Emm's famous little shock handles. Rear shock travel is 4.3 inches. Ride is a bit harsh in town, but at speed on the straight or in the corners the suspension does a good job of inspiring confidence.

The brakes are excellent. Drilled double discs handle the stopping chores up front and a drum takes care of the rear. One of our resident knee-scrapers declares the front binders rival Honda's industry-standard twin-piston units. A single finger pulling on the front lever hauls the bike down smartly.

Stopping in the wet? No problem. The brakes work as well during the 40th day of Noah's rainstorm as they do dry.

The R65LS is not particularly comfortable to ride around town. The intermittent vibes get to you, and the leaned-forward riding position necessitated by the low bar give you sore wrists and a crick in the neck. The footpegs seem mounted too far forward. And in stoplight getaways, any number of smaller displacement Japanese bikes leave it behind. But then, the LS is not supposed to be a town bike. It exists to ride the open road, where its excellent handling and dead-straight high-speed tracking come into their own. The forward-mounted pegs let you slide forward easily when you start doing business on a twisty section. Above 5,000 rpm the engine becomes almost uncannily smooth for a 650 twin and responds quickly to throttle input. The virtuous handling and braking make up for the lack of raw horsepower. Soon you find yourself moving along at quite a brisk speed, indeed—even if you're riding at night. The halogen headlight spreads its 60/55-watt beam in a good, useful pattern.

Still, is the bike worth the four-grand asking price? BMW has done a remarkable job of not only keeping its prices down, but of actually reducing them substantially, no mean feat in these inflation-harried times. In fact, the fancier LS costs no more than the standard R65 did in 1981, and *its* price had been cut about $200 over the 1980 price. Even so, the R65LS costs $1,000 to $1,500 more than the 650-cc Japanese fours and $1,700 more than Yamaha's 650 twin. If you want something exotic, Triumph's Royal will cost you about $300 less, and the even more exotic Moto Guzzi V50 Monza is $750 cheaper.

If the BMW were a perfect example of Old World craftsmanship, it might be worth what it costs. But our example suffered from a hanging-up choke and sticking throttle. Mileage, at an average of 45.6 miles per gallon, while not bad, was not nearly as good as we expected from a motor of this type. These problems are not major, and all would doubtlessly be fixed under warranty by the dealer—except low mileage, which may be a measure of how wide we held the throttle open. Still, we were disappointed to encounter them on a BMW, a bike that turned out to have niggling problems just as other bikes do.

The R65 is by no means the perfect demigod of motorcycling some BMW buffs might have you believe. It is simply a very refined flat twin, distinctively and functionally styled, with great brakes, excellent handling, and a high price tag. Whether you're willing to pay that price to get those qualities is up to you and your bank's loan arranger.

BMW R65 LS

Suggested retail price:	$3,995
Engine type:	Air-cooled horizontally opposed four-stroke twin
Valve arrangement:	OHV, two valves, operated by pushrods and rockers, threaded adjusters
Displacement:	649.6 cc
Bore x stroke:	82x61.5 mm
Compression ratio:	8.2:1
Carburetion:	Two, 32-mm Bing constant-velocity
Ignition:	Battery-powered, transistorized
Lubrication:	Wet sump, 2.6 qts.
Final drive:	Shaft
Front suspension:	36 mm BMW
Rear suspension:	Dual Boge dampers, adjustments for spring preload
Front brake:	Two single-action calipers
Rear brake:	Single-leading-shoe drum, rod-operated
Front tire:	3.25H18 RB2 Continental
Rear tire:	4.00H18 K112 Continental
Wheelbase:	56.0 in. (1,422 mm)
Wet weight:	452.5 lbs. (205.7 kg)
Best quarter-mile acceleration:	14.23 sec., at 90.2 mph
200-yd. top-gear acceleration from 50 mph:	67.3-mph terminal speed

BMW R100RS

Photography by Jim Brown & Dexter Ford
Motorcyclist, November 1982

*Fending Off the High-Tech Onslaught with Functional
Purity, Style, and Comfort*

To the uninitiated, the R100RS—like all BMWs—could easily be thought of as a
motorcycle for semi-retirees, a symbol, they say, of one's financial independence
and long-since dried-up adrenal glands. These observers see the RS singing the rich
man's song of the open road and not much else.

These people have simply spent too much time speculating about, and not enough
time riding, a BMW. There is a certain visceral quality about the R100RS that defies
metallurgical description or head-to-head comparisons with today's techno-wonders.
That quality stems from the Bavarian commitment to function first, the dedication to
building lightweight, uncomplicated machines with the kind of manufacturing quality
that begets durability, a high resale value, and the same esteem that, deserved or not,
surrounds the Mercedes-Benz.

Over the past few years, we've seen a tremendous diversification of the motorcycle
market, due almost entirely to the Japanese manufacturers. We've seen the raft of specials
gobbled up by the masses, we've seen hyperkinetic 1100s obliterate quarter-mile standards, we've seen luxo-cruisers that make short work of long-haul touring, and we've seen
the introduction of production-line turbo bikes, V-twins, and V-fours—and more glittering
gadgetry than you can shake a computer chip at.

Yet BMW has continued to sell its boxer twin, the same basic design that powered
Ernest Henne to a land-speed record of 134 miles per hour back in 1929. BMW has sur-
vived, for almost three-quarters of a century, without ever straying from its commitment
to functional purity. It hasn't sought to embellish its machines with gadgets for gadgetry's
sake. No symphonic radio systems or racy paint schemes here, thank you.

But this commitment has evolved into a Catch-22 situation for the West Germans.
Adorning their products with such enticements would probably broaden their market, or
at least help buyers justify the sticker price. But that's not BMW's style. BMW *has*, however, slashed the prices of some of its models. Our test bike, the R100RS, has not inflated

one penny in three years, and at $7,025, it is no longer the most expensive motorcycle on the market. (Harley-Davidson now has that distinction.)

The technical superiority of the Japanese machines can certainly be argued, but consider BMW's basic design fundamentals when applied to the R100RS. The Japanese have yet to build a large, lightweight engine that carries its weight as low as the 980-cc opposed twin. This low CG lends itself to a machine that makes snap directional changes with little effort and makes slow-going maneuvers easy. And at 544 pounds with bags (504 pounds dry), the RS is one of the lightest bikes in the 1-liter category.

By sticking to the same basic design year after year, BMW has been able to achieve a level of refinement that is just not possible on a first-year model. The

brakes are a prime example; on this year's R100RS they are better than ever. Bolting double-action Italian Brembo calipers in place of the old single-action German units has resulted in crisp, powerful braking action that gives the lightweight RS better stopping capability than anything in its class and has ended the need for prolonged break-in.

Long before the Japanese began fitting their sport machines, such as Honda's CBX and CX500 Turbo and Yamaha's XJ650 Turbo, with full-coverage fairings, BMW had enveloped the RS rider behind a functional, lightweight fairing. The sleek cowling positions the rider's hands, arms, torso, and lower legs out of the airstream. The low handlebar requires that the rider lean down to meet the machine and allows BMW to fit the RS with a low windscreen that directs the airflow over most riders' heads. Only six-footers noticed a slight buffeting at high speeds, but it was nothing like the beating dished out by the CBX fairing.

BMW's wind tunnel testing has resulted in a fairing shaped to reduce overall drag more effectively than the bikini-fairing-equipped R100S. By creating an aerodynamically slippery shape in the RS's fairing, BMW was also able to give the sporty RS excellent straight-line stability, a necessity for European riders who regularly blast along the autobahns at 100 miles per hour. By punching a clean hole through the static air, the RS fairing creates little turbulence to batter the sidewalls of the fairing. Instead, there is a relatively uniform stream of fast-moving air.

Stability is also enhanced by the downforce created by the fluted shape of the fairing and the midsection ridge on the sides, which acts like a race car's spoiler in creating downforce. This concentration on aerodynamics has also made the RS fairing less susceptible to crosswinds than most we've tried.

The horizontally opposed twin engine works well with the RS fairing. Both cylinders poke through openings in the fiberglass, where they are cooled by the airstream and are prevented from passing heat directly to the rider's legs and upper body. On the highway, little heat reaches the rider, but when cruising around town on particularly warm days, a lot of heat is transferred to the rider's feet, which are positioned inches from the cylinders.

Almost everyone complained that the trailing edge of the fairing's sidewalls swept back so far that his knees made contact with the edges. This was especially annoying under heavy braking when the rider slid forward and banged his knees.

Those who appreciate the function of the RS fairing will understand why its interior contains no storage compartments or bank of instruments; including the integral blinkers, quartz headlight, voltmeter, ignition switch, and quartz clock, the RS fairing weighs a scant 20 pounds.

Some may not like the RS's European seating position. Two of our testers felt that too much weight was placed on the arms and hands, especially during braking. Others more used to the European arrangement had few complaints. Everyone agreed that the wide, firm seat provided ample comfort for full days on the road.

For just such occasions, the 1982 R100RS comes with detachable saddlebags and an oil cooler as standard equipment. The cooler nestles into its own cavity in the front of the fairing just aft of the front fender. The lightweight saddlebags, located on removable chrome brackets, are beyond reproach. They carry the BMW stamp and replace the optional Krauser units available on last year's RS. They are made of high-density ABS plastic, and each is capable of carrying 22 pounds of luggage. These 20-liter bags will house a full-coverage helmet, yet are only a couple of inches wider than the width across the cylinder heads, so you needn't worry about cleaning them off when you're wedging your way through city traffic.

Each bag attaches to the brackets with a solid snap of a single metallic latch located at the rear, and each latch, including the two that close each bag, has a separate trapdoor that protects the locking tumblers. The pins in each bag's hinges can be removed to lay the bags flat for packing. Inside, there are elastic straps that keep the contents in place, and a double-lip sealing surface ensures that everything inside won't be as damp as everything outside.

The quality and overall craftsmanship of the bags, like most everything else on the RS, is top-notch. Everything fits perfectly, and the bags feel sturdy enough to stay that way for a long time. If you feel like lightening your load, the bags *and* bracketry can be removed in about 10 minutes.

Aside from the bags, the RS is fitted with a wide assortment of useful amenities: adjustable passenger pegs, extra padding in the rear section of the seat, a three-way-adjustable hydraulic steering-damper, a locking cable stored in the frame's center backbone, a tire pump, a fully equipped toolkit (including tire irons) that puts the Japanese tools to shame, a sealed storage area under the flip seat, a glove box located in the fiberglass tail section, and a set of honkers that, though they are louder inside the fairing than out, will still awaken most sleepyheads.

Most of these items are not new to the R100RS, but there are a few subtle, yet effective, changes that BMW made throughout its line in 1981. The most noticeable change is BMW's redesign of the flywheel/clutch assembly. In the past, BMW used heavy flywheels to smooth out the power pulses and protect the drivetrain. But fitting the driveshaft with a new ramp-coupler-type shock absorber in 1979 led the way to the lighter flywheel. The flywheel, now a stamped-out spider carrying the ring gear for the starter assembly, weighs 7 pounds, or roughly 40 percent, less than before. This change is noticed the minute you roll the throttle back on the RS; the engine responds quickly, gaining and losing revs like never before. At the drag strip, the RS clocked a time of 13.28 seconds at 98.9 miles per hour to make it the quickest BMW we've tested since 1977, when we recorded 12.48, 102.3 on an ess. In roll-on acceleration tests (performed by whacking the throttle wide-open in fifth gear at 50 miles per hour, 200 yards from the speed traps), the RS produced a terminal speed of 76.7 miles per hour. That makes it only .7 miles per hour slower in roll-ons than Suzuki's full-dress GS1100GK, which we tested last month.

These performance gains are also due in part to a number of other engine changes. The air box is bigger and features a new inlet system that allows the engine to breathe more air. In the exhaust system, a second crossover pipe is located just behind the oil sump, under the engine. The old BMWs used 40-mm-diameter tubing in their exhaust systems for optimum exhaust flow, but the noise produced by these pipes attracted the attention of Federal sound meters, and BMW was forced to use 38-mm tubing. With the new crossover, BMW claims to have attained its original flow characteristics and picked up the lost power.

The R100's aluminum cylinders no longer have heavy iron liners. In their stead are Nikasil-plated bores, which have shaved some 2.5 pounds off each cylinder. The Nikasil process requires BMW to bore the aluminum cylinders to size and apply silicon-carbide particles directly to the aluminum. The cylinders are then spun on their bore centers, and special diamond abrasives are used to grind the bores to their final dimensions. According to BMW, Nikasil is even tougher than hard chrome. And, aside from making the cylinder assemblies much lighter, the Nikasil dissipates heat much more efficiently than the old lined cylinder. The new cylinders also feature an air inlet in the exhaust ports, which works much like Kawasaki's air-suction system in cleaning up emissions. BMW then jettisoned the RS's breaker ignition in favor of an electronic breakerless system, which provides a more powerful spark. The rear wheel shaft-drive housing is also lighter and smaller, yet contains an additional 150 cc (now 350 cc) of 90-weight oil.

In all, BMW trimmed some 20 pounds off the already light engine and drivetrain. Our drag strip figures show the effect. On the open road, only a twist of the throttle is usually required to ease by traffic. If you want to *zap* slower drivers, downshifting is required. Passing on uphill stretches, especially at high altitudes, sometimes requires two downshifts. As long as you feed the shift lever a positive dab, the RS shifts through its five speeds smoothly. Clutch action is light and precise, though momentary slippage was evident during drag strip starts.

The 20-liter bags are rated at 22 pounds each and will house a full-coverage helmet. They detach in seconds, and their simple brackets won't interfere with rear-wheel removal.

The RS's beautifully crafted fiberglass fairing provides comfort and additional high-speed stability. The oil cooler is now standard, and the brakes employ Brembo calipers.

The RS requires such liberal downshifting because of its tall European-style gearing. At 60 miles per hour, the engine is loping along at 3,500 rpm, halfway through its power band. Though throttle response is crisp below 3,500, the Beemer doesn't begin to make real power until 4,000 rpm.

When cruising along at 55, the engine runs at what feels like a fast idle. This makes it difficult to keep it down to 55, but once, in the interest of mileage, we mustered all our adult restraint, and the RS returned 52.7 miles per gallon. At our average of 44.7 miles per gallon, the RS's 6.3-gallon tank will keep you in the saddle for half the day, or roughly 280 miles.

For those of us who liked the RS seating arrangement, the range was welcomed. Though it performs well around town, the RS is like a beer without its stein until it hits the open highway. There it kicks into full stride, devouring miles as it hunkers down on its soft suspension and slips you silently through the wind. Freeway expansion joints will set the RS into a gentle rocking motion, but not enough to spoil the ride. Larger lumps and bumps are absorbed, as if they never existed, into the BMW's famous long-travel suspenders.

Long sweeping roads are the RS's nirvana. There, the low center of gravity, light, neutral steering, and overall light weight let you flick the RS from left to right at citable speeds with little effort at the narrow handlebar. The relaxed manner and low-frequency rumble of the engine almost make a mockery of your fast pace. The long-travel suspension passes over large bumps that have other bikes airborne. Push the RS in tighter corners, however, and the sidestand or rear brake pedal hammers the ground. But combined with the fairly sticky Continental tires, the RS remains surefooted, even when the undercarriage is threatening to lever the wheels off the ground.

Two fingers draped across the front brake lever is all it takes to slow the RS down at any speed, and the lever transmits precise messages that keep you in touch with what's happening on the ground. There is also enough power available at any speed to skid the front tire using only two fingers. The rear brake reacts much like the front binders, but it faded during one particularly brisk downhill ride.

Other than the front fork, the RS chassis remains fundamentally unchanged since its introduction in 1975. The new fork, manufactured for BMW by Fichtel Sachs, features the same 36-mm stanchion diameter and a nearly 8-inch stroke, but each leg has fewer moving parts, a thicker wall section for additional rigidity, and Teflon rings in place of the old damper's metallic rings.

In the rear, a set of Boge dampers provides 5 inches of travel and offers a choice of three preload positions. A convenient handle makes adjustment easy. Both ends' spring rates are well matched to the damping rates and are also balanced well against each other. However, the rear shocks do not provide enough damping to mask the rise-and-fall effect of the shaft. This bobbing is only unsettling when the rider is uncertain with the throttle in a tight corner and the bike sinks on its suspension, robbing the rider of valuable ground clearance. With the rear shocks on their stiffest setting, more ground clearance is available, but the ride is not as plush. We used the stiffest setting when loading the saddlebags with gear, which helped the RS maintain its normal ride height, but the additional weight set up a slight wallow. Considering the price and BMW's functional dedication, the RS should come with more suspension adjustments.

When you finally pry yourself out of the seat, you find another problem: the sidestand is awkward to use and too short to be trusted. The centerstand should also be reworked; as it is, it takes a rupture-defying clean and jerk to pop the RS onto its stand.

But with the RS, you'll have plenty of time for bodybuilding, since you'll spend so little time on maintenance. Aside from oil changes and tapped adjustments, the new ignition system, shaft drive, and 5,000-mile service intervals will have you looking for something to do with your spare time.

Those who understand and appreciate the RS's functional disposition, the light, crisp action of its controls, the quality of its fiberglass and saddlebags, and the typical BMW craftsmanship of everything else will no doubt justify shelling out $7,025 and spend their spare time racking up the extra miles.

But the RS's sticker price will be too steep for those who prefer a more frenetic lifestyle. Swift traveling companions can be found in any Japanese stable for a less painful price. That in itself may guarantee the R100RS's exclusivity. But few motorcycles can balance sporty aspirations and long-distance touring capabilities like the RS—and most of those are BMWs. Fewer still can draw you to the open expanses, to the next county, or to the next state like BMW's R100RS.

BMW R100RS

Suggested retail price:	$7,025
Warranty:	12 months, unlimited miles
Engine type:	Air-cooled, horizontally opposed four-stroke twin
Valve arrangement:	OHV, two valves operated by pushrods and rockers, threaded adjusters
Displacement:	980 cc
Bore x stroke:	94.0x74.6 mm
Compression ratio:	8.2:1
Carburetion:	Two, 40-mm Bing constant-velocity
Ignition:	Battery-powered, inductive, two magnetic triggers
Front suspension:	36-mm Fichtel Sachs leading axle, 7.8-in. travel
Rear suspension:	Dual Boge dampers, 4.9-in. wheel travel; adjustments for spring preload
Front brake:	Two, double-action calipers, 260-mm discs
Rear brake:	Double-action caliper, 260-mm disc
Front tire:	3.25H19 Continental RB2
Rear tire:	4.00H18 Continental K112A
Rake/trail:	28.5 degrees/3.7 in. (94 mm)
Wheelbase:	57.8 in. (1,468 mm)
Seat height, unladen:	32.0 in. (812 mm)
Fuel capacity:	6.3 gal. (23.9 L)
Wet weight:	544 lbs. (247 kg)
Colors:	Red or silver-gray
Fuel consumption:	36.6 to 52.7 mpg, 44.7 mpg avg.
Average touring range:	281 miles
Best quarter-mile acceleration:	13.28 sec. at 98.9 mph
200-yd. top-gear acceleration from 50 mph:	76.7 mph terminal speed

11

BMW R80RT

Photography by Rich Cox and Paul Martinez
Motorcyclist, July 1983

Touring Exclusivity for a Smaller Stack of Bills

A BMW will make you a mellow man. To ride one is to take a sublime holiday from the frenetic pace of today's wonder bikes. It is a sort of hypo-kinetic, relaxing experience in modern leisure augmented by the certain mystique that has always surrounded the machines from Munchen. BMWs are stately controverters that seem to proclaim, "We don't care how the hell they do it in Japan; you can keep your four-valve Tilt-a-Whirl this and your anti-drive that. We'll move swiftly and silently down the open road, thank you very much."

But the BMW buyer has paid through the nose for his chauvinism. The sheer heft of BMW price tags has no doubt turned away more than a few potential buyers, especially those touring riders who saw the magnificent, but horribly expensive, R100RT as the only BMW of interest. For 1983, BMW has ruthlessly slashed the retail prices of its entire model line and enveloped the bikes in a three-year, unlimited-mileage warranty as further enticement. Yet those touring riders salivating over the R100RT still face a nearly $7,000 outlay.

In an attempt to broaden its touring line, BMW has designed a more affordable machine with all the fundamental attractions of the RT. BMW's main concern is to supply the buyer with the excellent RT fairing, the single component that really sets the RT apart from the big-bore cross-country crowd. In the R80RT, you also get the same chassis, ergonomic essentials, and running gear as the 1000. The boxer twin is the same horizontally opposed 797.5-cc mill used in the discontinued dual-purpose GS and the new street-going unfaired ST.

And, by shoehorning an existing engine into the chassis, BMW is spared the murderous expense of routing a new engine through the EPA exhaust sniffers.

The R80RT sells for $5,490, a full $1,500 less than the R100RT. That $1,500 savings came from the elimination of a few R100RT amenities. Buyers no longer get a voltmeter or clock in the fairing, the rear disc has been replaced with a rod-operated drum brake, the oil cooler has been dropped, and the hydropneumatic, self-leveling Nivomat rear shocks have been replaced with standard Boge units. Our R80RT was delivered with optional saddlebags. Yours won't be unless you pay an additional $450.

A bit of horsepower has also disappeared. BMW claims the R80RT peaks at about 50 horsepower, while the R100RT stops at 65. Even though the R80RT undercuts the 1000 by 18 pounds (with saddlebags), the 800 can't match the 1000's power-to-weight ratio. At low rpm, the difference is barely noticeable. Around town, the R80 zips along nicely and has plenty of grunt to jet you past traffic. Even in the midrange, the BMW makes enough power to zap traffic with little urging. Comparing the R80 with the leading 750-cc machines from Japan, however, brings the R80's shortcomings to light. Accelerating wide-open from 50 miles per hour in top gear (approximately 3,500 rpm), the R80 managed only 71.6

BMW's optional luggage is sturdy, light, large, convenient; a must for long-distance treks.

miles per hour after 200 yards. Current 750s typically run anywhere from 76 to 80 miles per hour. The R80's best quarter-mile run was a 14.57 at 85.87, which is substantially slower than the Honda VT500 tested last month.

This means that most high-speed passing requires at least one downshift, sometimes two. Around town, though, the R80 gives you a choice of at least two gears in which to cruise, thanks, in part, to a lower final drive ratio. The 800's ring and pinion gears have a 3.36:1 ratio in contrast to the 1000's 2.91:1; BMW made the change to shorten the gap between each of the transmission's five speeds.

Some testers regarded the gearing change as a no-win situation. Without the lower gearing, the bike would likely hedge during shifts in a moderate headwind. With the lower gearing, the engine has lost some of the relaxed, effortless feeling that makes BMWs so enjoyable. Other testers didn't seem to mind the lower gearing at all, citing the engine as the smoothest BMW has ever produced.

Aside from the low-rpm rumble common to all Bimmers, the 800 is indeed supremely smooth—smoother than the R100RT. That stands to reason, since the 800's pistons are substantially smaller than the 1000's; and when you're dealing with such large pistons, reducing their reciprocating mass can make a big difference. Even at high engine speeds, it's difficult to detect any vibration through the handlebar, seat, or pegs, and the images in the mirrors remain clear.

The 800's smoothness is remarkable because at 60 miles per hour (where the engine spins at just over 4,000 rpm), the R80 is turning almost 550 rpm faster than the R100RT.

BMW R80RT

Suggested retail price:	$5,490
Warranty:	Three years, unlimited miles
Recommended maintenance intervals:	5,000 miles
Engine type:	Air-cooled, horizontally opposed four-stroke twin
Valve arrangement:	OHV, two valves operated by pushrods and rockers, threaded adjusters
Displacement:	797.5 cc
Bore x stroke:	84.8x70.6 mm
Compression ratio:	8.2:1
Carburetion:	Two, 32-mm Bing, constant-velocity
Final drive:	Shaft and bevel gear, 3:36.1
Front suspension:	36-mm Fichtel Sachs, leading axle, 7.8-in. travel
Rear suspension:	Dual Boge dampers, 5.9-in. wheel travel; adjustments for spring preload
Front brake:	Two, dual-action Brembo calipers, 260-mm discs
Rear brake:	One, dual-action Brembo caliper, 260-mm discs
Front tire:	3.25H19 Continental RB2
Rear tire:	4.00H18 Continental K112A
Wheelbase:	57.7 in. (1,465 mm)
Seat height, unladen:	32.0 in. (813 mm)

Fuel capacity:	6.3 gal. (23.8 L)
Weight (with bags):	539.5 lbs. (235 kg) wet; 519.0 lbs. (235.4 kg) tank empty
Fuel consumption:	31 to 40 mpg, 36.1 mpg avg.
Average touring range:	227 miles
Best quarter-mile acceleration:	14.57 sec., 85.9 mph
200-yd. top-gear acceleration from 50 mph:	71.6-mph terminal speed

This higher rpm level had a predictable effect on mileage; our 800 averaged only 36 miles per hour. An R100 delivers about 45.

The R80 engine also differs from the 1000 in that it uses 32-mm constant-velocity Bing carbs, in place of the R100's 40-mm units, and smaller valves. The 80 uses 42-mm intake valves and 38-mm exhaust; the R100 utilizes 44-mm intake, 40-mm exhaust. The rest of the engine remains the same and incorporates the refinements that found their way into production in 1981; Nikasil cylinder lining and a lighter clutch/flywheel assembly.

Like the other late-model BMWs that have received driveline streamlining, the R80's clutch and driveline components work exceptionally well. Action at the clutch lever is very light and precise, and engagement takes place over a narrow enough sweep of the lever to allow two-fingered operation without squashing unwary digits. Though the shift-lever throw is rather long, positive gear engagement requires little effort. The bike did, however, mysteriously pop out of second gear on several occasions.

Aside from that, there were few complaints about the drivetrain's action. From throttle to contact patch, the system is surprisingly slop-free and void of the routine clunking associated with many of today's shaft drive scooters.

One area in which the BMW loses points to the other shaft systems is in shaft-induced rise and fall. Sudden on/off throttle transitions have the Bimmer hopping up and down on its suspension, which can cost you precious ground clearance in a tight corner. This phenomenon is worse on a BMW than on most shafties because of the German application of lightly damped, long-travel suspension. The solution is to know where you're going and to be smooth with the throttle; don't shut off in midcorner. Bumping spring preload in the rear to the stiffest of the three settings will give you far more cornering clearance than the limpest position, but it also tends to accentuate the rise-and-fall effect.

We rode our BMW through four states—some 1,800 miles—and were perfectly comfortable with the preload at its stiffest setting. We packed essentials for a week on the road in the saddlebags. In every situation we encountered, the rear dampers performed exceptionally well. They could use a bit more rebound damping, perhaps, to control the shaft's effects, but aside from that the ride was exemplary. Over California freeway slabs, the shocks isolated the rider from jolts and prevented the hobbyhorsing that plagues most everything on freeways in Southern California.

Through the high-speed desert of Arizona, the R80 remained wobble-free, and when called upon to set a brisk pace through the twisting canyons of Utah's Zion National Park, the BMW complied happily. Even when traversing menacing bumps at high speed, the suspension was content to soak it up without passing a jolt to the rider. The high-mileage Continental tires, however, were not designed to be pushed hard through the turns and were less than inspiring when the pace got really hot. At more responsible speeds, the tires worked well.

Spring and damping rates up front are spot-on. The fork never bottomed, despite a full load of luggage and a hefty tank bag. It delivered a cushy, stiction-free ride, a ride that compares to the very best Japanese offerings.

The twin Brembo calipers up front are extremely powerful, capable of locking the front wheel at any speed with only a two-finger coaxing. Action at the lever is precise and rather abrupt until you are used to it. Thanks to a change in pad structure in 1981, it no longer takes hundreds of break-in miles before the binders begin to work, and they continue to work well even when abused or sopping wet. The rear drum does an adequate job of stopping, but requires more lever pressure than the R100RT's disc.

A fast pace requires smoothness on the rider's part and an active shifting boot, but very little body English. Quick transitions require a minimum of countersteering, and, no matter what the speed, steering remains light and precise. This is partially due to the Bimmer's low center of gravity and relatively light weight. Honda's 750 Interceptor, which weighs 550 pounds, is 11 pounds heavier than the fully armed R80RT.

The seating position lends itself to hot-dogging in the twisties, but is far better suited to the open road. The handlebar is high compared with sporty BMWs and sweeps back to put you in a more upright position behind the fairing. From a distance, the seat looks like a torture rack—thin, flat, firm. It is, however, one of the most comfortable seats we've encountered, one that we sat on for 130 miles at a time without any posterior discomfort. There is no step to limit your movement, and the seat's narrowness allows you to move easily from side to side. It also allows shorter riders to plant both feet on the ground. The footpegs also contribute to the seating comfort. They are not positioned far enough forward to put pressure on your tailbone, nor back far enough to cramp your legs.

What makes the R80RT really comfortable is the protection provided by the fairing. The lower section completely envelopes your legs, while trapping heat from the engine to warm your toes. On hot days, it gets a little warm down there, but never uncomfortable. Aside from a breeze on your arms and head, the fairing completely isolates the rider

OFF THE RECORD

● With the R80RT, BMW offers a more affordable alternative to the R100RT. The R80RT gives you all the things that make the R100RT attractive, but with a smaller price tag. Like the R100RT, the R80RT is far more comfortable than you would expect from looking at the thinly padded seat, and I found myself perfectly content in the saddle for 130 miles at a time. Racking up miles has always been a BMW forte, and the R80RT has been designed to further that tradition.

Along with the reduced price, however, you also get a reduction in horsepower. In the low-rev range, there is plenty of power to launch you away from stoplights and drive-through tellers, but on the open road the R80RT lacks the long legs of the R100RT. Passing traffic often requires two downshifts, and even at legal speeds, the engine transmits a sort of urgency uncommon to BMWs. It remains smooth and quiet—perhaps more so than all but a handful of other machines—and it can keep pace with much larger bikes, but it doesn't have the leisurely feel of the R100RT. However, it still eats up the miles, feels light, handles very well, and fits the sport/touring bill the way a BMW should.

— Ken Vreeke

● I am hooked on the BMW R100RT—the biggest of the German tourers. It has just enough power to keep me happy, and the rest of the package meshes nicely with my idea of touring. The R80 has much the same basic personality, but unfortunately, it lacks the power I need. A good 550 will tear up the BMW in a speed contest and, to me, that's an unacceptable state of affairs in an 800-cc motorcycle, particularly one that sells for $5,490. The whole BMW mystique falls flat on its face when the machine is straining on uphills and tops out at 95 miles per hour on the flat. Touring on a BMW is supposed to be effortless and relaxing. Touring on the R80 is an exercise in gear shifting and engine revving, a constant search for power that isn't there.

—Jeff Karr

If you don't agree with Japanese machinery or it doesn't agree with you, BMW may be the Great Alternative. It's different from Japanese machinery—different, without being worse. Too often, "different" means "bad." But BMW manages to go its own way, without going a way that almost nobody wants to go. The 800 is my favorite BMW, smoother than either the 650 or the 1000 and with enough power for any reasonable human.

BMW should have quite a few good years in the near future. With its three-year warranty and price-competitiveness created by Harley's tariff, BMW could become a much more popular choice for riders looking for an alternative.

—Art Friedman

● With seven hefty road brutes in tow, it was always with a sigh of relief and with the anticipation of a few highway larks that I drew the BMW—the only bike on the tour which tipped the scales at near a quarter-ton. To me, it has the best seating position, best handling, and the most pleasing engine of the few tourers left with motors you can still hear and feel while bowling along at 60 miles per hour. I'm told that you have to make a paradigm shift when reviewing a BMW, much like the diplomatic pouch you casually slip over your head when roasting a Harley. Of course, the sidestands and centerstands still have flecks of primeval ooze clinging to their castings. Of course, the gas cap decides to lunch itself in Pivnik, Utah. Of course, the windscreen turns the world into an outtake from *The Beast at Fifty Fathoms*. And, of course, the price tag for this cobbiness is astronomical. The buck is weak against the mark—so what's a fella to do? At least BMW has now given us a shot at the RTs, some of the best touring bikes ever made, and for a cool grand less. With the tariff cafuffle looming, the price of admission could finally blow that paradigm shift right out of the water. A BMW for the price of an Oriental scoot? Tough choice, *mein Herr!*

—Paul Gordon

from the onrushing wind. The mirrors are mounted on little deflectors that angle the air away from your hands, and even in freezing climates, a thin pair of winter gloves will keep your hands warm.

Our only complaints center around the windscreen. It is adjustable for height and angle through two twist-knobs, but there doesn't seem to be any position that prevents helmet buffeting. Our testers ranged in height from five foot, six inches to six foot, three inches, and all of them cited the buffeting as an annoyance. Below 50 miles per hour, the screen works well, but at 55 miles per hour and above, things get a bit noisy.

None of us could live with the black piping around the screen's edge because it interfered with vision. Even with the piping removed, it is difficult to see through the screen. Near its edges, there is a good deal of distortion, and peering below it—where the plastic is wave-free—requires a hunchback posture. Looking over the screen, even when it is in the lowest position, requires stretching. Our screen also scratched easily, despite the use of a special plastic polish during bug removal.

The rest of the fairing, however, is faultless. There are two locking storage compartments (operated by the ignition key) that are large enough to store pocket-sized items. Two vents, located at hip-level within the cowling, operate with a twist of a knob and direct air at your legs or upper body depending on how they are adjusted. The fairing is solidly mounted and seems impervious to all crosswinds.

We highly recommend the factory luggage to anyone serious about touring. The ABS plastic bags are tough, well constructed, convenient, large, and waterproof. They can easily house a full-face helmet, feature sturdy hinges, latches, and brackets and can handle 22 pounds of junk in each side. Each bag can be removed in seconds through a latch, which does require some fiddling to unlock in the dead of night.

Some more complaints: The sidestands and centerstands fitted to the R80 are the worst in the business. With luggage, it honestly takes two people to safely hoist the R80 onto its centerstand. The bike must be counter-leaned past vertical to lower the long sidestand. Also, the clutching mechanism in our gas cap gave out when the cap was over-tightened, and it took a BMW mechanic and a drill to remove the assembly. Luckily, we had enough fuel in the tank to make it to a nearby dealer, who was very familiar with the problem. The fix was covered by the warranty.

That said, we can say that anyone can find happiness with BMW's R80RT. You're not going to outgun the Japanese competition, but then again, on the R80RT you probably won't want to. The R80RT is pleasant, very comfortable, light, durable, quiet, and a more precise handler than any big touring bike available, save the R100RT. It is indeed a successful alternative to the high-kinetic record-breakers offered by many manufacturers. BMW's latest RT is the kind of bike that turns a one-hour ride into a weeklong vacation.

The RT cockpit has few amenities, but keeps you toasty and dry in the foulest climes.

12

BMW R80ST

Photography by Paul Gordon & Rich Cox
Motorcyclist, October 1983

The Poise and Polish of the Sporty ST Evidences BMW's
Winning Formula: Give the Yanks What They Want.

Regard the BMW. Its peculiar balance of litheness and mass, the unique symmetry of its shape, the simplicity of its design, and the refinement of its finish make it a contemporary classic. From the smoothness of its frame welds to the brush strokes in its hand-laid pinstriping, the BMW positively reeks of Old World elegance and exclusivity.

But don't be fooled. The machine you see before you is far from a sclerotic old aristocrat struggling to survive. It is instead a shrewd blend of venerable tradition and financial viability. Aside from Honda, BMW is currently the only major motorcycle manufacturer enjoying profitable growth and bright prospects for the future. It owes its good health to an astute tailoring of product to market demand. Customers assailing dealers with cries of "Don't ever change" may be a short-term boon, but their loyalty is ultimately the kiss of death to a company striving to stay afloat in the post-boom marketplace. Though BMW has left its basic boxer power plant virtually unchanged for six decades, the company has carefully sifted rider feedback and constantly adjusted the style, design, and price of its machines to keep the marque's market niche strong and well fortified.

It may seem that BMW has fended off the onslaught of overmuscled Japanese upstarts by bending the wills of a few well-heeled buyers to its cause. But the new R80ST is a prime example of the company's increasing dedication to serving the demands of the lucrative U.S. market. It is the end product of a circuitous evolution, but the 798-cc ST is perhaps the most Americanized BMW to ever come down the autobahn.

The ST's bloodline can be traced directly to the R80/7, a sort of R100 "stripper" intended to snare those riders either unwilling to shell out the 1,000-cc machine's stiff asking price or uninterested in matching its performance. Over the years the R80/7 managed to build an enviable reputation as a middleweight workhorse. It was comfortable, reliable, and many felt it had a smoother, more pleasant motor than its bigger, more expensive brother. In 1981, however, the R80/7 was pulled from the export manifest, and replaced by the most radical motorcycle BMW has ever produced, the single-shock dual-purpose R80G/S—"G" for off-road and "S" meaning street in Beemerese.

However, while the G/S racked up scores of victories in European cross-country competition (most notably a pair of first-place finishes in the grueling Paris/Dakar rally), the idea of a 400-pound dirt bike appealed to few buyers not infected with chronic wanderlust. "After all," one BMW spokesman admitted recently, "who wants to ride a $5,000 trail bike in the woods?"

Stateside, the G/S received the same lukewarm reception in the showroom, but, in the hands of American buyers, the bike underwent a curious transformation. Owners tossed the 21-inch front wheel in favor of a 19-inch rim shod with street rubber, and the white-and-orange "trail bike" was even introduced to the road-racing circuit. Blessed with light weight, good ground clearance, and loads of low-end torque, the G/S began making a name for itself as a creditable pavement scratcher.

The trend did not go unnoticed in the boardrooms of BMW, and the G/S, while still available in its old dirt duds, was modified for all-street use. It is now offered to the public in the form of the R80ST.

The new ST really represents nothing more significant than the combining of all that was good about the old R80/7—namely the simplicity and smoothness of its motor—with the modified monolever chassis of the G/S. What is most remarkable about the ST is BMW's own unabashed affection for it. During a recent visit to the company's North American headquarters in Montvale, New Jersey, not a word was spoken about the traditional BMW virtues of reliability, low maintenance, and comfort. Instead, spokesmen glowed about the ST's flickability, engineers praised its high-speed stability, and technicians touted its racetrack prowess. One high-ranking employee pointed with pride to a heavily modified ST with an entire winter of labor and thousands of dollars invested to turn it into a hard-core café racer. All this enthusiasm for a bike that any fast-running 550 could snuff handily with one cylinder tied behind its back. Why? It was obvious that the long-standing BMW values of light weight and agility were being observed in the ST, but talk of racetracks and lap times was something new. At BMW, the ST is almost universally seen as a superlative handler, perhaps the best Munchen has ever produced.

Most obvious in the change from G/S to ST is the switch from a 21- to a 19-inch front wheel while a tire-hugging plastic fender has replaced the high-mounted, dirt-type mudguard of the G/S. For a number of reasons, spoked wheels were retained on the ST. The lightness and greater flexibility of wire wheels has been gospel in the engineering labs at BMW for years, but buyers demanded the low maintenance and contemporary look of cast spinners, and here the marketing department has always prevailed.

In designing the ST, however, with lightness at a premium, 40-spoke wheels with Akront rims were chosen. Spoked wheels may indeed require a little wrenching now and then to keep them running true, but a shiny new rim can be laced up for one-fifth the cost of replacing a damaged $400 cast wheel should a mishap occur. Many riders also appreciate the aesthetics of spoked wheels, and the ST's are beautifully crafted.

The front rim on the R80 is the same size as those affixed to the rest of the BMW line, from R65 to R100, a 1.85 shod with a 100/90-19 Metzeler Perfect tire. Out back, however, a wide 2.50 rim replaces the G/S's 2.15 unit, giving a super-wide footprint for the low-profile 120/90-18 Metzeler skin. The new Metzelers provide an extra margin of security when cornering at speed. They feel much more sticky and predictable than the high-mileage Continentals.

Other changes are more subtle. Spring rates have been stiffened, and the ST's wheel travel, both front and rear, is substantially shorter than the G/S's, still the ST front fork strokes a lanky 6.8 inches, while the swingarm travels 6 inches at the axle. BMW has never been drawn to the advantages of pneumatic preload in its front suspension components, so the ST has preset rates in the fork, while a three-tiered preload collar adjusts the gas-charged Bilstein rear shock. There is no provision for damping adjustment.

BMW's use of lightly damped, long-travel suspension is just the ticket for around-town riding. The stictionless fork and supple rear end soak up small and large bumps without transmitting any discomforting jolts to the rider, and the lightness and precision of the ST's steering make it a breeze to toss around. Similarly, the ST floats over freeway expansion joints and rain grooves with genteel stability, and 80-mile-per-hour cruising finds it settled down into an easy, loping pace that is both spritely and sedate. Engine pulses are more noticeable than the tingle produced by a modern multi, but is a pleasant, relaxing vibration that will appeal to those who prefer the roughness of corduroy to the textureless smoothness of satin.

The ST shares with all BMWs a predilection for the open road where its cushy ride and calm engine make it the mount of choice for long-distance touring. But, when hammered down a twisty back road at high speed, the ST's springy suspenders get all ungimballed. Inadequate rebound and compression damping in the rear make the shaft drive's rise and fall a limiting factor entering and exiting fast turns, and the spongy front fork produces excessive dive under hard braking. The Beemer moves around on its suspension more than other current bikes. The ST represents a step forward in suspension technology for BMW, but, in fast turns, it still feels like a heavy dirt bike balanced on long, slender legs. Pressed to perform at ten-tenths, the BMW becomes very sensitive to rider input and rides like a runaway horse best given its head rather than a firm hand at the controls. Full-goose crazies found themselves levered off their line by the sidestand in left-handers and the frame-mounted cylinder protection bars on the right, long before the Metzelers ran out of traction.

But c'mon. No one, not even a demented Yankee, buys a BMW to exorcise his or her speed demons. It's like asking Pavarotti to perform the splits—an intriguing exercise perhaps, but more revealing of the underlying motivations of the viewer than any real deficiency in the subject himself. So let's be fair. The ST is without doubt the most competent high-speed corner carver in the BMW fleet. BMWs, even the best-handling of the breed, are designed for devouring highway mileage in the easiest, most relaxing manner, and at this the ST excels.

First of all, the downsized power plant does indeed feel smoother than any BMW engine in recent memory. The 798-cc motor shares most of its major components with the 1,000-cc mill, but the bores are slimmed down 10 millimeters to 84.8 mm, necessitating a reduction in carb and valve sizes. The trio of "80s" in the BMW line—the G/S, the fully faired RT, and the ST—are all filled with 32-mm Bing constant-velocity carburetors in place of the R100's 40-mm mixers, and 2 millimeters have been shaved from the intake and exhaust valves which measure 42 mm and 38 mm respectively. Otherwise, the tried-and-true two-banger remains the same. Pushrods actuate rockers on a pair of overhead valves, and lash is taken up with threaded adjusters in a half-hour maintenance

You won't find an R80ST in my garage. I was tremendously aggravated by the bike's forward-sloping, slick-surfaced saddle, which sent me sliding forward every time I closed the throttle, hit a bump, or touched the brakes. Not only did that put me in an uncomfortable position, it banged my shins against the carbs, sometimes painfully. And it happened all the time, two or three times a block when I was in traffic.

Of course, once one of a bike's features begins to aggravate you as much as the slip-'n'-slide saddle did me, you begin to find all sorts of things that annoy you. Soon I was angry at the stands, the turn signal dash lights that became invisible in harsh sunlight, the fact that I kept missing second gear, the rear suspension action, the high-effort braking, and the up-and-down reaction of the chassis when you change throttle settings.

Although I'm normally inclined to view BMWs as bikes which are a viable alternative to the Asian horde, I certainly don't like the ST, even though it does have my favorite BMW engine.

—Art Friedman

I respect BMW for remaining unaffected by the technology wars that spur the Japanese to new heights of engine performance and handling, but I have to admit I'm not in love with the R80ST. It is light, it steers well, and it's a BMW at a reasonable price, but a BMW for a reasonable price is still very, very expensive. I can get used to the violent wrenching the shaft delivers on the application of throttle, but I'm not sure why I'm supposed to. I can deal with the lurching the ultrasoft suspension lets the chassis go through, but that doesn't mean I like it.

I don't think I can get used to the pointed seat, the tacky styling, or the perennially unusable BMW sidestands and centerstands.

The R100RS is nice enough and dramatic enough in styling and performance to help me overlook the shortcomings of the basic BMW design, but the R80ST is not, I'm afraid. If I wanted the German motorcycling experience, I'd buy a GPz550, and with the thousand or so dollars I'd saved, I'd fly back to Munich and take a week's tour of the Alps.

—Dexter Ford

Over the years I've managed to convince myself (and not without crushing a few sour grapes) that I'm just not a BMW kind of guy. Even in my dotage I intend to ride briskly, and the Beemer's placid pace and weirdly cockeyed drivetrain put me off fast riding, while the price puts me off my food.

But the BMW image in this country is currently undergoing a real change. Under the Butler & Smith regime in the 1970s, the marque was hobbled by stingy warranties, poor parts availability, and lousy service. But, since taking over in 1980, BMW has strived hard to make its product popular, and it is succeeding. Sales are up to 4,800, from a low of under 2,000 in 1980, and spokesmen project a U.S. market of 10,000 units within five years. With the ST's lightness, smoothness, and good handling manners, I have to admit the company is headed in the right direction. And for a measly $4,190—hell, that's what interceptors are going for in California—there might just be a BMW in my future after all.

—Paul Gordon

procedure every 5,000 miles. The ST incorporates all the modifications introduced into the 1981 BMW line: a lightweight flywheel, single-plate clutch assembly, and Nikasil aluminum cylinders, which have their bores impregnated with crystals of silicone carbide for tighter tolerances and a super-hard finish.

The factory rates the 800's output at 50 horsepower versus 65 for the 1000. The ST pulls with unhurried but earnest enthusiasm from 3,000 rpm, and its power builds smoothly and progressively. One or two strokes of the long-throw shift lever are required to keep the ST humming when passing uphill with a passenger aboard, but the ST is definitely quicker than the fully faired RT, both in roll-on and acceleration contests. It tops out at about 110 miles per hour.

On the highway the ST pots along at double-nickel velocity in top gear with the tach needle indicating a little over halfway to the 7,500-rpm redline, which is a trifle busier than the bigger Beemers at cruising speed. When modifying the R80/7 to G/S

BMW R80ST

Suggested retail price:	$4,190	**Rear brake:**	Single-leading-shoe drum, rod-operated
Warranty:	36 months, unlimited miles	**Front tire:**	100/90H 19 Metzeler RILLE 16
Number of U.S. dealers:	257	**Rear tire:**	120/90H 18 Metzeler Perfect ME99A
Recommended maintenance intervals:	5,000 miles	**Rake/trail:**	30 degrees/5.07 in. (129 mm)

Suggested retail price: $4,190
Warranty: 36 months, unlimited miles
Number of U.S. dealers: 257
Recommended maintenance 5,000 miles
intervals:

ENGINE
Type: Air-cooled, horizontally opposed Four-stroke twin
Valve arrangement: OHV, two valves, operated by pushrods and rockers, threaded adjusters
Displacement: 797.5 cc
Bore x stroke: 84.8x70.6 mm
Compression ratio: 8.2:1
Carburetion: Two, 32-mm Bing constant-velocity
Ignition: Battery-powered, inductive, two magnetic triggers
Lubrication: Wet sump, 2.4 qts.
Charging output: 280 watts AC
Battery: 12-volt, 16 AH

DRIVETRAIN
Primary transmission: Helical gears, 1:1
Clutch: Dry, single-plate
Final drive: Shaft, 3.36:1

CHASSIS
Front suspension: 36-mm leading axle, 6.8-in. travel
Rear suspension: One Boge damper, 6-in. wheel travel, adjustment for spring preload
Front brake: One, double-action Brembo caliper, 260-mm disc

Rear brake: Single-leading-shoe drum, rod-operated
Front tire: 100/90H 19 Metzeler RILLE 16
Rear tire: 120/90H 18 Metzeler Perfect ME99A
Rake/trail: 30 degrees/5.07 in. (129 mm)
Wheelbase: 57.7 in. (1,465 mm)
Seat height, unladen: 33.0 in. (838 mm)
Fuel capacity: 5.1 gal (20 L)
Weight: 452 lbs. (206 kg) wet; 421lbs. (191kg) tank empty
Colors: Red or silver
Instruments: Speedometer, odometer, tripmeter, tachometer; lights for turn signals, neutral, high beam, generator failure, and low oil pressure

PERFORMANCE
Fuel consumption: 31 to 52 mpg, 41.5 mpg avg.
Average touring range: 212 miles
Best quarter-mile acceleration: 13.74 sec., 93.5 mph
200-yd. top-gear acceleration from 50 mph: 73.0-mph terminal speed
RPM at 60 mph, top gear: 3,991
Calculated speed in gears at (redline): 7,500
First 38 mph
Second 58 mph
Third 80 mph
Fourth 100 mph
Fifth 112 mph
Speedometer error: 30 mph, actual 26.4; 60 mph, actual 53.9

	1983 BMW R80ST	1983 YAMAHA XJ900	1983 BMW R80RT
Price	$4,190	$3,699	$5,490
Wet Weight	452 lbs.	537 lbs.	540 lbs.
Quarter-Mile Time	13.74 sec., 93.5 mph	11.90 sec., 113.2 mph	14.57 sec., 85.9 mph
Average Fuel Consumption	41.5 mpg	41.3 mpg	36.1 mpg
High-Speed Pass, Terminal Speed	73.0 mph	78.0 mph	71.6 mph
Average Touring Range	212 miles	240 miles	227 miles

specs in 1981, the old final drive reduction ratio of 3.2:1 was increased slightly to 3.36:1. This shorter ratio has been retained on the ST, which, compared with the 1000's 2.9:1 ratio, accounts for approximately 550 more rpm at 60 miles per hour. The faster-spinning engine gives the twin a little more grunt for passing, but it takes its toll in increased fuel consumption. Our ST's mileage ranged from a best of 52 miles per gallon to 31 miles per gallon. With the 5.1-gallon gas tank, the ST has an average range of 212 miles between necessary stops.

The act of traveling that distance is greatly eased by the addition of a new seat this year. The old G/S saddle, while admirably soft and supple at first, had an annoying habit of collapsing into a butt-numbing torture rack after only a few months of service. Happily, that situation has now been remedied by BMW's return to good old Dupont foam rubber for lining the saddle pans. While breaking in the new seat is an excruciating experience for the first thousand miles or so, the initial agony is well worth the years of solid support afforded by the foam. The seat has also been reshaped slightly for added comfort.

The riding position on the ST is just what the times demand, that is, a conservative posture with one's weight placed squarely on the spine. If the seat were poor, this would result in exquisite pain after a few hours, but, as it is, the ST is pleasant to ride for long distances. The high handlebar has a comfortable bend, the pegs are in the right place, and passengers report the rear half of the stepped saddle rivals the cockpit of the most luxurious tourers for comfort and roominess. The upswept exhaust pipe, shielded by plastic and metal shrouds, posed no comfort problems except to one tester who swore he felt the bike listing slightly to the left to balance its offset weight.

The single Brembo disc up front took about 500 miles of constant use to burnish in, and, while it does an adequate job of hauling the Beemer down from speed, it cannot match the stopping power of the twin-disc R80RT.

While we've now tiptoed into negativity, we might as well clean the slate of niggling annoyances: The single horn is too weak to be heard, the turn signal indicator lights aren't bright enough, and, during the road test, our ST's left fork leg began to weep 20-weight tears. But by far the biggest bone we have to pick with the ST concerns its standing apparatus. The spring-loaded sidestand is a spindly, malevolent device always ready to catch you unaware and pitch your pride and joy on its ear, while the equally unstable center-stand is a masterpiece of the chiropractor's art, requiring two healthy he-men and a length of Ace bandage to operate correctly. After years of suffering with one infernal contraption after another, we feel the stands attached to the current crop of BMWs would be better tossed into the ocean and the unsold inventory of bikes left to lean against the responsible engineers until a workable solution is reached. The stands are currently the most serious flaw in an otherwise well-executed piece of design.

But, all in all, we must conclude that the ST, with its 36-month warranty, high-quality optional saddlebags, and $4190 price tag, is as competitive in this market as any BMW to date. The ST couldn't hope to be a take-no-prisoners back-road straightener without major chassis work and more power. Still, it will capture a lot of hearts just being what it is—a lightweight, torquey sport/tourer that wears the magic blue-and-white BMW crest, tailored to American taste.

BMW K100 FOUR

Photography by Rich Cox & Ken Vreeke
Motorcyclist, February 1984

13

Completely New, Completely BMW

Sixty years have passed since the introduction of BMW's venerable boxer twin. In that time, man has unveiled secrets of the universe, launched himself toward the stars, and invented devices such as the fully automated robot, the four-slice toaster, and the microchip. We have become expert on such matters as disposable income and the dangers of plutonium, while the masters at BMW have held steadfast to their seemingly arcane belief that people still yearn for old-world craftsmanship and returnable investment.

Many view BMW's age-old boxer as the result of corporate tightfistedness and the hard-headed refusal of some people to dangle their lot into the fires of current technology, for fear of getting royally burned by the Japanese.

This convenient manner of thinking simply happens to be dead wrong. BMW has never built mainstream machines and probably never will if the motorcycle you see before you is any indication. Scheduled to arrive in the United States in 1985, the BMW K100, the sporty K100RS, and the touring K100RT siblings represent a new era in BMW tradition that began on the Bavarian drawing boards 10 years ago. In 1976 Suzuki introduced the revolutionary GS750 four to combat the Kawasaki and Honda fours; AMF still owned Harley-Davidson; Triumph motorcycles were plentiful; Johnny Cecotto won Daytona on Yamaha's only 4-cylinder, the TZ700; a BMW boxer twin won the Superbike race at Daytona; Hodaka proudly displayed its Thunderdog; and, significantly, the Honda Gold Wing was in its second year of record sales.

During this time, the winds of change blew through the BMW design center and teams of engineers molded modern motorcycles, while marketing wizards desperately tried to predict nebulous future trends and select one design from the many.

The visionary musings of one Stefan Pachernegg, a young Austrian engineer who cut his design teeth at Puch before signing with BMW, focused on building an engine that would not only meet the performance criteria set forth, but also further BMW's tradition of serviceability, reliability, and uniqueness in what would surely become a highly sophisticated and Japanese-dominated market. Drawing from BMW's great wealth of technology, Pachernegg produced an engine that closely paralleled BMW's current automobile engines.

Other designs were built and tested by various engineering teams. A horizontally opposed flat four was ready for introduction in the early 1970s, only to be scrapped by the arrival of Honda's nearly identical Gold Wing. Also a V-4 and a triple, et al. were tried. And while some designs had major flaws, others showed promise. Pachernegg pushed for the K100 project, and in an act of sheer clairvoyance, BMW decided to give it the green light over the alternate designs. If

BMW had decided banked on the V-4, the company would have found itself repeating the flat-four debacle and customers who buy BMWs to avoid the mainstream might have aimed their dollars elsewhere.

Yet one look at the K100 tells you that although it branches rather far out on the family tree, its roots are firmly entrenched in rich BMW heritage. This new motorcycle with blatant modern overtones has been spared the filigree and festoonery which often accompany contemporary offerings from the Orient. It is BMW through and through, as it is: supple, stark, dignified, comfortable, maneuverable, light, and uncharacteristically fast. From its Muth-designed bodywork to its single-shock Monolever rear suspension, this motorcycle begs for long, hard rides by those with rich enough tastes and deep enough pockets to afford it.

Aside from its unique appearance, there is a hidden genius in the K100. For example, turn indicators pop in and out easily in the event of a parking lot tip-over; the rear wheel, with a swingarm on only the right side, can be removed in about six minutes; the taillight dislodges from the tail section without tools in about two minutes; the valve cover, on the left side of the engine, comes off in minutes to expose the double overhead camshafts and adjusting shims on top of buckets, a special tool is required for quick shim adjustment without camshaft removal; and the crankshaft, the 2-piece rods and the pistons can be pulled out from the right side of the engine once the lower-end cover has been removed. All of this can be accomplished, without removing the engine from the frame, which makes quite a handy workstand. More remarkable still, the aforementioned disassembly can be performed using no more than the owner's manual and the standard, tucked-in-the-tail BMW tool kit.

Though the K100 promises the low-maintenance tradition of the boxers, this ironically is the kind of motorcycle you want to take apart. Every little piece, from the self-centering case bolts, to the beefy Asllen head chassis bolts, to the non-stressed Nylok nuts, seems foolproof and designed to make even the worst hack a proficient fiddler.

If the engine resembles a car engine on its side, it's because that is fundamentally what it is. The single-piece forged crankshaft, located off center to the right and supported

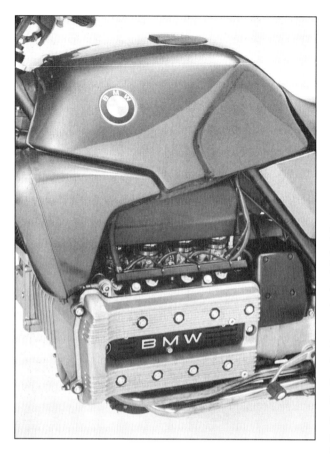

A removable plate in the center of the valve cover hides and protects the plug leads.

by five sturdy automotive-type plain bearings and seven crank webs, spins clockwise while the large, single-plate dry clutch, powerful 460-watt alternator and auxiliary jackshaft, all driven directly by a spur gear at the rearmost end of the crankshaft, spin in opposition to compensate for the torque reaction in longitudinal crank engines. This system makes the K100 engine virtually torque-reaction free.

Power is fed directly through the clutch, 5-speed transmission and lightweight damper-equipped hollow drive shaft to the rear hub where it makes its one and only 90-degree bend through 2.91:1 bevel gears before launching you on your way. This straight shot of power to the rear hub avoids the power loss that occurs with more complex driveline deviations. The patented Compact Drive System is also free of the bothersome lash that always accompanies the opposed twins.

In the boxer, the shaft's engine coupling was located nearly an inch and a half in front of the swingarm pivot, which meant the driveshaft had to become longer and shorter in relation to the swingarm as it moved through its suspension arc. To accomplish this, a sliding spline coupler attached the driveshaft to the rear-wheel gearset. Slip-fit clearances had to be added in an already convoluted driveline and the result was more free play and subsequent clunking during sudden power fluctuations.

The two pivots in the K100 are now concentric and move in unison, thus negating the need for sliding splines. With two large dampers incorporated in front of the clutch and behind the gearbox, driveline shock has been kept to a minimum and the system must be ranked among the most glitch-free we've tried.

In addition to these internal changes, the old tubular driveshaft housing/swingarm is now cast aluminum and heavily webbed for additional torsional rigidity. The long engine, however, necessitates a shorter swingarm than the previous boxers' to keep the wheelbase down to 59.7 inches, which is two inches longer than the R100. Honda and Suzuki have long known the advantages of a lengthy shaft to combat rise and fall during throttle transitions, and while we have to admit the K100's rear end antics are more exaggerated than the best shaft-equipped bikes we've tested, they are less pronounced than the boxers'.

There are two other gears driven by the crankshaft's rear gear. One, above the clutch, spins a 460-watt alternator, powerful enough to provide juice for every accessory known to mankind. The other turns an auxiliary jackshaft just below and parallel to the crankshaft, that powers the oil pump and water pump located at the front of the engine.

This latter shaft will play a far more important role in another motorcycle which BMW plans to introduce next year. Based on the K100, that machine will have only three cylinders and displace 750 cc. The jackshaft will do double duty as a balancing shaft to quell secondary vibration. The 750 is top secret and its existence is officially denied, so you didn't hear about it here.

Exclusivity aside, the K100 had to meet certain performance criteria, namely the ability to produce 90 horsepower without straining, zero to 60 miles per hour acceleration in four seconds, 120-miles per hour cruising speeds and solid yet nimble handling—all without busting the weight scales. BMW achieved all it set out to do with the K100, except perhaps attain the rather lofty cruising speed. Our bike was wound tight at 120 miles per hour, though taller gearing has been fitted to the K100RS and is available in Europe as an option to the K100 and K100RT.

Void of coolant and oil, the longitudinally mounted DOHC, 987 cc in-line engine weighs in at 168 pounds. It hangs from the tubular frame rather than being cradled, and bolts solidly to serve as a stressed member without the intervention of rubber engine mounts. Though the engine is wide and somewhat cumbersome in appearance, it locates its center of gravity low in traditional BMW fashion. And despite being wide, our most ardent asphalt scratcher was never remotely close to banging the cases on the ground during hard cornering, an improvement on the ground-up valve covers we returned on a number of previously tested boxers. However, if you drop this baby at speed, it will slide down the road on rather large and expensive engine components unless someone finds a place to hang protective engine guards.

Power-producing engine components follow current design practices. The longish 70-milimeter stroke and 67-milimeter bore lay the foundation for a smooth power curve, and BMW claims the engine reaches 85 percent of its maximum torque output at 3,500 rpm, building steadily to its 8,600 rpm redline. Camshafts, driven from the front end of the crankshaft by a single, automatically tensioned roller chain, ride against adjusting shims above bucket tappets which control 34-milimeter intake and 28-milimeter exhaust valves. The valves lie in different planes within the compact combustion chamber to create additional turbulence around the centrally located spark plugs. The cam lobes ride slightly off center against the shims, ensuring the shims rotate within the buckets with each actuation of the valves. This distributes shim wear more evenly and prolongs valve adjustment intervals.

To keep the engine aslight and short, fore and aft, as possible, the cylinders had to be compact. A shallow 19-degree valve angle not only provides greater latitude in valve timing but guarantees that the combustion chamber can be made small as well. BMW also used its Scanimet, nickel-silicone carbide, coating to line the cylinder bores rather than the recently disposed iron liners. This coating provides greater thermal conductivity than iron liners, takes up less space, since close bore centers are of paramount importance, is much lighter, and far more durable. Flat-top pistons provide a clean surface for efficient burning and set compression ratio at 10.2:1.

Airbox access is hassle-free on the simple, yet porky, right side of the 987cc engine.

Removing four bolts sets the rear wheel free for roadside repairs in about 10 minutes.

Instrument pod is informative and uncluttered. Handlebar switches take some getting used to.

To cut frictional losses, BMW has liquid cooled the K100 engine. Coolant circulates through the aluminum cylinder head and is routed through a large 18-row radiator mounted in front of the engine and adorned with a kidney-shaped cowling. An electronic fan, located behind the radiator and triggered thermostatically, kicks in automatically at 215 degrees F.

Centerpiece in the K100's new engine is the Bosch LE-Jetronic digital fuel-injection unit, a variant of the injection system BMW has been using in its cars for years. Designed specifically for the K100, the LE-Jetronic system utilizes a computerized brain located under the seat to set duration, and thus quantity, of the injection by monitoring air temperature and pressure within the intake port, coolant temperature and engine speed. An electronic fuel pump, immersed within the K100's aluminum fuel tank, ensures delivery of a steady stream of fossils to the injector units.

An electronic Bosch ignition system, triggered at the front end of the crankshaft, is mounted just behind the steering head under the fuel tank. In addition to providing spark, this system serves as a rev limiter by retarding ignition advance to slow engine speed at 8,600 rpm. At 8,750 rpm, the black box switches off the injection system entirely until the engine drops back down to proper operating revs. It is an effective system of extending engine life, though the shut-off comes rather unexpectedly as there is little engine noise, vibration or sudden surge of power at high revs to inform the rider he is about to be restrained. A watchful eye on the electronic tachometer is required to maintain a brisk pace.

BMW's first four delivers performance heretofore unheard of in BMW's lineup. It dispatched the 1/4 mile in 12.40 seconds at 108 miles per hour and produced a linear power curve that surpasses most contemporary transverse fours. In our top-gear passing tests, the K100 accelerated to 80.5 miles per hour from 50 miles per hour in 200 yards. By comparison, the R100RS only managed 76.7 miles per hour, and Yamaha's XJ900 Seca could muster only 78.0 miles per hour in the same tests. During one testing excursion, we brought along a Suzuki GS850G and faced it off against the K100 in roll-on tests. The K100 showed a slight advantage over the GS from about 3,000 rpm to about 7,000 rpm, when it really began to leave the GS behind. There is no burst of power at high revs, nor is the K100 engine particularly cammy. Rather, it feels as though the engine gets the best of its slightly heavy flywheels at high revs. Horsepower continues to build impressively as the engine nears redline.

If there is an Asian similarity in the K100, it is that the engine doesn't devour miles in great breathless strides like the big boxers. Instead, there is a definite Oriental sense about the motor, a kind of urgency that will find the seasoned BMW rider searching for another gear. And it's not that the engine necessarily works harder than the phlegmatic boxer did at strato-cruise speeds. It doesn't. At 60 miles per hour, the K100 is spinning at an easy 3,800 rpm, just 300 rpm more than the R100RS at the same speed. But the boxer's lazy lope, which stirred your senses with the relaxed, muffled clicking of happy valve gear and subdued engine rumble, has been replaced with an extremely quiet power plant that impresses you only with a high-frequency tingle through the rubber-mounted handlebar, seat and thick rubber footrests. The tingling sensation is not particularly bothersome.; it is just unusual for a BMW. The K100 is not overextended at high speeds; it simply hums a different tune than the boxer. Its battle cry is more banshee-like.

This is in keeping with BMW's desire to preserve countenance amid more sporting aspirations. And BMW is banking that the trade-off is worthwhile. We think it is. The K100 is faster in every way than all previous BMWs and is far more glitch-free and easy to ride at all speeds. It can't even be compared to the boxer but rather begs comparison with current leading-edge Japanese machinery.

Aside from a flat spot in the power curve just above idle, the K100 responds immediately to throttle inputs. There is a rather large gap from first to second gear; the K100 leaps with ease, but the other four cogs are closely spaced and offer the rider a wide choice of gears for a given turn. The shifting action ranks tops with us. With such linear power, the rider can more or less shift when he feels like it, rather than knuckle under to the engine's demands. The single-plate clutch is smooth, predictable, sturdy, and requires little effort at the lever to operate. However, the point of engagement is rather narrow, like the boxer's, and requires an acquired touch to prevent lurching starts. Some of our testers never got the hang of it and pogoed from almost every stoplight. Others more accustomed to riding BMWs had few problems.

The typical but now somewhat subdued rise-and-fall effect of the BMW shaft takes some getting used to as well. Sudden on-off throttle transitions have the chassis bounding up and down on its suspension and can present problems if

Integrated taillight pops out in seconds. Note rack and passenger grab handles.

You might expect the engine to be excessively wide, but it's not. Note sturdy fork.

The valve cover comes off quickly to expose the K100's compact valve gear. A special tool allows rapid replacement of the adjusting shims without camshaft removal.

you ride erratically through corners. The massive 41.4-milimeter fork and single rear shock are lightly sprung and lightly damped to provide a smooth ride; few machines can match the suppleness of the K100's suspension components. But this also provides little resistance to shaft-induced gyrations. You have to control the shaft effect yourself; the motorcycle won't do it for you.

The K100's fork is the most compliant and sturdy unit ever slid under the BMW crest. You will be hard pressed to bottom the front end since it has over seven inches of travel. Even though the nonadjustable fork is fitted with light springs, more rebound damping would slow extension during sudden throttle transitions.

BMW was obviously serious about producing a stable front end as evidenced by the unusually large 22-milimeter-diameter hollow axle and four widely spaced pinch bolts that clamp it in place. There is no need for a fork brace on this motorcycle.

A set of double-action aluminum Brembo calipers squeeze two large 285mm stainless steel discs up front that are slotted for additional cooling and to allow an avenue for water dispersal. Brake pads are semimetallic in compound for consistent braking action in the wet. Having ridden the K100 for over 300 miles in rain, we can attest to the effectiveness of the brakes in inclement conditions. They are powerful yet require only a two-fingered effort at the lever to lock the wheel at speed.

The front brake lines, devoid of extraneous anti-drive apparatus, exit the master cylinder under the handlebar and out of harm's way. The single line then passes through the steering head where it splits and dives to the calipers. This method, also used to hide all the K100 wiring within the frame tubes, provides additional protection while resulting in clean, uncluttered lines.

There is another 285mm disc at the rear, and like the front brake, it provides powerful, predictable action with little effort, though it is prone to initiating some hopping in the rear wheel when used in harness with hard engine deceleration. This only happens during extreme braking on rough road surfaces and was only experienced by a minority of our testers. Part of the problem stems from the rear shock unit itself, which lacks both sufficiently stiff springing and enough damping under the circumstances.

The rear end is set up just like the front. Soft and lightly damped, the Monolever system provides admirable compliance to bumps of all sizes. In an effort to control the shaft effect, BMW has limited rear wheel travel to 4.3 inches. Preload can be adjusted to any one of three positions through a ramp-type collar; we found the middle position the most versatile. At its softest setting, the suspension is smooth on the highway but sinks more than we like during hard cornering. The stiffest position is best suited to two-up riding.

While the 540-pound (wet) K100 is, on balance, a most versatile speed merchant, it shines brightest on long, fast, twisting roads. With a rather long wheelbase or nearly 60 inches, steep 27.5-degree steering-head angle and 3.9 inches of trail, the K100 is at once light-steering, responsive and unflinchingly stable. You can wait until the last possible second to dive the K100 into a fast corner, and then proceed the way you would dare on a leading Japanese weapon. The suspension settles evenly and predictably into a corner, and steering remains dead neutral at all lean angles. Most impressive is the fact that you can brake spiritedly while banked way over, and the K100 displays no tendency to stand back up. It stays right where you put it.

The entire crankshaft assembly can be pulled out of the engine once the right side cover has been removed. A handy fiddler could probably do it in under an hour.

Low-speed corners require more accurate control over the throttle and subsequent shaft effect for smooth transitions, but the K100 can get in and out of a tight turn on the tail pipes of the best sport/touring machines available. You may, if you push hard enough, hear the centerstand tang and footpegs graze the tarmac, but nothing touches down solidly enough to shake your confidence.

The K100 displays such good road-holding manners partially because BMW fit the machine with a wide 2.5-inch front wheel and wider 2.75-inch rear wheel, both shod with large and sticky Pirelli Phantom tires. We don't know if the K100 will be delivered to the U.S. next year with this same rubber, but we know that in Europe this year both Metzeler and Dunlop skins are also fitted at the factory.

Exploiting the K100's sporting prowess will get you about 37 miles down the road for each gallon of fuel. But a more stately pace on the open highway can easily return 49 mpg. And it is not until you settle into an easy interstate pace that you begin to notice the sundry items that tie the K100 more closely to its Bavarian roots. The instrument panel, for instance, is modern yet purposeful. Two large analog dials keep you informed of your highway speed and rpm, while a small LCD indicator keeps you appraised of gear selection. There is also a small LCD clock nestled between the speedo and tach. Standard warning lights are fitted for oil level, battery charge and water temperature, and there is a red warning light that switches off after using both brakes to tell you that your brake system is still in working condition. Another light remains on as long as the handlebar-mounted choke lever is activated, and there are two warning lights that signal fuel level. All of this fits into an uncluttered, easily read instrument panel.

Building a motorcycle that encompasses the almost polarized characteristics of sporting and touring machines is a lofty ambition. Machines that have tried to unite the two often create a fragile coexistence that falls into a gray area of the marketplace. In this land of the choke-hold speed limit, we don't need machines capable of nine-tenths cornering that are also stable, comfortable, quiet and underextended at 110-mph cruising speeds. Maybe in Europe, where speed limits are set at redline in top gear, the sport/touring juxtaposition makes good sense, but in America it is more sensible to have a ten-tenths cornering machine that is adequate at 55 mph, or a less frenetic tourer that rides like a cloud on the open road.

Therefore, sport/touring machines in America must be something special to stand out. I have long felt that BMW knows exactly what that special something is, and the K100 furthers that belief. It is fun of a unique sort. It's the difference between sipping 30-year-old brandy while tugging on a fine cigar in front of a warm fire at the yacht club and knocking back the beers in the garage with your buddies. You can still get roaring drunk; you just get there a different way.

—Ken Vreeke

Idling there, it deceived me. Its four-cylinder sound was so conventional that I forgot what I was dealing with. As soon as I let out the clutch, I was forcefully reminded. The bike lurched forward. I pulled the clutch in and let it out again. Another lurch. Then I remembered: this is a BMW; it has a narrow clutch engagement point.

I had been briefed on the handlebar switches earlier. Let's see, down on the right to signal right. Up with the right thumb to cancel. Down on the left for left signal. Up on the ... oops, that's the horn. Up on the right to cancel. Hmm. There is still a light glowing on the dash. What is it trying to tell me? Is that a fan? No, it's a choke. Turn the choke off. Good, at least the choke lever is in a conventional location.

The shifting is smoother than before, but you have to turn the throttle a long way to reach WFO. Instruments are easier to read too. Let's take the winding road home.

A little nose dive when using the decent brakes, but the shaft effect has been largely disposed of. Less flywheel effect, driveline clunk and engine torque reaction too. The low-end power is almost automotive. Typically soft BMW damping. Nice, reasonably precise, light steering. Lighter than I expected. Comfortable and confident.

Here comes the freeway. Nice ride at this speed, but a bit of buzz in the pegs. I don't like the bar angle at all. Hope they change it

for the U.S. It passes easily. Oops, honked the horn accidentally again. The lights sure brighten things up tonight, but some running lights would be nice.

Time to head for home. Boy, did the guy on the R100S do a double take. Hi, I'm home. The handle makes centerstanding a cinch, and the stand has a wider stance too. Good deal. Turn the key off and ... you mean I still have to fumble for the fork lock in the dark? Come on!

All in all, impressive. I'll be most interested to see the RT version. Should be deluxe.

—Art Friedman

I'm very glad BMW chose to put its time and development money into the K100; it's good for the motorcycle business for European and American companies to show their technological muscle now and then. The Japanese are advancing the state of motorcycle technology at an unreachable pace, but it's nice to see at least one Western company trying some new ideas on the buying public.

As a piece of sculpture, the K100 is unrivaled; the design of the bodywork, the glorious aluminum castings and the perfect candy-apple red finish make the K bike worthy of inclusion in any museum's industrial design section. It's the first motorcycle I've seen in the past 10 years I would not hesitate to call beautiful.

I have problems with some of the functional aspects of the K, however. The shaft effect is still there, very definitely, making hard changes in the lower gears violent and unsettling. Even though suspension travel is shorter than on the boxers, the rebound damping is still ultra-limp; this puzzles me substantially, because more rebound is the one fix that would help tame the errant shaft.

The riding problems I have with the K could be easily fixed. The next question is the price: Is the K100 worth three GS850s? If I were a rich man, the answer would be yes. The GS850 was made to use, to ride, to leave out in the rain. The K100 is to own. I can't think of a sweeter machine to admire.

—Dexter Ford

I'm drawn to the K100 more as a lover of machines than as a motorcyclist. Something about the way the BMW's pieces fit together brings to mind my classic old Hoover vacuum cleaner. And as odd as that may sound, that's a favorable association. The BMW's bodywork is quite nice, but the engine and driveline are at the core of what makes the K100 so appealing to me. The motor is more than engineered, it is styled. The various internal pieces are wrapped in contoured aluminum castings, all finished with a natural aluminum matte surface. Someone in Germany wanted the K100 engine to have a certain look and a definite personality. They succeeded. My old Hoover has the same sort of attention to form—sure it looks dated now, but the lovesome designer had for the damn thing when it was on the drawing board is still obvious today.

Today's Japanese engines aren't consciously styled in this way. The internal engine components seem to have been arranged in space, then dipped in hot, gooey aluminum. In the finished piece, you can see every shaft, boss and stud, even as they lie buried in the metal that covers it all. A Japanese motor has no secrets from the viewer.

The BMW offers a snapshot of the way things used to be; back then, the functional starkness of today was considered merely uninspired design. A designer should go at least a little out of his way to pretty up the lines of the machinery, the logic ran. BMW has done that with the K100. The best part is that under those artful castings lies very modern technology.

—Jeff Karr

The self-canceling turn-indicator switches (one on each side) operate within the sweep of the rider's thumbs so that he need not loosen his grip to use them. They are manually canceled by lifting the right thumb. Dual horns, mounted in the louvered headlight nacelle, are operated by the left thumb and are loud enough to startle the most narcoleptic driver. Some of our testers could not get used to the unusual switches and each lane change was a symphony of frantic jabs and horn-honking buffoonery. Others found the system sensible and easy to use. The headlight is large and powerful enough to replicate a swath of daylight on a moonless night.

While the seating position could be labeled European in the way it cants the rider into the wind, it is supremely comfortable on the open road and diabolically purposeful in the swervery. The handlebar is short and stubby but doesn't put undue pressure on the rider's arms. The seat is deep and wide enough to comfortably support a rider through a nonstop 250-mile tank of gas, and the footpeg location is back far enough and sufficiently low to allow quick maneuvering without cramping the legs on long rides. Overall ergonomics could best be described as comfy for both rider and passenger. There are even integrated grab handles in the seat for the passenger. The K100 is the most comfortable BMW ever offered, and the faired RS and RT promise to be even more luxurious.

BMW aficionados will be happy to note that the fuse box, previously housing cheesy porcelain fuses in the headlight, has been moved behind the left side panel, is easily accessible, and also houses Bosch's new plug-type glass fuses.

All electronic components and connectors are housed in weather-resistant compartments under the seat and tank, and there are two large storage areas that can keep gloves and belongings dry while still holding the tool kit, tire-repair kit and hazardous-duty first-aid kit.

And, yes, BMW also redesigned the side- and centerstands. A spring-loaded folding handle located below the left side panel on the frame tube allows the rider to pop the K100 up onto its centerstand with ease. Now located farther back than the old boxer stand, the centerstand lifts the rear wheel off the ground rather than the front and no longer generates hernias. The sidestand, still spring loaded, is cast, not stamped, and can

BMW K100 FOUR

Suggested retail price: NA
Warranty: 36 months, unlimited miles
Number of U.S. dealers: 257
Recommended maintenance intervals: 4650 miles

ENGINE
Type: Water-cooled, longitudinal in-line 4-stroke four
Valve arrangement: DOHC, 2 valves operated by buckets, adjusting shims on top
Displacement: 987cc
Bore x stroke: 67 x 70mm
Compression ratio: 10.2:1
Carburetion: Bosch LE-Jetronic fuel injection, 4, 34mm venturis
Ignition: Battery-powered Bosch digital system, electronic
Lubrication: Wet sump, 3.8 qt.
Charging output: 460 watts
Battery: 12V, 20AH

DRIVETRAIN
Primary transmission: Straight cut gears, 1:1
Clutch: Dry, single plate
Final drive: Shaft, 2.91:1

Gear	Internal Ratio	mph per 1000 rpm	mph at redline (8300)
1	4.50	6	48
2	2.96	9	73
3	2.30	11	94
4	1.88	14	115
5	1.67	16	130

CHASSIS
Front suspension: 41.4mm BMW, 7.3 in. travel
Rear suspension: Single BMW damper, 4.3 in. wheel travel; adjustment for spring preload
Front brake: 2, double-action Brembo calipers, 285mm discs
Rear brake: Double-action Brembo caliper, 285mm disc
Front wheel: 2.50 x 18 in.; cast aluminum
Rear wheel: 2.75 x 17 in.; cast aluminum

Front tire: 100/90V18 Pirelli Phantom MT29
Rear tire: 130/90V17 Pirelli Phantom MT28
Rake/trail: 27.5∞/3.9 in. (101mm)
Wheelbase: 59.7 in. (1516mm)
Seat height, unladen: 32.7 in. (831mm)
Seat height, with 160-lb rider: 30.2 in. (774mm)
Fuel capacity: 5.8 gal (22L)
Weight: 540 lb (244kg) wet
506 lb (229kg) tank empty
Colors: Red or silver
Instruments: Speedometer, tachometer, odometer, tripmeter, LCD clock, LCD gear indicator; warning lights for oil level, battery charge, water temperature, brake failure, high beam, fuel level, choke on, neutral, turn signals
Speedometer error: 30 mph, actual 29.6
60 mph, actual 60.0

PERFORMANCE
Fuel consumption: 37 to 49 mpg, 43.0 mpg avg.
Average touring range: 249 miles
Average 200-yd. top-gear acceleration from 50 mph: 80.5 mph terminal speed
Best 1/4-mile acceleration: 12.40 sec., 108.2 mph
Projected best 1/4-mile acceleration*: 12.27 sec., 109.5 mph

*Projected performance with test-session weather conditions corrected to sea level standard conditions (59 degrees F, 29.92 in. of mercury).

	1984 BMW K100	1983 Yamaha XJ900 Seca	1983 BMW R100RS	1983 Suzuki GS1100ES
Price	NA	$3699	$7025	$4350
Quarter-mile time	12.40/108.2	11.90/113.2	13.28/98.9	11.33/119.7
Wet Weight	540 lb	537 lb	544 lb	568 lb
High speed pass, terminal speed	80.5 mph	78.0 mph	76.7 mph	85.5 mph
Average fuel consumption	43.0 mpg	41.3 mpg	44.7 mpg	42.6 mpg
Average touring range	249 miles	240 miles	281 miles	247 miles

be operated from the saddle by long-legged riders. Those of us of dwarf proportions need both feet on the ground to avoid sidestand disaster.

While other manufacturers adhere to wild and intimidating marketing tactics to lure the buying dollar, BMW has chosen, as always, to coddle the buyer, to provide refuge from a stormy marketplace that once displayed some kind of order. In the K100, BMW has flown in the face of monkey-see, monkey-do design trends and produced a machine that is utterly unorthodox and positively oozes stately and sporting character. It is an assemblage of high-quality components waltzing in harmony with no invisible barbs or treacheries for which we can find few unkind words. Yes, we would like more damping. Yes, we would like less shaft effect. And, yes, a more convenient fork lock would be nice. But these shortcomings are not enough to spoil the enchantment of the K100.

This is a machine of quality and strength, with broad-range muscle that purrs and devours miles with seven-league strides. It is more raffish than any boxer could ever hope to be, yet priced in the same ball park. It can scoot through a corner or troll along the open road the way few machines can, and if we had to find some complaint, we would be hard pressed to do more than rebuff the Bavarians for not giving America the K100 right now. It is completely new, but it is also completely BMW.

We would like to extend a warm thanks to the brave folks at Century BMW (1811 West Main Street, Alhambra, CA 91801) for allowing us to cruise, scoot, dash, bash and otherwise thrash their own K100 during the road test. They are a hearty lot.

14

BMW K100RT

Photography by Dexter Ford & Rich Fox
Motorcyclist, September 1984

The Sport-Tourer, European Style: Fast, Elegant . . . And Completely Different

Consider the plight of a motorcycle engineer at BMW. He works for a company committed to making unique, exclusive, upper-crust motorcycles, machines with a reputation for high-speed grace and irrefutable reliability. Problem is, the company has also been committed to the same engine design for the last 63 years: the ancient air-cooled, aircraft-engine-derived, flat, pushrod twin first bolted together in 1921 by Martin Stolle. As recently as the middle seventies, the boxer was still strong enough to make BMW a threat in production-based Superbike racing—but it's the eighties, and there are some very worthy competitors two oceans away coming up with new, and very effective, engine designs year after year, often just for the sake of innovation. Even if he has the skill and luck to build a motorcycle that can outperform the quickest and fastest of the new generation of Japanese superbikes, the German designer can be sure the Japanese will come at him, four-valve heads blazing, to send him and all his expensive engineering down to defeat the next year.

So the task of devising a fresh, new engine configuration, one BMW could rightfully call its own, was a complex one. It had to produce 90 horsepower, but with the components stressed lightly enough to go 100,000 miles without major work. It also had to be simple enough and accessible enough to make service easy and inexpensive when it *is* needed. In addition, the engine had to mate easily to a drive-shaft system, as much a BMW trademark as the whirling-propeller insignia on the tank.

The first designs envisioned by the BMW engineering brain trust were liquid-cooled flat twins and fours. A BMW motorcycle has to be light, lighter than its competition, and the boys in Munich found flat fours bulky and heavy, and the twins deficient in power production. Vs were considered, of course, both longitudinal and transverse in orientation, but the bugaboos of their high CG and complicated intake systems eliminated them. Also, BMW knew the Japanese were working on their own V-4s, and BMW was not keen to grapple Honda on Honda's home court.

In 1977, Josef Fritzenwenger had the engineering flash that was to shape the K589 project. Longitudinal in-line fours had been considered, but mounted conventionally with the cylinder head on top, they were simply too tall and long to fit into a normally proportioned motorcycle. Fritzenwenger opted to flop the engine on its side, with the head to the left and the crankcase on the right, and the rest is recent history. The idea was new, would look distinctive and had many of the advantages BMW was searching for. The crankshaft would already be spinning parallel to the drive shaft, so a power-robbing 90-degree joint could be avoided. The center of gravity would be low and access to engine internals unequaled. If the need arose, one could pop off a cover and yank the crank.

The first proof-of-concept prototype was not a BMW engine at all; it was the all-aluminum engine of a Peugeot 104 automobile, shoehorned into a cut-up mule chassis. The resulting hybrid was low, not especially wide and quite long; heartened, the engineers started designing the new-generation BMW from whole cloth.

The K series was first conceived as a four-cylinder version displacing up to 1300cc and a subsequent triple pumping between 800 and 1000cc. This was the era of the CBX, remember, before excess had been recognized as essentially wretched. The big-guy prototypes built, with SOHC and two-valve BMW car-type cylinder heads, were heavy, bulky and incredibly long. The project stalled until January '79, when a new management team reevaluated the concept; even then, the proposal to build a UJM-style chain or shaft-drive transverse four was considered and for the last time rejected.

On February 20 of that year, the board of BMW Motorrad GmbH made its final decision; the new K was to be a smaller, flopped four with a maximum capacity of 1000cc, producing no more (or less) than 90 horsepower, with a very broad torque curve. If the Japanese couldn't be conquered, they could be neatly circumvented; if you can't beat them, make up a new game.

The new head of the motorcycle engine department, Martin Probst, was uniquely qualified to mastermind the K's power-plant development, being one of the two men responsible for the world-winning four-cylinder BMW Formula Two engine, an engine now finding its way, in turbocharged form, into Formula One cars as well. The engine got much smaller, and the single overhead camshaft, with eight attendant rocker arms, gave way to the conventional (in motorcycle circles) DOHC design, with each cam smacking its valves with a solid bucket-and-shim lifter.

The inherent problem of torque reaction in a longitudinal engine design was sidestepped in the K series in much the same way Honda handled it in the Gold Wing. In

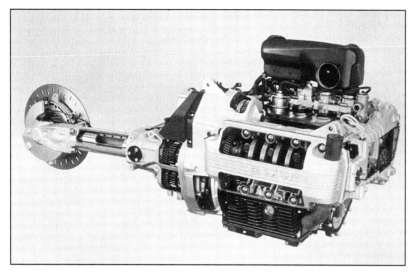

The patented Compact Drive System is the integrated package of the engine, transmission and rear suspension drive-shaft unit; the single-sided swingarm pivots in tapered roller bearings from the rear of the transmission housing. The engine uses a deep wet sump to collect oil; the lubricant drops to a level below the crankshaft, minimizing oil-fling friction losses.

The left side cover unbolts to reveal the valve train; the adjusting shims can be removed and replaced using a special tool, with no need to disturb the cams. Single-row roller chain provides the motion; spark plugs are revealed by removing a simple plastic cover.

the Honda, the massive permanent-magnet AC generator is geared from the crank to spin in the opposite direction, negating any rocking force the spinning crank might apply to the chassis. In the K100, the power from the crankshaft is transferred by large 1:1 helical gears to a jackshaft located below and inboard of the crank. The clutch is driven directly by this shaft, through a torsional damper composed of a star-shaped interior member held in place by rubber shock absorbers. The front of the shaft also motivates both the oil and water pumps, and in the expected 750cc triple version of the same basic engine, it may also function as a balancer shaft. The 460-watt alternator is geared to the crankshaft's helical gear at a 1.5:1 ratio, to ensure full charging at low engine speeds. With all these objects spinning backward relative to the crankshaft, the characteristic BMW dip to the right under throttle has been eliminated.

The crankshaft itself is a steel forging, with five 45mm-diameter plain main bearings and seven precisely balanced crank webs. The position that would have been occupied by an eighth web is used instead for the spur gear that drives the main jackshaft. Connecting rod big ends also employ plain bearings, each 38mm across; piston pins are plain as well and 18mm in diameter.

Martin Probst's car-racing experience shows in the K100's cylinder-head design; the two valves are angled only 19 degrees from the cylinder axis, the time-tested "Cosworth numbers" that determine valve inclination in most four-valve heads. Even in a two-valve design, the resultant fashionably flat combustion chamber allows a high compression ratio without resorting to a domed piston, which can interfere with breathing and squander energy, heating the piston instead of the expanding gases. The tiny 12mm spark plugs are located as close to the center of the chamber as possible, making shoehorning efforts a little easier.

The K100 engine was designed to displace 1000cc in four-cylinder trim, but no more; the cylinder walls are now only 9mm apart, just enough to keep the engine assembly acceptably rigid. To keep the engine short, the cylinders are undersquare: bore is 67mm, stroke is 70mm. There are no iron cylinder liners; like recent air-cooled BMWs, the aluminum/silicon/magnesium cylinders are treated with a wear-resistant nickel/silicon process known as Scanimet.

The two camshafts each run in five plain bearings and are driven by chain from a separate side shaft also geared to the crank. BMW is no stranger to four-valve heads—many of its race-car engines are four valvers, so the engineering expertise was sitting right there in Munich, ready to be tapped. In the interest of simplicity and reduced maintenance costs,

Maintenance access is the best of any motorcycle we've ever tested; the crankshaft and connecting rod big ends are revealed by removing the right side cover. The helical gear at the rear drives the secondary shaft, which drives the clutch, oil pump and water pump.

however, a two-valve setup, with intake poppets 34mm across and exhaust valves of 28mm, was chosen. This leaves room for BMW to easily upgrade the K series with four-valve heads if buyers ever demand more power.

Carburetors were discarded for the K project and replaced by the same Bosch LE Jetronic electronic fuel-injection system used on many BMW autos. Fuel is supplied to electrically controlled injector valves at 35 psi, and the valves are opened for a variable amount of time to give the proper mix of fuel and air in any operating circumstance. To assess operating conditions, sensors feed the EFI computer data on engine speed, throttle position, engine temperature and, by use of a movable flap in the intake tract between the airbox and throttle bores, air density and temperature. There's also a cut-off feature built into the system; at engine speeds above 2000 rpm, fuel supply is cut off completely when the throttle is closed, for improved mileage.

Unlike many of the EFI systems used on motorcycles, there is no "limp home" mode built into the computer. If a sensor goes out, it's possible the EFI system will stop completely on the K bike, apparently BMW's engineers have enough faith in the Bosch system to rely on it absolutely.

The ignition system of the K is just as sophisticated as its fuel injection; there are no vacuum lines, no centrifugal advancers; in fact, there are no moving parts of any kind. A vacuum switch tells the ignition computer whether the engine is running at full or partial load; the length of the signal from two Hall-effect generators located at the front of the crank tells the computer how fast the engine is turning and also lets it know the exact

A single spring and damper unit, adjustable for spring preload only, holds the rear end up; the saddleboxes mount neatly to the H-section aluminum bracket above the passenger peg.

crank position at any given time. With all this data, the computer can tell the plugs exactly when to fire for maximum power with minimum emissions. And if the rider overrevs the engine, the ignition is gently retarded at 8600 rpm, and the fuel injection system cuts out at 8750 rpm if the rider persists.

With the K100, BMW didn't only want to design a new engine, the new machine was conceived as a whole from start to finish, with each piece designed as part of an integrated whole. The engine, clutch, transmission and final drive system are one complete modular package; it would be easier to take the upper frame with the tank, seat and front suspension parts off the drive package than to separate the engine from the transmission and rear end. The engine is a structural part of the chassis, and the elaborately cast one-sided swingarm/drive shaft assembly pivots in tapered roller bearings mounted in the rear of the transmission case. The old boxer had a U joint located ahead of the swingarm pivot, forcing designers to incorporate sliding splines into the system to accommodate changes in shaft length as the swingarm moved through its travel. The K100 U joint is located on the same axis as the short swingarm, so the splines, and attendant driveline lash, are unnecessary.

The gearbox is a triple-shaft design, planned with help from Getrag, a German transmission manufacturer. The input shaft transfers power to the secondary shaft via 1:1.994 helical gears, and the secondary spins the mainshaft in one of five different gearbox ratios, ranging from a 2.26:1 first to a 0.838:1 fifth. The 2.91:1 final drive unit (2.81:1 on the RS) is fairly conventional, but it has the rear brake disc incorporated to allow easy rear-wheel removal and also carries the electronic sensor to inform the electronic speedometer.

With the patented Compact Drive System (the engine/transmission/rear end assembly) such a solid piece, the frame's function is quite simple: it ties the steering head onto the drive system using straight steel tubing, with relatively light extensions to provide mounting tabs for the seat, rear fender, tank and fairing. The well-supported steering head pivots the fork assembly on tapered roller bearings; rigidity is ensured by the huge 41.4mm fork tubes and the 22mm steel-tubing axle. The fork sliders are also designed to keep the front end as flex-free as possible, with two widely separated pinch bolts holding each end of the axle. The front fork is not air adjustable, nor are there any damping changes available. Gunter Schier, the man in charge of BMW's chassis development, has said, "It is not the job of the rider, but of the manufacturer to tune the bike correctly." In fine Bavarian tradition, the travel of the fork is long, and the springing and damping are very light. With 7.3 inches of travel available, the chassis can pitch forward and aft freely under hard acceleration or braking, but there is no provision for any kind of anti-dive system. As Stefan Pachernegg, the head of K100 development puts it, "The best thing you can do with these anti-dive systems at the moment is to leave them out."

The rear Monolever system is just a bit more adjustable than the front; spring pre-load is changeable, but only in three rather coarse increments. The single shock is bolted in a disarmingly simple manner between the frame and swingarm; on our RT version it is necessary to remove the right luggage box before it's possible to use the tool kit's spanner to adjust preload.

A motorcycle with the K100's putative sport-touring credentials should come stock with the best in brakes, and the K's 285mm Brembo-squeezed discs, two in front, one in back, measure up to the task. Along with the increased power of the four comes the demand for more traction; cast aluminum wheels, 2.50 x 18 in front and 2.75 x 17 rear, allow realistically wide and sticky rubber to be used. The German-spec K100 we sampled in February came shod with Pirelli Phantom tires; our American-spec K100 RT is equipped with Metzeler Perfects. There will be, we are given to understand, K100s coming with high-quality Dunlops and Michelins as well.

K100s will come in three distinct flavors. The basic machine, labeled simply the K100 (tested in our February issue), has no fairing at all; an elaborately styled headlight cover is the only distinct body part it carries; two sizes of BMW-designed clear fairings will be available as options. The two higher-ticket incarnations of the new Beemer breed, the RS and RT, use exactly the same aluminum tank, side covers, seat assembly and rear fender section. The RS uses a relatively small, frame-mounted fiberglass fairing to keep the wind off the rider's midsection; its low bar and limited rider protection make it the sportiest model. It has mirror assemblies with built-in turn signals and a stubby windscreen with an adjustable wind deflector to allow the rider to tailor the airflow around his head.

Suspension settings for all three models are the same, notwithstanding their different weights and intended usage; the RS has a slightly taller final drive ratio to allow speed-crazed autobahners to wring out the last few kilometers per hour available. Also, the RS and RT have rubber-insulated front engine mounts, whereas the plain jane K100 mounts are all rigid. The RS and RT rear mounts are still quite rigid, so any major engine movement will be felt; a day spent riding all three versions back to back revealed that individual differences between bikes had more effect on the perceived vibration than did the absence or presence of rubber mounts.

The subject of this test, the RT, is the touring incarnation of the K100 concept. When Americans think of BMWs, they tend to think of them as the ultimate long-haul sport-tourers, the perfect marque to board when a lot of ground has to be covered, not necessarily at legal speeds. In Europe the RT will be seen as the top-of-the-line auto-bahn blitzer, so it needs all the high-speed competence it can muster, along with ample luggage capacity and enough wind and weather protection to make 100-mph cruising pleasant. BMW had no intention of creating a "battleship," the term its engineers use to describe American-style Gold Wings, Ventures and Voyagers.

The new RT fairing owes nothing to the older design used on the boxers. It's lower, and its lines are much more angular; the windshield curves up at a very shallow angle and stops no more than a foot from the rider's face. BMW's engineers spent a great deal of time in the wind tunnel getting the fairing's protection up and keeping the drag down.

They decided to keep the windshield low, and the rider's space free of buffeting by directing a stream of high-velocity air up and over his head. With this aim, the rear of the windshield has a kick-up lip and a second clear plastic lip above it to contain the airstream. The lower section of the fairing wraps over the engine cases to give the best possible leg protection. The glass outer panels are backed up with black plastic inner panels; there are two large storage bins inside the fairing for gloves, tapes or maps. Turn signals are built right into the lines of the upper fairing piece.

The rear luggage is made by BMW, not Krauser, and the boxes are molded of black pebble-grain polypropylene, with a tasteful BMW crest stuck on the side. The boxes open quickly and easily, with two lockable latches, one on the top and one to the rear. The boxes are hung on beefy H-section aluminum brackets; one flick of a finger pops open a third latch at the front of each box, freeing the unit for motel entry. The boxes are quite large, and intelligently shaped; a full-face helmet fits into each. Our only complaint about the luggage design concerns the snap-on brace intended to hold the outside half of the box horizontal while open. The material of the boxes is too pliable to hold the brace firmly, and any weight distorts the box until the snap unsnaps, unloading your dainty underthings onto the asphalt.

Each of the three K models comes with its own distinct handlebar; other than that, the riding positions are very close to one another. The RS has a short, low bar that forces the rider to crouch considerably, the plain model has a medium-rise bend that allows the rider to stay upright and still lean into the wind. The RT bar is a long, high, tiller affair, reminiscent of the bar used on the GS1100E in '83. We tried the RT bar on a naked K100 and found it almost unbearable without the fairing's wind protection. Behind the RT's carefully designed windbreaker, though, the bar provides an appropriately Teutonic, upright posture. The new RT's glasswork is much smaller and lower than the old one's, representing a significant departure from the concept of a full fairing, as far as BMW is concerned. By manipulating the airstream effectively, the idea was to give almost the same protection as the old RT but without the penalties in drag.

The protection is there, from the rider's neck down, and there is a delightful lack of buffeting, even at the RT's indicated top speed of 135 mph. The trade-off is in noise; the two-tiered windscreen sends a shot of accelerated air right at the top of most helmets' face shields, setting up a roar at 50 mph that will have you checking the speedometer in disbelief. With a good, tight-fitting face shield and earplugs, there's no problem—but a one-day trip without plugs left one staffer's ears ringing for the next two days. In an effort to reduce noise, we removed the top lip of the windscreen (when you turn the clear plastic bolts to remove the lip, they break off before they unscrew, so this fix is a one-way street). The improvement was dramatic. Buffeting didn't seem to rise substantially, but noise was cut almost in half according to our admittedly unscientific ears.

We also learned quickly that the RT is not an ideal summer tourer. Some quirk of ducting apparently sends heated air from the radiator into the tunnel under the fuel tank, heating the tank to the point where it's painful to touch on a hot, fast day's ride.

The K model starts easily, once you figure out the hieroglyphics on the various handlebar buttons. There's the standard-issue BMW choke lever atop the left switch pod; the Bosch fuel injection is ready to keep the bike running soon after it starts, so there's no point in riding around for a half hour with the injector throats closed down. With the choke either on or off, the first 100 feet have the K bike stumbling a bit.

As on previous BMWs, the range of engagement of the auto-type, single-plate clutch is quite narrow. The pull is deceivingly light, but with the substantial flywheel effect inherent in the engine assembly, it's difficult to move away from a dead stop smoothly the first few times. There is also a large dose of shaft-produced rise and fall going on at the rear end in the lower gears, so a rider's first few launches in stop-and-go traffic may be on the lurchy side. The long-travel suspension does little to resist pitching of the machine, so braking, or even a sudden roll-off of the throttle, sends the nose down without hesitation.

The RT was never made for inner-city grocery shopping; it was designed for covering ground, hour after hour, on fast and convoluted roads. Once the gearbox is in third gear or higher, the jerkiness and awkward chassis movements caused by the unchecked shaft largely disappear. Steering, with the long RT bars, is light and precise; the substantial gyroscopic effect of the 18-inch front wheel is noticeable, but a little extra pressure on the inside bar can have the RT diving into a corner with real authority. The naked K100 we tested before maintained its steering neutrality in cornering, but our RT tends to stand up slightly. A pound or two of pressure on the inside grip lets the bike

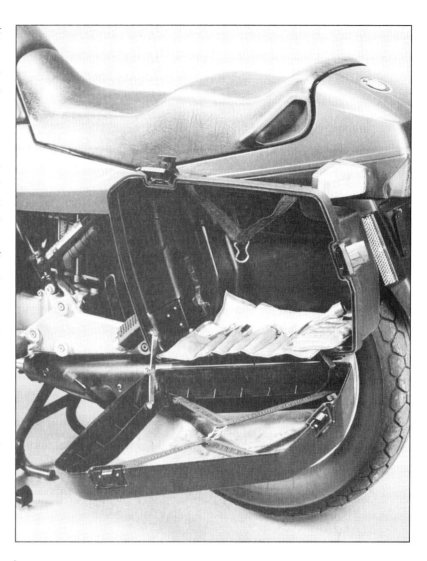

The RT's luggage boxes are pebble-grained polypropylene; the bags open using the lockable latches on the top and rear and detach from the bike with a flip of the front latch.

track with precision on your chosen line. The stand-up tendency could be corrected with a minor weight shift to the inside, but the rear edges of the fairing lowers effectively keep your legs captured; confirmed knee draggers should opt for the less-restrictive RS package.

The long and fluid travel of the suspension units allows the wheels to follow road undulations easily. The front fork is smooth and gratifyingly stiction free; even with stiff-sidewalled Metzelers mounted, the ride at the front is excellent. The huge fork tubes, large diameter axle and beefy forged triple clamps all combine to make an admirably rigid assembly. With the rear preload set on the softest setting, the RT rides well on the roughest freeway or coarsest back road. The soft setting allows the chassis to move around excessively during hard cornering or violent maneuvering, so for faster work we clicked the preload collar to the middle setting.

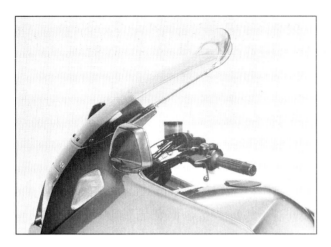

The windscreen is molded clear plastic; the lip at the top is designed to direct a blast of high-velocity air over the rider's head, but for tall riders at least, it only increases noise.

As long as enthusiasm stays below the nine-tenths level, the RT performs well as a sporting machine. The steering is precise and predictable; the triple Brembos, though a bit sensitive in the first few millimeters of travel, haul the bike down well from high speeds without excessive lever pressure, and cornering clearance is excellent. The number of times we touched the K100 down on an unrehearsed road can be counted on one hand. Either footpeg will contact the road in an extreme lean; the sidestand will graze the road on the left if you press on regardless.

Two problems keep the K100 RT from being a top-echelon handler, however. The soft damping and springing are fine for a smooth ride, but the RT is just too loose on its wheels when the curves start coming up quickly. The chassis is rigid, so it won't wiggle and wallow like the boxers when the speed gets into triple digits, but it is nearly a full-time chore to keep track of the bike's pitch attitude. The lack of rebound damping at the rear, combined with the long-travel front end, make the bike vault violently forward under braking. The machine dives enthusiastically the instant the brakes come on, and with the cut-down American-spec seat, the rider slides forward helplessly until his knees bottom out on the fairing. European versions and some early U.S. bikes have a seat about a half-inch taller, without the downward slant that slides the rider noseward. BMW has apparently cut down the seat for short-legged riders, but the taller seat works much better once the bike is moving.

With adjustable air, preload and damping at the front and adjustable damping at the back, relief would be just a poof and a click away, but the BMW people have decided they will do the tuning, and for some riders (as anyone could have predicted) they got it wrong.

The RT must be handled carefully during fast cornering because of the ample shaft effect caused by the relatively short swingarm. The ground clearance is there, so the old boxer problem of grinding the valve cover when the throttle is closed in mid-corner is gone. But any sharp throttle input puts the chassis through some long-excursion gyrations that will keep the rider from making any aggressive action until the movement dies out. Once you've mastered the shaft's behavior, it's possible to get the K bike down the road smartly, but it takes quite a bit of orientation time before you're riding smoothly.

But the engine does a lot to make up any time lost to the suspension. As advertised, it starts making power early in the rev band and feels almost unstoppable as the analog tach winds past six grand. In first and second, the engine easily overwhelms the shaft; it's possible to pop the front wheel a good foot in the air by twisting the long-travel throttle quickly, and a hard first-to-second shift launches the rear end up at the rider's rump. The engine is strong; its 81.1-mph roll-on speed, measured 200 yards from a 50-mph rolling start in top gear, puts it ahead of some very torquey company. It beats the Yamaha Seca 900, at 78.0 mph, the GS1100G Suzuki, at 79.3 mph, and all the full-dress battleships.

The RT's quarter-mile performance was hampered by two glitches. First, the barely controlled shaft sent the rear suspension to full extension with a bang the instant the clutch

At my first gas stop on the BMW two attendants ran right over to see the new K100 RT, and one of them kept telling the other that these are the Cadillacs of motorcycles. I had to tell them that it's really not that bad. It's not great, but a Cadillac? That's mean.

The Beemer handles around-town chores just fine but is a disaster in the canyons. Where it really shines is flying down a fast, gently winding road. But for me the bike just has too many little quirks about it. For that price I would buy three leftover 1981 GS850Gs which I feel is a better bike anyway, and then two friends could ride with me.

—Brent Ross

I'm not real crazy about the parts of the K100 RT that make it an RT: the seat sends me sliding forward every time I brake hard, and the fairing is there waiting to bash my knees. The wind-tunnel-designed windshield may work well for plastic human mock-ups, but I have ears I want to use in 20 years, and the noise the windshield generates is literally deafening.

I'm much more partial to the RS model of the new K bike; I'd rather have my head out in the free airstream than have it bombarded by the blast from the RT's windshield venturi. I'd spring for a slightly higher set of bars to replace the RS's roadracer stubs, order the optional saddle boxes (just like the RT's) and go riding.

—Dexter Ford

BMW has slid nicely into the Modern Age with the K100. It is a clever application of current technology that has a good chance of remaining as perenially unique as the boxer twin did. Compared to those old twins, the K model is substantially superior in almost every performance respect. But in most subjective ways it is uncannily similar. One long ride tells you BMW hasn't changed its idea of how a motorcycle should feel.

For me, that is a drawback. Most of the things that make the K100 feel like the rest of the BMWs happen to grate on me. Call me crazy, but I don't enjoy weak clutches, limp suspension, odd switches and extreme shaft effect. None of those quirks is in any way tied to the basic concept of the K100, but they are an integral part of every motorcycle BMW builds.

I'd love a debugged BMW K100, but I doubt BMW will ever build one.

—Jeff Karr

BMW's compulsive need to be different has brought it to a fairly happy juncture with the K100 RT. The engine has the attractions of the in-line four with the low CG and shaft-drive compatibility of the Honda Gold Wing.

Although several of the details—the aggravating turn-signal switches, the excessive wind noise and the sloping saddle—annoyed me, I found the bike basically well conceived and enjoyable. But there is one important fault: vibration. It is doubly annoying because a simple solution is staring you right in the face in the form of the jackshaft, which with better supports could be used as a balancer shaft. If rumors of a K75 triple are true, it is already being done on that bike, so why have a flagship that buzzes?

BMW's habit of holding onto designs and refining them should pay big dividends with the K100 RT because the basic design is so suitable for a dressed motorcycle.

—Art Friedman

was released, either breaking traction at the rear or forcing a lurid wheelie. Second, the close proximity of the windshield to the rider's face kept him from moving as far forward as he normally would to keep the front wheel on the ground. The RT's best was a respectable 12.47 at 107.3 mph; our dragstrip rider figures the RT could get under 12.4 with the windshield out of his way.

The changes made to the K100 to meet U.S. smog limits were supposed to reduce horsepower about five percent, but it didn't show on our RT; its times, with about 32 pounds of extra fiberglass and plastic, were very close to those delivered by our bootlegged German-spec K100 in February. Corrected for temperature, pressure and humidity variations, the German K100 ran 12.27 at 109.5 mph at Carlsbad, while the RT ran 12.36 at 108.5 mph.

BMW K100 RT

Suggested retail price: $7500
Warranty: 36 months, unlimited miles
Number of U.S. dealers: 257
Recommended maintenance 4650 miles
  intervals:

ENGINE

Type: Water-cooled, longitudinal in-line 4-stroke four
Valve arrangement: DOHC, 2 valves; adjusting shims on top of buckets
Displacement: 987cc
Bore x stroke: 67.0 x 70.0mm
Compression ratio: 10.2:1
Carburetion: Bosch LE-Jetronic fuel injection, 34mm venturis
Ignition: Bosch digital system, electronic
Lubrication: Wet sump, 3.8 qt
Charging output: 460 watts
Battery: 12V, 20AH

DRIVETRAIN

Primary transmission: Spur gear, 1.944:1
Clutch: Dry, one-plate
Final drive: Shaft and bevel gear, 2.91:1

Gear	Internal Ratio	mph per 1000 rpm	mph at redline (8300)
1	2.315	5.8	48
2	1.523	8.8	73
3	1.183	11.3	94
4	0.967	14.7	122
5	0.859	15.6	130

CHASSIS

Front suspension: 41.4mm BMW, 7.3 in. travel
Rear suspension: BMW damper, 4.3 in. wheel travel; adjustment for spring preload
Front brake: 2, double-action Brembo calipers, 285mm discs
Rear brake: Single-action Brembo caliper, 285mm disc
Front wheel: 2.50 x 18 in.; cast aluminum
Rear wheel: 2.75 x 17 in.; cast aluminum
Front tire: 100/90V18 Metzeler Perfect ME77
Rear tire: 130/90V17 Metzeler Perfect ME99A
Rake/trail: 27.5°/3.9 in. (101mm)
Wheelbase: 59.7 in. (1516mm)
Seat height, unladen: 32.0 in. (813mm)
Seat height, with 160-lb rider: 31.3 in. (794mm)
Fuel capacity: 5.8 gal (22L)
Weight: 595 lb (270kg) wet; 560 lb (255kg) tank empty

Colors: Maroon or gray/green
Instruments: Speedometer, tachometer, odometer, tripmeter, LCD clock, LCD gear indicator; warning lights for oil level, battery charge, water temperature, brakes, high beam, fuel level, choke on, neutral, left and right turn signals
Speedometer error: 30 mph, actual 27.4; 60 mph, actual 58.0

PERFORMANCE

Fuel consumption: 29 to 46 mpg, 37.6 mpg avg.
Average touring range: 218 miles
Average 200-yd. top-gear acceleration from 50 mph: 81.1 mph terminal speed
Best 1/4-mile acceleration: 12.47 sec., 107.3 mph
*Projected best 1/4-mile acceleration: 12.35 sec., 108.5 mph

*Projected performance with test-session weather conditions corrected to sea-level standard conditions (59 degrees F, 29.92 in. of mercury).

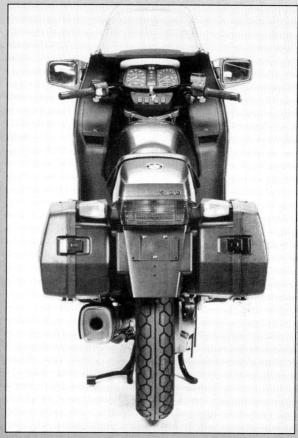

	1985 BMW K100 RT	1984 Honda VF1100S Sabre	1983 BMW R100RS	1984 Harley-Davidson FXRT
Price	$7500	$4548	$6900	$7699
Quarter-mile time/mph	12.47/107.3	11.19/121.3	13.28/98.6	13.90/92.4
Wet Weight	595 lb	601 lb	544 lb	654 lb
High speed pass, terminal speed	81.0 mph	79.0 mph	76.7 mph	77.3 mph
Average fuel consumption	37.6 mpg	34.7 mpg	44.7 mpg	46.1 mpg
Average touring range	218 miles	201 miles	281 miles	194 miles

The motor is certainly strong at the top end: during one of our test rides, we had the opportunity to run the thing almost flat-out for the better part of an hour along a deserted secondary highway. With the rider sitting bolt upright, as the fairing and riding position dictate, the RT whistled along, mile after mile, at an indicated 135 mph. The ride was noisy but turbulence-free inside the fairing's protection bubble. This wild ride got the mileage for that leg down to 28.6 mpg, compared to a freeway average of over 45 mpg.

In day-to-day riding, the engine is impressive; the torque builds smoothly, with no noticeable steps or flat spots from idle to redline. Throttle response is less than immediate, though, blipping the throttle to equalize gear speeds while downshifting is just not possible because the engine won't rev up fast enough. We suspect the culprit is the air-density measuring flap in the airbox; the flap must first move out of the way before the engine gets any air, and it feels like the flap is a bit slow.

Our RT, and at least two of the other K100s being tested in the L.A. area at this time, are not as smooth and vibration-free as expected. There is a definite buzz in the handle-bar at 3500 rpm, followed by random buzzes that circulate through the tank, the seat and the footpegs from there all the way to redline. BMW, in the person of Stefan Pachernegg, is aware of the problem but as yet has no solution. "Some of them are worse than others," says Pachernegg. "We don't know why at this time." Our RT vibrates more through the left footpeg than the right, so we believe the design or assembly of the exhaust system is partly at fault.

Another separate problem involves the muffler heat shield. On the early production bikes given to the press, the shield is held in tension by a spring that keeps it from vibrating. Our spring broke, allowing the shield to vibrate loudly at about 2000 rpm. According to Pachernegg, the breakable spring will be replaced by silicon-rubber mounts that should prove buzz-free.

The unique switch assemblies of the K100 series were worked out painstakingly—the Institute for Automotive Studies at the Technical University at Aachen was consulted for the design of the system. In place of the almost universal left-thumb-operated turn signal switch, there's a thumb button, hidden under the body of the switch housing, on both the left and the right. Unlike the similar Harley-Davidson system, the turn signals stay on after being pushed once; they self-cancel after both 10 seconds and 210 meters. If you want to turn off the blinker yourself, there's a separate switch; you move your right thumb upward to hit another nearly hidden button. If you try to cancel the left turn, signal by moving your *left* thumb up, as you might logically do, you'll get a 100-decibel surprise; the button above the left blinker is the horn, and for once it's downright effective. The rest of the hand switches are easier to fathom; the light switch, with its autobahn-replica flashing mode, is in the expected place on the left switch housing, and the combination starter/kill button, odd though it is, sits in full view on the right side housing.

The owner of a K100 who rides the bike regularly will probably acclimate himself nicely to the new switch system, but for us riding the K in city traffic was, even after two weeks of steady riding, an exercise in frustration. It's hard to get it through your head that you can't stop an electrical function by hitting the same switch that started it—and once you've gotten past that learning hurdle, it's hard to remember that to turn off the *left* signal, the *right* thumb is supposed to be lifted and in a very awkward way. Also, having the horn activated by an almost-invisible button is hard to justify; when you need it, you really need it, and there seems to be plenty of room on the left switch housing, right above the light switch, to have it in clear sight and easy thumb range.

As a staff, we would like the opportunity to buy each and every BMW engineer a drink in appreciation for the side- and centerstand. The stands on the boxers were almost unimaginably poor; these are jewels of technological progress by comparison. The side-stand is about the right length and can be easily reached with a toe without leaving the saddle. It's linked by a cable to the clutch lever; when you pull in the clutch, the side-stand pops up with a resounding clang. Of course, if the bike is leaning on the stand, the clutch lever isn't going to budge; and if you yank the clutch lever hard enough, you can break the clutch actuating arm. It's obviously nice, once you've learned how the system works, to pop up the stand as you leave without groping around with your foot; it also makes it virtually impossible to ride off with the stand still down. However, you're forced to find neutral or shut off the engine before you toe the stand down.

The centerstand is not quite as sophisticated, but it's accessible and effective; to avoid possible damage to the seat caused by ham-handed riders clawing for a handhold, there's a neat folding handle under the left side seat-support tube to help get the bike airborne.

The major instruments, the speedo and the tach, are large analog dials on all the K100s. They are both electronically informed; the speedo gets its signals from the aforementioned magnetic sensor at the rear wheel. There's an LCD gear indicator and all kinds of nice warning lights to watch; in fact, instead of a fuel gauge, there are two warning lights, one that flashes when seven liters remain in the tank and a second that flashes on when you're down to four liters, or just over one gallon. An LCD clock is also standard.

We had one problem with our K100: if left on its sidestand, it smoked heavily when started. Oil is apparently draining into the combustion chambers through the ring gaps; Stefan Pachernegg has hinted that BMW may pin the rings against rotation to prevent the problem, but he didn't say when the change might take place.

Compared to its almost homogenized Japanese brethren, the K100 RT is, literally, in a class by itself. It's a fully loadable tourer that can give certain sport bikes fits on a twisty road. It's an island of opinionated engineering afloat in a sea of sanitized-for-your-protection motorcycles that have been market researched to a fare-thee-well. BMW surveyed its owners' clubs before the K100 was revealed, asking which engine configuration they preferred for the new BMW. Over 90 percent chose the flat-twin arrangement over the others listed—including the flopped straight four. A survey conducted *after* the release of the bike showed that, surprise, 90 percent of the owners' club members were now behind the K100 arrangement; the company had essentially ignored the wishes of its customers, but then the customers changed their minds to suit the engineers.

The K100 RT is a fresh, brilliantly engineered departure from the accepted norms of the motorcycle industry, and for an elite minority of buyers, nothing less will do. Instead of falling into Japanese-dominated performance wars, BMW has chosen to focus on what it sees as reasonable, manageable performance goals, meeting them with designs it expects will still be in use in BMWs 20 years from now.

Because the K100 is so unambiguously engineered by men with very definite and unique opinions, the motorcycle stands apart from everything that has come before. It is a product of zero-based engineering; the designers started with nothing and built a completely new machine based on their best ideas. They were forced to challenge a group of Japanese manufacturers whom other European (and American) makers view invincible; and if the early deposits for K100s are any indication, they're going to be very successful.

15

BMW K100RS

Motorcyclist, December 1984

The Best K Bike Yet

Just as with the old boxer twins, the RS designation has been saved for the company's flagship sport bike. Changes between the K100RS, the RT and the standard K100 are slight. All use the same liquid-cooled 987cc four-cylinder motor and have their fuel metered by Bosch fuel injection. Since the power plants and drivetrains are the same on all models and we dealt with the mechanics of them in depth in our September issue, we won't repeat ourselves here on those subjects. In fact, the entire motorcycles are identical with a few exceptions, the major difference being the type of fairing or lack thereof, as on the standard K100. Each model also gets its own handlebars.

The RS has a much lower and more swept-back fairing than the RT and is missing the lowers found on the RT. Fairing-mounted mirrors on most sport bikes rarely offer a view of anything other than your arms, but the ones on the RS provide an excellent display of the world behind and are virtually unaffected by vibration. The mirrors are an integral part of the front turn signals; the units are designed to pop off if the bike is knocked over and can simply be snapped back into place.

Another trick feature of the fairing is found along the top edge of the windscreen—a small adjustable wing that can be positioned to deflect the windblast according to the rider's preference. By tilting it all the way forward, the airstream is deflected over the rider's head, creating a quiet, almost indoor atmosphere in which to travel.

Seating accommodations are very nice. The RS is not quite as comfortable as a loafer seat in the back row of a movie theater, but for high-speed sport-touring the BMW's position works better. The seat is well padded and offers good support, although it slopes forward, sending the rider sliding onto the tank whenever the brakes are applied. We might add that it's a hot gas tank too, an oddity shared with the RT and caused by an excess of engine heat being transferred to the tank—and the fuel. Low, very narrow bars help keep you leaned in behind the small RS fairing in true European fashion. Footpegs are placed fairly rearward, and the footpeg-to-seat relationship is comfortable for even the tallest riders.

All K bikes come with something out of the past: a hinged seat with a large storage compartment underneath. The K bikes also come with a pretty serious tool kit, a tire repair kit and even a first aid kit.

Also found on all the BMW water-pumpers is one of the most incomprehensible turn signal setups yet. If you want to indicate a left turn, you must search for a hidden button on the left bar; then if you want to switch it off before it self-cancels, you press a cancel button on the right bar. To indicate a right turn, it is necessary to find another mystery button on the right bar. To interrupt the signal before its time expires, you must push up on the same cancel button on the right bar. But don't push up on the button on the left; that's the horn. Fortunately, the light switches are much easier to use.

Most of the four-cylinder BMWs we've seen smoke terribly for several miles after being left on their sidestands for more than a few minutes. We suspect this is the result of oil from the crankcase running up through the piston-ring end gaps and into the combustion chamber. On some occasions the smoking does not occur at all, either because the ring end gaps have all spun to the top so oil cannot leak past or because the oil level in the sump has dropped enough so it cannot run into the cylinders while the bike is leaned over on the sidestand.

If the smoking problem persists, the easiest solution is to use the centerstand. The folks at BMW have finally fixed the poor side- and centerstands which have troubled the old twins for years. The sidestand no longer folds up when the weight is taken off it, and there is a small hinged handle on the right side that folds down and helps to hoist the bike onto the centerstand.

Suspension problems are the RS's biggest shortcomings. All the K models use the same spring and damping rates, although the different bikes are not the same weight and they bias their weight differently. The fork has no provisions for any adjustment whatsoever, and only spring preload can be varied at the rear. With its long travel and light damping and spring rates, the RS soaks up the biggest bumps without upsetting the motorcycle. But maneuvering smoothly through traffic is nearly impossible with lots of shaft effect jacking the bike up and down whenever the throttle is opened or closed and with the fork bottoming every time the front brakes are applied suddenly. This, coupled with a narrow clutch engagement, makes the BMW tricky to ride smoothly in town, but it can be done after much practice.

Long, swooping roads winding their way through the countryside are where BMW's K100RS comes into its own. On roads like these, the Beemer can make very good time if the rider is so inclined. With strong midrange power, the RS accelerates rapidly without the need for shifting. On the open road the RS's around-town awkwardness vanishes.

The steering is slow due to the narrow bars, yet precise, and the bike has a slight tendency to stand up once leaned over. Our RS came shod with Metzeler Perfects which were well up to the task, allowing all of the RS's plentiful ground clearance to be gobbled up. Brembo calipers with 285mm discs are used, two up front and one in back.

The rear brake fades quickly during hard riding, rendering itself useless. But up front the dual discs work much better. Fading was never a problem. Feel is not the best, but boy, will they haul speed right down.

Final drive ratio on the RS is a little taller than on the other two—2.81:1 compared to 2.91:1. All internal spacings go unchanged. Since the RS has taller gearing and more weight than the standard K100, we were expecting slower ETs at the strip and a slightly less

BMW K100RS

Engine type:	Water-cooled, longitudinal in-line 4-stroke four
Valve arrangement:	DOHC, 2 valves; adjusting shims on top of buckets
Displacement:	987cc
Bore x stroke:	67.0 x 70.0mm
Compression ratio:	10.2:1
Carburetion:	Bosch LE-Jetronic fuel injection, 34mm venturis
Charging output:	460 watts
Battery:	12V, 20AH
Front suspension:	41.4mm BMW, 7.3 in. travel
Rear suspension:	Single BMW damper, 4.3 in. wheel travel; adjustment for preload
Front tire:	100/90V18 Metzeler ME77
Rear tire:	130/90V18 Metzeler ME99A
Rake/trail:	27.5°/3.9 in. (101mm)
Wheelbase:	59.7 in. (1516mm)
Seat height, unladen:	32.0 in. (813mm)
Fuel capacity:	5.8 gal (22L)
Weight:	554 lb (251kg) wet
Fuel consumption:	32 to 50 mpg, 41.0 mpg avg.
Average 200-yd. top-gear acceleration from 50 mph:	82.4 mph terminal speed
Best ?-mile acceleration:	12.59 sec., 107.9 mph
Projected best ?-mile acceleration*:	12.37 sec., 110.0 mph

*Projected performance with test-session weather conditions corrected to sea-level standard conditions (59 degrees F, 29.92 in. of mercury).

buzzy motor. Our predictions were right on one count: the RS is slightly slower, turning in a 12.59 as opposed to the standard's 12.40—both right in step with the 550-class times. However, at speeds above 40 mph, the RS lets it be known the motor is hard at work by shaking every part of itself which comes in contact with the rider. The footpegs are the worst offenders.

During the Beemers stay at *Motorcyclist*, one staffer had an unpleasant experience: the rear wheel came loose while he was riding on the freeway. He was able to stop before it fell all the way off, but it is a problem that should never occur. The rear wheel is held on by four automotive-style tapered lug bolts that secure the wheel to the Monolever. Two of the bolts fell completely out and the other two had backed out about halfway. Other machines use lock nuts, cotter pins or locking tabs to secure wheel components. The K bike has none of these. If the bolts are not properly tightened—as must have been the case when the machine was delivered (although it went a couple of hundred miles before the problem developed)—there is nothing to keep them from loosening and falling out. Our test bike's wheel was reassembled with lots of Loctite. If we owned it, the bolts would have been drilled and safety wired. If we were BMW, we would make a change—and fast.

Like the other Beemers, the K100RS fits in its own little niche. It's not competition for Ninjas or FJ1100s, although its styling might suggest that. It's more laid-back and civilized. It shares the strengths and weaknesses of the other K models, and like them is ripe for some refinement. However, like them, it will in all probability be around for years to come, thereby maintaining its reputation and value.

16

Photography by Mike Gaspar
Motorcyclist, August 1985

BMW R80RT

The Old Boxer—with Some Fresh New Moves

We don't have to tell you that BMWs are up-market motorcycles. You'd have to be fresh off the shuttle from Phobos to be ignorant of the Bavarian marque's elevated status—and elevated price tags. Like French champagne, Swiss watches, Swedish women and American refrigerators, German vehicles seem more highly valued than those from other locales, even when there are no measurable performance differences. With the new but familiar R80RT, though, BMW is trying to mitigate the actual cost of owning a classic German touring bike. At $5700 the RT is the least expensive full-fairing, saddlebag-equipped tourer on the market. It also costs $240 less than a similarly equipped R80RT would have cost in 1983, the difference due mostly to the strength of the dollar against the German mark.

Until very recently the motorcycle arm of the Bayerische Motoren Werke was known for brilliant conservatism in engineering; the boxer-twin engine has been around for more than 60 years, after all, with very few basic changes. The K100 changed all that—and forced BMW to discontinue the legendary R100 twin series, for fear that buyers would undercut K100 sales by stubbornly continuing to buy the proven twins.

But the boxer twin lives, as a half-second glance at the lead photo of this test reveals. The R65 and R80 series remain, and the R80RT, the last descendant of the formidable R100RT sport-tourer, has received a face-lift for 1985 that borders on the radical for a firm as rooted in tradition as BMW.

To understand touring BMWs you have to understand their natural habitat. The German road system is a wonderful combination of twisting, convoluted mountain roads, tiny cobblestoned village streets and flank-speed autobahns. To please German riders, a tourer must be nimble, as lightweight as feasible, comfortable at high speeds and low speeds and finished in a style that denotes restraint and class above all things. The plastic gadgets and electronic toys Japanese/American tourers are encrusted with are viewed as unnecessary, and vaguely embarrassing, by the Germans. To ride an R80RT is to float, serene and slightly aloof, above both the road and the tacky, hard-sell paint jobs, feature lists and high-tech speed-first flash being thrown across the ocean by Japan, Inc.

From 50 feet away it would be very hard to tell an '85 R80 from an '84, but a closer look reveals a number of definite refinements. The dual-shock rear suspension is gone, replaced by a single-shock Monolever system much like that used on the K series and the dual-purpose R80 G/S. The Boge spring/damper unit adjusts only for spring preload; a very long adjustment extension on the top of the shock reaches under the right side cover to bolt to the frame. Unlike the R80 G/S, the RT's shock bolts to the ring-gear housing instead of farther forward on the swingarm/shaft cover tube. Inside the housing is another, more subtle improvement: the stub axle and ring gear now run in a tapered roller bearing instead of the earlier needle bearing.

The front suspension has also been rethought, with 38.5mm fork stanchions replacing the old 36mm tubes, and a new aluminum fork brace bolted on above the front fender. For even more rigidity, the axle is now a large-diameter tube. The front brakes are the same as those used on the much heavier and faster K100: twin 285mm discs with double-action Brembo calipers. The rear binder is a Simplex drum incorporated into the ring-gear housing, actuated by a rod.

The rest of the motorcycle is amazingly close to the R80RT we tested, and liked a lot, in July of 1983. The engine is the same pushrod opposed twin; the only difference is a refinement of the rocker arms, which are set to tighter tolerances than before, and now have nylon inserts to quell rocker noise before it bounces up to the rider's ears from the exposed cylinders. The exhaust system is new. The old one was interconnected between the head pipes; the present one is also, but there's a large resonance chamber added between the pipes just ahead of the chromed mufflers, and it's claimed to give the 797.5cc engine more torque at the bottom of its operating range.

The frame is very similar to the old one, except for some larger tubes in the rear section and the juggling of mounting hardware necessary to accommodate the new Monolever. The fairing is unchanged, but the adjustable windshield is considerably shorter than before, so that all but certifiable dwarfs look over, rather than through it. As one might expect, the new RT feels very much like the old RT, and that's not intended as criticism. The engine thrums quietly to life with the choke open, and then immediately requires closing the choke to its half-open position. Blipping the throttle with the clutch in makes the bike want to tilt slightly to the right, due to the torque effect of the longitudinal running gear.

The clutch is delightfully light and delicate in response, and the drivetrain is relatively slop-free, especially for a shaft-drive design. And why shouldn't it be? After all, BMW has been working on the same shaft-drive system since the time your father was born. There is, or course, the usual shaft-induced rise at the back end under throttle that BMWs are known for. The long-travel, soft suspension units let the chassis tilt fore and aft freely with changing braking and power applications, giving an excellent ride over rough surfaces or undulating pavement, but making the rider's task a little more difficult on a challenging, twisty road. Clicking up the rear shock's preload tends to stabilize the motorcycle's movements on its legs; the ride gets firmer with the preload up, but never to the point of harshness. With the preload set soft, the dampers seem underendowed with rebound damping, but clicking the preload toward the stiff end seems to take up the slack, even though there is no change in the actual rebound-damping setting.

The riding position is excellent, a straight-up-and-down posture that kept most testers fresh for hours on the flat, thin and yet surprisingly comfortable saddle. One dissenter, however, felt the saddle was too hard. The shorter windshield was adopted, we suspect, to counter criticism about the difficulty of seeing through the old screen; now the problem is turbulence. The rider's helmet is always being blasted at highway speeds, making earplugs a necessity on a long tour. A taller shield could be easily fitted, making the RT as comfortable as, say, the new Suzuki Cavalcade, but as it is the RT is missing one of the main benefits of a full-fairing tourer.

The engine of our RT wasn't as smooth and buzz-free as we remembered other 800cc Beemers. The mirrors were never clear, and there was almost always a perceptible tingling in the handlebar and the footpegs. However, Joe Minton got the machine running smoothly with a few twists of a wrench—the bike had been delivered to us with its carbs badly out of sync. The transmission was not up to the usual BMW standards either; the lever was prone to sticking up after an upshift, and it would occasionally pop back out of third gear a second or so after a shift from second.

The centerstand is new, and it works well—it's finally as good as the worst modern Japanese centerstand. The sidestand, however, is still an awkward reach, and the bike's soft suspension makes its stance on the sidestand precarious. The fork lock is still located down on the steering head; one forgetful staffer climbed aboard the bike, started the engine and confidently attempted to ride away, only to have the fork lock dump him and the bike down a steep driveway. An ignition-mounted fork lock would have prevented the mishap, and the cost can't be all that high if every 250cc Japanese dual-purpose bike comes with the nice setup.

For a tourer, the RT is a fine sport bike, and vice versa. The steering is light and responsive, and the new, more rigid fork turns rider inputs into results with less random motion than before. The RT is the lightest touring bike available, lighter than most 750cc sporting fours, and its low center of gravity makes it feel even lighter than it is. With the suspension jacked up, ground clearance is quite adequate, as long as the rider remembers to keep the gas on to keep the bike from lowering on its suspension in the middle of a corner.

The front Brembos are powerful; it takes a few stops before the rider learns to treat them with the care and precision they require. The flat twin's power is always there, if not particularly overwhelming, and the flat torque curve makes engine management

BMW R80RT

Suggested retail price:	$5700
Warranty:	3 years, unlimited miles
Recommended maintenance intervals:	5000 miles
Engine type:	Air-cooled, horizontally opposed longitudinal four-stroke twin
Valve arrangement:	OHV, 2 valves operated by pushrods and rockers, threaded adjusters
Displacement:	797cc
Bore x stroke:	84.8 x 70.6 mm
Compression ratio:	8.2:1
Carburetion:	2, 32mm Bing constant-velocity
Final drive:	Shaft and bevel gear, 3.36:1
Front suspension:	38.5mm Fichtel and Sachs, 7.3 in. travel
Rear suspension:	Single Boge damper, 4.8 in. wheel travel
Front brake:	2, dual-action Brembo calipers, 285mm discs
Rear brake:	200mm Simplex drum
Front tire:	90/90-18 Metzeler ME11 Perfect
Rear tire:	120/90-V18 Metzeler ME99A Perfect
Rake/trail:	28.0°/3.8 in. (97mm)
Fuel capacity:	6.3 gal (24L)
Weight:	521 lb (236kg) wet; 443 lb (219kg) tank empty
Fuel consumption:	32 to 46 mpg, 38.2 avg.
Average touring range:	241 miles
Best ?-mile acceleration:	14.07 sec., 91.6 mph
Average 200-yd. top-gear acceleration from 50 mph:	73.7 mph terminal speed
Projected best ?-mile acceleration*:	13.99 sec., 92.4 mph

*Projected performance with test-session weather conditions corrected to sea-level standard conditions (59 degrees F, 29.92 in. of mercury).

At the risk of sounding reactionary, I have to say that I like BMW's twin better than its four. Although BMW's compulsion to be different can still make me crazy (the layout of the left switches, for example), the twin's simplicity, pleasant power and basic smoothness (just keep the carb synchronized) make it unique in a more genuine and practical manner than the four. I have always felt that the 750 and 800cc boxers are the best of the twins.

The changes made this year have generally improved the R80, so at least I am happily backward.

—Art Friedman

I thoroughly enjoyed the Paris/Dakar R80 G/S I used in Tunisia last year, and the new R80RT, though much different in appearance, is functionally quite similar. I've often mused that one of the Japanese companies should make a sport-touring bike based on a 750-to-850 "standard" model, with a fairing roughly comparable to those on the Honda and Yamaha turbos and enough luggage capacity and easy-maintenance features to make it a viable long-term people mover.

The RT is the closest thing running to that basic tourer I keep talking about. It needs a prettier, higher windshield, better engine and gearbox quality control and adjustable suspension. But even as it is, it's a pleasant relief from the huge, boring land yachts on one side and the hyper-frenetic sport bikes on the other. The R80RT is like finding a good jazz station on the radio just when you'd resigned yourself to a choice between an endless opera or a Cindy Lauper retrospective.

—Dexter Ford

The R80 stands as a touchstone of reality in a decade when almost all bikes are specifically aimed at a narrow category. The Beemer may be leaning a bit toward the touring side of the sport, but remains simple and light enough to stay out of the full-dress niche.

If you feel a need to label the RT, try to find one which doesn't limit the bike to too tight a slot. Sport-tourer comes closer than any other classification, but I think smooth, stable and comfortable should be included.

—Nick Ienatsch

undemanding. In the hands of a smooth rider, the RT is perfectly capable of hurting overconfident Japanese sport bike riders emotionally. The machine can be made to wallow around when cornering at speed, especially if the rear spring preload is set too low, but the precise steering, light weight, wide bars and great brakes combine to make the RT quite capable in eight-tenths riding.

But it's on the open road, preferably a sweeping, sun-drenched back-country highway, that the R80RT does its best. The engine has to work harder than the old R100RT's did, and the shorter gearing of the 80 makes the engine feel more frantic at any given speed, but the feeling of a carefully refined, well-oiled machine inhaling the road beneath it, in almost effortless dignity, is still there. That's why the classic R80RT still exists.

17

BMW K75S

Photograhy by Jim Brown, Jeff Karr & Mike Gaspar
Motorcyclist, November 1986

The "S" Stands For Suspension

We first saw the S a year ago in Prien, Germany, at BMW's international K75 press introduction. Compared to the standard C, the S radiated sportiness; its sleek sport fairing, narrow handlebar and Pirelli Phantoms promised a bit more sporting competence than we'd come to expect from K bikes. We were disappointed to learn, however, that the striking, gun-metal gray S on display was a nonrunner, brought to Prien for photo purposes only.

The C model proved to be a competent sport-tourer, even while navigating the demanding roadways of the Alps. At a less-than-hectic pace, the C was stable, smooth and confidence-inspiring. Pushed harder, though, the bike revealed its shortcomings. A softly sprung, underdamped suspension and an overdose of shaft effect made back-road sprinting difficult. We expected BMW to adhere to its policy of fitting each model with identical suspension components and to give the S model the same spongy legs of the other triples. Our assumption was happily shattered at the S model's U.S. introduction in Williamsburg, Virginia, and during this test. BMW has done an about-face in its supension thinking and blessed the S with what the company calls an "aggressively tuned sport suspension."

The sleeker, racier look of the S comes by way of a new computer-designed, wind-tunnel-tested sport fairing with a color-matched engine cowl. The fairing is slimmer than the unit on the K100RS and does an acceptable job of fending off the windblast, the brunt of which hits the top of an average-sized rider's helmet. The rushing air is a bit noisy, but not a major annoyance. The narrow windshield is low and out of the rider's vision, which is good because it is relatively thick and almost impossible to see through. The engine cowl helps make the K75S more slippery and directs cool air to the power plant at the same time.

The engine in the S boasts no new technological tricks; it's the same 740cc power plant found in the C and T versions. The water-cooled, six-valve triple is flopped on its side, the pistons moving horizontally and perpendicular to the direction of travel. Balance weights on the output shaft keep the engine's inner workings smooth and thump-free, while BMW's Compact Drive System, consisting of a Monolever swingarm and shaft-drive unit, delivers power to the rear wheel by way of a slick-shifting five-speed transmission.

The frame of the S is constructed of steel tubing and uses the engine as a stressed member, following the K100 pattern. Instrumentation and handlebar controls also remain unchanged. The bar-mounted switches and controls are confusing to the uninitiated, and even after spending lots of time aboard all types of K bikes, none of us has become totally comfortable with them. The horn is the toughest to learn; you must lift your left thumb up to activate the horn. The horn's bark is fairly loud, but the button's placement is a sore spot.

Along with the fairing's redesign and addition of the engine cowl, the critical eye will immediately notice the smaller 17-inch rear wheel and the 285mm disc it carries. The wheel, lifted directly off the K100s, accommodates a rear tire 10mm wider than that fitted to the C and T. The 18-inch front wheel is identical to the one on the other K75s, as are the dual Brembo discs bolted to it.

It's the S's suspension that distinguishes it from the other triples—and, for that matter, from all previous Beemers. The K75 fork has been criticized heavily since the bike's introduction last year. On straight routes, the fork works well, offering compliance and smoothness. But when asked to handle the rigors of aggressive cornering, the fork's 7.5 inches of soft, spongy action does not provide adequate control or confidence. BMW engineers addressed the problem by reducing the fork's travel almost two inches, from 185mm to 135mm. In addition, each fork leg now contains a stiffer, progressively wound spring, tightly wound coils at the bottom and looser windings on top. Only the left leg contains a damping unit; the right leg's oil is for lubrication only.

Damping rates have been upped at the rear to match those in the fork, and a slightly stiffer spring is also used. Only three preload settings are offered, with no provision for rebound- or compression-damping adjustments. As with the other K75s, some damping adjustability would prove useful.

When you reach for the narrow handlebar on the S, you discover an altogether different feel than on the C. The S-model bar positions your hands only 14 inches apart. The rider's view of the cockpit is similarly narrow. The instrument pod sits between the fiberglass panels of the fairing and looks as if it *belongs* there, the way a tachometer belongs in a Porsche 911. The windshield is low and lean, enhancing the feeling of slimness. Grips are soft foam and comfy. The mirrors offer a vibrationless rear view, although the C is better in this respect because of its wider handlebar.

To start the S, just flick the fast-idle lever to its max setting and hit the button. After a minute or so, the lever can be thumbed off, and the bike idles nicely. Excessive smoking is still a problem after the bike is parked on its sidestand for any length of time; using the centerstand and parking on level ground avoids the problem, since it doesn't encourage oil to leak past the ring-end gaps. Once warm, the three-cylinder power plant runs cleanly, though throttle response is typically slow due to the engine's heavy flywheel inertia. Because of their unique balancing system, which utilizes counterweights on the output shaft, three-cylinder BMWs are considerably smoother than the K100 models, and as smooth as anything on the market.

Now this is more like it. Badly sorted-out suspension and shaft-drive systems get my technological hackles raised. In my estimation, previous BMWs were not the pinnacle of the suspension tuner's art. The long-travel, relatively undamped suspenders on the boxers were weird, but manageable because the bikes were light and the power limited. On the Ks, it's been another story. The lurching and pitching that goes on under heavy throttle or braking makes them much more awkward and difficult to ride than they should be. They had the worst-controlled shaft-drive system in motorcycling—until the S.

Without a lot of sacrifice in terms of ride quality, the S is more stable, eminently flickable and generally much more trustworthy when the road is coming at you like a roller-coaster track. This is a whole new motorcycle—even though the only changes are different bodywork and revised springs and dampers. Previous K bikes left me cold, but I now find myself hot for one very red K75S.

—Dexter Ford

You wouldn't expect a 25 percent reduction in displacement to make a motorcycle more fun to ride, but that's what has happened with the K-series BMWs. The character of this engine in big and small sizes is nearly the same, only the small one reaps the benefits of another couple of years of refinement. Though the little bike is in fact slower, it doesn't feel that way on the road. Instead, the sensations are of utter smoothness, clatter-free operation and flexibility. I'm happier going a touch slower on the 75 than I am making better time on the big bike. Maybe the BMW people should saw off yet another cylinder and see how that works.

—Jeff Karr

The K75S needs a sports-disclaimer tag—it's a sport bike only in relation to other K-series BMWs. Don't buy this bike expecting to run with other three-quarter-liter sport bikes. We tried it this month, and the 700 Interceptor didn't even bother to downshift; it just left.

If you like BMW Ks for their smoothness, looks, pedigree, luggage capacity or any other quality and want a sportier version of those attributes, the K75S won't disappoint you in any way. It's a sport bike, but a BMW sport bike.

—Nick Ienatsch

Funny how a couple of small changes can make a machine 100 percent better. I've logged a lot of miles on the BMW triples and enjoyed almost every minute. The C and T are very good motorcycles, and although they're both limited in what they're able to do well, I've been enthusiastic about them.

But the S is much better. This bike retains the C and T's good qualities and due to its exceptional suspension, offers a surprising amount of sporting ability. I love the looks of the S, and besides, it's a rather unique piece. I said a couple of issues ago that for my money the Concours was just about the most practical and competent motorcycle made. Well, I'm allowed to change my mind. The Concours is a super machine, but for me, the K75S is better.

—Mitch Boehm

On the road, the S feels noticeably different from its C stablemate. Steering is a bit heavier, both in slow, tight situations and at speed, because of the narrower handlebar and wider rear tire. Banking the S into a turn takes substantially more countersteering force, and that effort increases right along with speed.

Fork compliance remains almost as good as on the C, but the rear damper unit offers a slightly harsher ride, especially at the number two and three preload settings. However, when set in the softest position, the rear end delivers a compliant ride that's smooth and comfortable for everyday riding.

But the tauter suspension pays high dividends when the pace quickens and the road snakes. The stout 41mm fork dives less radically when pitched into a turn, increasing control and tire-traction feedback. The decrease in travel also helps; when the bike

BMW K75S

Suggested retail price:	$5950
Warranty:	36 months, unlimited miles
Engine type:	Water-cooled, longitudinal, in-line, 4-stroke triple
Valve arrangement:	DOHC, 2 valves; adjusting shims on top of buckets
Displacement:	740cc
Bore x stroke:	67.0 x 70.0mm
Compression ratio:	10.5:1
Carburetion:	Bosch LE Jetronic Fuel-injection
Final drive:	Shaft, 3.2:1
Front suspension:	41mm BMW, 5.3 in. travel
Rear suspension:	One BMW damper, 4.3 in. wheel travel; adjustment for preload
Front tire:	100/90-18 Metzeler ME33 Lazer
Rear tire:	130/90-17 Metzeler ME99
Seat height, unladen:	31.5 in. (800mm)
Fuel capacity:	5.5 gal (21L)
Wet weight:	522 lb (237kg)
Color:	Red
Instruments:	Speedometer, tachometer, odometer, gear-position indicator, clock; lights for fuel level, turn signals, high beam, neutral, low oil level, choke, battery, coolant temperature
Average 200-yd. top-gear acceleration from 50 mph:	74.4 mph terminal speed
Best 1/4-mile acceleration:	13.77 sec., 96.9 mph
Projected best 1/4-mile acceleration*	13.25 sec., 100.8 mph

*Projected performance with test-session weather conditions corrected to sea level standard conditions (59 degrees F, 29.92 in. of mercury).

pitches forward under braking, it dives less, keeping a more consistent attitude during braking and throughout a turn. This stability makes riding the S quickly less precarious and loads more fun.

At the rear, the tauter spring rate and greater damping resistance also contribute to greater stability. The second of the three pre-load settings is optimum for aggressive or two-up riding; the third position sacrifices compliance and allows the spring to override damping. The rear damper helps control the K's nasty shaft effect as well. The shaft's tendency to raise and lower the chassis according to throttle setting is a major flaw in the C's sport manners, but that glitch is noticeably reduced in the S.

The S works significantly better as a sporting machine than any of the other K bikes, triples or fours. The suspension allows a much quicker pace on twisty, bumpy routes or flat-out, sweeper-infested roads, and the S can be flicked into corners with confidence and without any wallowing or head shake. And if you enter a turn too hot, chopping the throttle and braking suddenly isn't the traumatic experience it would be aboard the C. The Metzeler ME99 and Lazer tires on our test machine worked superbly in the dry as well as in the wet, offering a smooth ride and predictable traction.

Give the S room to stretch its legs and generate some velocity and everything falls into place. This means keeping the tach needle in the upper portions of the rev range, though. The motor's power spread is very linear, and there's an abundance of low-end and midrange grunt, but if it's quick acceleration you want, look to the upper reaches of the rev range.

The S uses the same engine as the entire K75 family but outperforms the T model by .3 second at the dragstrip, posting a 13.77-second quarter-mile time. It's faster in the roll-on test as well; our S reached 74.4 mph, while the best the T could do was a stifled 68.4 mph. The S is heavier than the T since it carries the heavier rear wheel and disc as well as its sport fairing. The S's suspension and lower bar make it simpler to launch, however.

Because of the S's sporting emphasis, brakes became even more important. The dual Brembo grabbers up front work adequately at a normal pace, but at serious velocities the front system is prone to fading and not quite strong enough to haul you down in a hurry. The rear unit, however, is excellent: not at all grabby and easy to control.

All this emphasis on the S's sporting credentials doesn't mean it has lost its long-haul capabilities. On the contrary, the S is an extremely competent machine for putting away the miles, even with two aboard. The seat is the same design utilized on the C and 100RS, and most staffers gave it high marks. It's flat, fairly wide and comfortably firm.

The S model's seat-peg-bar relationship also lends itself well to sporty touring; even though the bar is narrow, it's not as low as those on some current sport bikes. The pegs are set low and fairly rearward to strike a balance between a full-fledged sport bike and a forward-pegged tourer. It's safe to say you won't be hoping for gas stops while touring on the S.

Our test machine flaunts excellent attention to detail. The paint is smooth, glossy and chip-resistant. Body panels fit snugly. The 5.5 gallon fuel capacity is good for approximately 170 to 200 miles. Engine maintenance on the K series is a study in simplicity; a complete teardown can be performed while the motor sits cozily in the frame.

The $5950 price isn't exactly pocket change, but it buys quite a bit of motorcycle. The K75S is a versatile machine, fully capable of being flailed on the back roads and still taking you and a partner cross-country in relative comfort. The S's suspension improvements are terrific, and they give the bike the sporting competency to back up its radical look and S designation. The S is, by far, the finest-handling factory BMW we've ridden. It took a year to get our hands on a K75S, but it has been well worth the wait.

18

BMW R65

Photograhy by Michael Pons & Jim Brown
Motorcyclist, April 1987

I f the skyrocketing cost of today's motorcycles has you running for cover, consider this: In 1980, the suggested retail price for a BMW R65 was $4275. Today, 7 years and a bundle of improvements later, the price has dropped to just $4100. That's *good* news, Beemer-philes.

That bundle of improvements, first seen on the '85 R80 and grafted onto the 650 version last year, includes parts and designs lifted directly from the K-bike mold. In place of dual rear dampers you'll find a monolever, single-damper rear-suspension system that, according to BMW, saves almost four and a half pounds of unsprung weight over a conventional dual-shock swingarm design and increases rigidity as well. Eighteen-inch K-bike wheels grace both ends, and to these are bolted K-bike brakes: a single disc with a double-action Brembo caliper up front and the K75C's drum unit in back. The front fork is of the K design as well, although fork-tube diameter is 38.5mm instead of the 41.4mm tubes on the 750 and 1000.

The venerable boxer power plant, a horizontally opposed, air-cooled twin, has seen many years of use — 64 to be exact. Designed by BMW engineer Max Friz in '23, the engine has been gradually refined and improved over the years though the basic design remains intact. The fact that BMW continues to utilize a rather dated design isn't terribly surprising when one considers the mill's virtues: simplicity, fuel efficiency, durability, a decent amount of power spread over a broad range and a low center of mass.

In 650cc trim, the latest boxer engine shows off no new technological tricks. Bore and stroke are the time-honored 82.0 and 61.5mm, the compression ratio is half a point higher than that of the R80 at 8.7:1, and pushrods move each cylinder's 40mm intake and 36mm exhaust valves. The cast-aluminum cylinders are lined with a Nikasil coating and, according to BMW, are virtually wear-free. Two 32mm constant-velocity Bing carburetors feed each cylinder while a transistorized breakerless ignition system provides maintenance-free sparking. The dry clutch is an automotive-type, single-plate unit, and there are five speeds.

The R65's chassis saw a major renovation last year. The tubular-steel, double-downtube frame kept its 28-degree rake and 4.7-inch trail, but suspension at both ends is derived from the K-series machines. The rear damper's preload settings adjust through four steps, but there is still no damping adjustability. The rear offers 4.8 inches of travel. There's also no adjustability in the braced, 6.9-inch-travel fork.

Braking action on our test bike was exceptional; both front and rear brakes were powerful but controllable, and surprisingly, more than one staffer rated the R65's brakes better overall than the triple-disc systems found on the K75S and full-liter K bikes.

Our test machine started fairly readily when cold with a flick of the bar-mounted choke lever and a stab at the starter button; 30 seconds or so and the choke lever could be thumbed off and the bike ridden away. The engine's output is impressive because of the way the available horsepower is delivered. The power seems perfectly linear; there's useful power from the basement all the way to the 7300-rpm redline, making the bike easy to ride in most situations. However, we encountered a major carburetion glitch on

The R65's 18-inch cast aluminum-alloy wheel carries a single 284mm disc squeezed by a double-action Brembo caliper. It's an excellent combination.

Like its K-bike brethren, the R65's rear end has some shaft effect but less than any of the larger BMWs. Four-way adjustable damper lacks compliance.

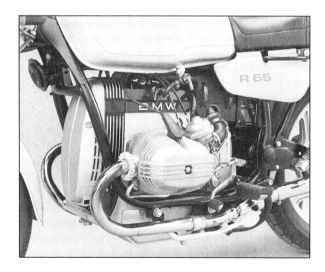

BMW's air-cooled opposed-twin design is a bit dated, but its ease of serviceability, broad power spread and the low CG it offers are traits that remain important.

our California-spec bike. At steady throttle settings between 2500 and 4000 rpm, the machine surged and hesitated almost as if it were running out of fuel. Carburetion was crisp above and below the two points and at larger throttle settings where the needle circuit wasn't as dominant, but the problem area lies in a frequently used rpm range. BMW says that raising the needle slightly helps matters, but that doing so violates California's strict emissions laws.

The problem wasn't severe enough to keep us from enjoying the R65's gentle road manners, however. In a time when motorcycle ergonomics follow either the race-replica crouch or the laid-back cruiser layout, the boxer's standard riding position is refreshing. The handlebar is wide and reaches out to greet you like a friend shaking your hand. The seat is flat, fairly wide and more comfortable than anything found on the K machines. The slightly staggered footpegs place your feet directly under you, the most comfortable position at most speeds. The Bing carburetors

I tend to like boxer BMWs, though not usually as they are delivered from the factory. The R80G/S Paris-Dakar dual-purpose bike is the only one I've liked recently just the way the boys from Berlin screwed it together. The R65 brings back memories of the things I've appreciated in the BMW twins I've ridden over the years, but I'm afraid I'd much rather spend $4000 on a cherry 1975 R90S (a burnt orange one) and the parts to upgrade it, than on a newer, slower, plain vanilla 650. If I wanted a slick new European twin, I'd zip right down to my local Cagiva dealer for a 650 Alazzurra—and save $400 or so in the bargain.

—Dexter Ford

I like the R65 because it's one of the few remaining middleweights with the comfort and versatility of a standard-style machine. After riding it for a while, I can adjust to most of its foibles and eccentricities, except the awful surge between 3000 and 4000 rpm on the California model. Actually, it's more like a bad miss. The R65 is otherwise enjoyable to ride, free of the limitations and drawbacks of a sport bike or cruiser.

The only problem is that, for a lot less money, I can get a Yamaha 600 Radian, with most of the same virtues, better performance, no foibles, no surge—and no shaft drive. And that's exactly what I would do.

—Art Friedman

It's pretty obvious why BMW twins have endured over the years. The boxer engine is simple, easy to work on and, in 650cc trim, plenty powerful for just about any type of use. The chassis improvements made last year give the bike more secure and competent manners and add a touch of modernism to the bike's traditional makeup. If I planned on spending lots of time aboard an R65, I'd install a small fairing or windshield to cut down the windblast, but other than that, the bike suits me fine. After a steady diet of high-tech Japanese machinery, this Beemer is a very nice, very traditional change of pace.

—Mitch Boehm

don't seem to crowd the rider's feet quite as much as before, and vibration, a problem on previous R65s, is properly subdued now.

A relatively uncompliant fork and rear damper take some of the smoothness out of the ride, but that tautness pays dividends when the pace quickens. The 454-pound (wet weight) R65 will never threaten a good Japanese middleweight on a twisty road, but its torquey motor, fairly taut suspension and above-average Conti SuperTwin tires make the bike ready for an occasional series of corners. It dives less than other Beemers during braking and exhibits less shaft effect as well.

Some minor problems remain. Although BMW redesigned the centerstand a few years back to provide a much wider, more solid stance, the sidestand is still spring-loaded and snaps back when the machine's weight is shifted off the stand. This is a good safety feature, but it can be inconvenient; it may even result in a parking-lot tip-over. Handlebar controls are a bit quirky as well, even though their design is completely different than those fitted to the K bikes. The horn's bark is loud enough to wake the dead,

An alloy fork brace integrated into the front fender keeps the 38.5mm fork tubes relatively flex-free. Ribbed Continental works well in wet conditions.

BMW R65

Suggested retail price:	$4100
Warranty:	3 years, unlimited miles
Recommended maintenance intervals:	5000 miles
Engine type:	Air-cooled, horizontally opposed 4-stroke twin
Valve arrangement:	OHV, 2 valves, operated by pushrods and rockers; threaded adjusters
Displacement:	650cc
Bore x stroke:	82.0 x 61.5mm
Compression ratio:	8.7:1
Carburetion:	2, 32mm Bing constant-velocity
Ignition:	Transistorized breakerless
Primary drive:	Helical-cut gears
Clutch:	Dry, single-plate with diaphragm spring
Final drive:	Shaft, 3.36:1
Front suspension:	38.5mm telescopic fork, 6.9 in. travel
Rear suspension:	Single BMW damper, 4.8 in. wheel travel; adjustment for spring preload
Front brake:	1, double-action caliper, 284mm disc
Rear brake:	Single-leading-shoe drum

Front tire:	90/90-18 Continental TK22
Rear tire:	120/90-18 Continental TK44
Rake/trail:	28.0°/4.7 in. (119mm)
Wheelbase:	57 in. (1447mm)
Seat height, unladen:	31.8 in. (807mm)
Fuel capacity:	5.8 gal (22L)
Wet weight:	454 lb (206kg)
Instruments:	Speedometer, tachometer, odometer, tripmeter; lights for turn signals, neutral, high beam, low oil pressure, generator
Speedometer error:	30 mph, actual 26.5 60 mph, actual 53.3
Fuel consumption:	40 to 52 mpg, 46.0 mpg avg.
Average 200-yd. top-gear acceleration from 50 mph:	68.6 mph terminal speed
Best ?-mile acceleration:	14.77 sec., 88.8 mph
Projected best : ?-mile acceleration*	14.34 sec., 91.5 mph

*Project performance with test-session weather conditions corrected to sea level standard conditions (59 degrees F, 29.92 in. of mercury).

but the button, found at the bottom of the switch housing on the majority of the world's motorcycles, is on top, making it difficult to reach in a panic situation. What's more, the turn-signal switch, normally found in the middle of the housing, is located at the bottom. Also, the speedometer on our test machine was hopelessly optimistic, and the under-seat storage compartments are large and waterproof, but they rattle over bumps.

But high quality and intelligent features abound. Almost 6 gallons of fuel can be pumped into the R65's tank, offering an average touring range of about 230 miles. The mirrors are spaced widely apart, and although vibration muddies their images at certain rpm levels, they offer a fairly good view to the rear. A simple, accessible design means easy maintenance; the rear wheel can be removed in about a minute, and engine maintenance, such as routine valve adjustments, is just a valve cover and a feeler gauge away.

Many of the reasons for buying a boxer are emotional. The high-quality paint and hand-striped tank and bodywork have a strong message for many riders, and to them, the traditional, simple design is far more alluring than four-valve heads, wraparound bodywork and 160-mph top speeds. With motorcycle prices escalating wildly, the R65's $4100 price tag seems more reasonable than ever. And since the 650 version almost equals the R80 in terms of horsepower, the R65 makes a very strong bid for those considering a European twin. Perhaps the world has arrived at the point where the R65 has been all along, waiting for us to finally see things its way.

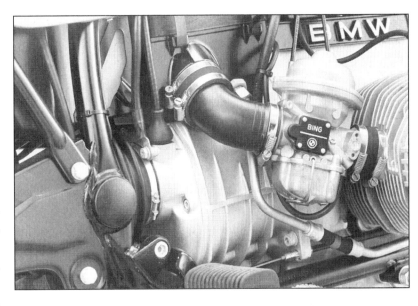

Carburetion on our bike was off between 2500 and 4000 rpm. The problem is an overly lean needle setting required to keep California air regulators happy.

The controls on the left handlebar take some getting used to. The turn-signal switch's action is vague, and the horn button's placement is out of the ordinary.

There are no gizmos or gadgets here, just a simple tachometer, speedometer and BMW's usual array of lights. Dual switches make adding power accessories easy.

19

BMW K75

Photograhy by Mike Gaspar
Motorcyclist, December 1988

Short People Just Got One More Reason to Live

The BMW K bikes have been controversial from the start. The motorheads from Munich had to tread a fine line between their legendary but dated boxers and the hordes of technologically stunning Japanese machines flooding the world market; the K100 and K75 are the result. The liquid-cooled German machines have their rabid fans and their rabid detractors—but until now their fans have almost all been tall.

Every K bike until now, you see, has had a seat height more typical of a dual-purpose machine than a street bike. According to BMW's designated spokesman, Rob Mitchell, a substantial minority of BMW fans liked the K75, but weren't going to buy one until it came in their size. The letters have been coming in steadily for years, and this year BMW responded. In the words of a BMW spokesperson: "We decided to see if they'd put their money where their mouths are."

The official designation of this K75 is simply that—the K75. Around BMW, and around our editorial offices, it's called the Lowboy, but it's actually the replacement for the original standard-issue K75C we first tested back in 1985. Except for cosmetic details the bikes are mechanically identical, but a whole new seat assembly has taken about 2 inches off the seat height—and the C off the end of the name.

The K75 line now includes the S model with its swoopy frame-mounted fairing, wider 17-inch rear wheel, rear disc brake and tauter sport suspension, and the K75T with its tall bar-mounted clear fairing, double-divot seat and mechanicals identical to this test machine. The base model shares a drum brake and a slightly narrower 18-inch rear hoop with the T. Engine specs are the same through the entire K75 lineup.

The engine is, of course, a truncated version of the original K100 flopped four. The triple has one cylinder lopped off the front, and its engine-speed jackshaft has a pair of counterweights to overcome the essential imbalance of a triple, but otherwise the twin-cam, two-valve, fuel-injected design is the same. In order to get more power out of the smaller mill, BMW took certain hot-rodding liberties with the 75: compression ratio is higher, at 11:1, the cams are a bit hotter and the intake tracts are slightly shorter.

The result is a smoother, slightly slower engine than the full 1000. Until this year the K100 was quite a buzzy engine; new, lighter pistons have cured most of the problem in the '89s. K bikes have also been known to smoke horrendously after a stint on the sidestand; '89 K100s (and the '88 ABS RS) have a new pinned-ring design that nearly eliminates the smoke screen. Here's the bad news: the K75s, all of them, will soldier on with the old ring setup for the remainder of the '88 model run, and ours smokes just as badly as any K100 ever did. According to BMW you *can* replace the pistons on any older K bike with the new smokeless pinned pistons. BMW doesn't recommend it, due to possible difficulties in breaking the glaze in a worn-in Scanimet-surfaced bore. Our aftermarket tuning sources, though, see no practical problem in making the switch—as long as the bike is already out of warranty. Remember, K75 pistons have taller crowns than K100 slugs; wait for the '89-spec K75 pistons which will, according to BMW, use the pinned-ring design.

The new riding position involves a new seat, but the frame is the same; theoretically, you can also interchange the seat-area parts with those on an older K75 (or K100). The handy glove box under the old seat is gone, as are the painted side covers. A black pebble-grained plastic shroud fits over the rear of the stock tank and reaches down between the rider's thighs to cover the holes left by the missing side panels. The new seat has the same basic layout of the old C and S pad, but it's obviously much lower in the pilot area. Our tallest tester, a burly 6-footer, found the new arrangement too low, but the medium-sized staffers judged it quite comfortable.

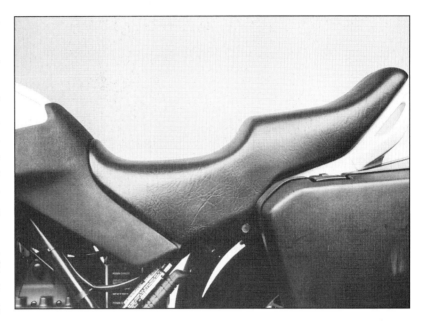

The new seat tapes out at 29.7 inches from the ground, 2.2 inches lower than the original C model's perch. Side panels, seat hinges and underseat bin are gone.

The front Brembos are crisp and responsive, but the soft fork allows lots of dive under hard use. Fading is rare, but possible during repeated stops.

The counterbalanced triple is unchanged inside, but now comes with a black paint treatment found previously only on high-zoot K100RS and Motorsport models.

Tire changes, as on all K bikes, are greatly simplified by the one-sided Monolever swingarm and shaft design. The K75 has a drum, not the S model's disc.

The seat feels hard upon first squat, but as the miles roll on, it works swimmingly. The acid test of a low seat height around our offices involves a certain 5-foot managing editor named Marcie; the K75 is low, but not near low enough to let her touch anything but her toes. The new seat seems right for people above 5-foot-4, all the way to about 5-foot-10.

The new K75 differs slightly from the earlier C model in cosmetics; the engine is painted black, and the heat shield on the muffler is chromed, not black as before. The slick handlebar-mounted fairing with its integrated turn signals is still here, making the K75 look quite a bit more sporting than its Everyman market position would lead one to expect. The handlebar is a relatively tall bend; we adjusted ours to the rear to bring the rider's hands down lower to the dished seat, and suspect that most seriously short riders will opt for a lower bar.

Riding position notwithstanding, the new K75 is exactly the same as the first one ever built. Its tall, soft suspension is perfect for relaxed, tasteful riding, from long-haul touring to everyday commuting. The 41mm fork is sprung and damped very loosely, letting everything short of a cinder block pass underneath without disturbing the rider; this works great on freeways, on gnarled city streets and on endlessly twisting roads, so long as the rider keeps his excitement level down. The rear shock, acting on the rigid Monolever swingarm, doesn't offer the same amount of travel, but it too is biased toward a relaxed riding style. Neither suspension system offers damping adjustability, though the rear Boge shock has three preload settings.

With the short driveshaft and gooey suspension, shaft effect is abundant. If you stick to the K75's laid-back riding profile, everything stays in line, but large or violent throttle movements bob the chassis up and down like a dog with a piece of meat. The new Paralever system, introduced on the R100GS this year would fix it, but we don't expect to see it on base-model K100s soon, let alone the even baser K75. Starting is not a problem, but if you left the Beemer on the sidestand last night, you'll leave your driveway in a blue cloud this morning.

The engine is smooth, but a rider's first few miles likely won't be. Throttle response is slow, due in part to a boggy fuel-injection system, in part to massive amounts of flywheel inertia. Also, the clutch takes up quite suddenly, and out near the end of its travel. This and the shaft effect make for lurching, bobbing departures until the rider (and the bike) is up to speed.

BMW triples are my favorite K bikes, but I don't fit this new standard model very well. The new seat is comfortable, more so than the previous designs, but the extensive reach to the handlebar it creates for the rider definitely is not. A poor tire choice also plagued our test unit; the 48-series Michelins offered minimal traction and a harsh ride, and they squirmed on rain-grooved freeways like a freshly landed trout. This bike still has a few of the traits I love about the BMW 750s—a smooth engine, supple suspension parts, easy drivability and well-designed luggage—but together they're not enough to make me like the bike more than the motorcycle it replaced—the K75C.

—Mitch Boehm

Riding the K75, especially our white one, gives me a much greater understanding of our presidential candidates. It's competent, it's unexciting, it's inoffensive; doesn't it sound as if I'm describing Bush and Dukakis?

If the little K were a person, it'd be the perfect neighbor. It wouldn't throw loud parties, it'd keep its lawn clean and its mailbox painted, and its son wouldn't wear a safety pin in his nose.

Yup, the K75 works fine, for the most part. You shouldn't try to corner hard on it, just as it would be a little silly to take George Bush to an Oingo Boingo concert. Excess enthusiasm with the throttle tends to upset the chassis, just as Mike Dukakis would get all unhinged if you wheelied up on a V-Max to take his daughter to the prom. For the regular grind of daily motorcycling, the K75 is hardly there for me. After a few days of commuting I can't remember one definite impression it's made on me—much like the incessant drone of Georgie and Mikey beaming out at me, month after month, from the evening news.

There's one other definite similarity. All three blow clouds of smoke too thick to see through.

—Dexter Ford

I'm really missing something here. I always thought life should progress smoothly forward, getting progressively better if possible, while avoiding past pitfalls or mistakes. Then this BMW K75 comes along. I've witnessed the new oil-control rings on the K100RS Special that remedied the fumigation problem, but this rig comes with the old rings everyone's castigated for four years. Modern street tires work unbelievably in the dry or wet and offer excellent life, yet the K comes with a set of tires I know the BMW test riders didn't choose, unless they were on the outrigger bike. The K75S suspension garnered unanimous approval from the press and public, yet we're back to underdamped, undersprung mush on the standard 75.

The new, low K75 disappoints me only because I realize what it could easily be. I hate to mention the aftermarket in yet another BMW "Off the Record," but that's where many Beemer riders must turn to finish what the factory started. Will '89 be the year BMW moves forward with all of its bikes? I hope so; we've seen the sophisticated components that will make a wonderful BMW. Now we need to see them all on one bike.

—Nick Ienatsch

This machine reminds me of the bike I was enamored of 15 years ago: It's a 750 triple, it wiggles in rain grooves like a snake that swallowed a joy-buzzer, and it produces enough smoke to kill every mosquito in the county. Of course, my Kawasaki Mach IV was quicker in the quarter and handled better in corners.

The K75 has all the basics for making a nice motorcycle; I'm surprised that a company with the sense to produce the first ABS motorcycle can also offer a bike with such outdated tires and rings so obviously in need of pinning (which has now been done to the K100). A serious motorcyclist might put up with a change of tires, but most would balk at pulling the pistons. The old saying "Don't sweat the small stuff" is fine unless you are competing against someone who does.

—Art Friedman

As with the K100, power is evenly spread throughout the engine's usable rev range; the hot-rod parts theoretically make the K75 peakier, but it's hard to notice a difference. Shifts are positive, but the high-mass flywheels make matching engine revs to road speed difficult, and the abundant shaft effect comes into play instantly if you misjudge a downshift badly, bouncing the chassis around enthusiastically and possibly sliding the rear tire. This chassis is not made for lightning starts, hard-edged riding technique or an impatient throttle hand.

The new K75 has one other cosmetic trick up its pipe; the earlier C, S and T models had a matte-black heat shield on the muffler, but the base bike now uses chrome.

The braced, 41mm BMW-made fork is unchanged from the C model. Its long (7.3-inch) travel and soft springs and damping make for a smooth but mushy ride.

With the moderately wide, high handlebar, steering is easy and predictable. In most day-to-day riding our five-speed K75 performed well, and in the areas in which it fell short it did so because of one simple change: the tires. BMW is very tough to pin down when it comes to tire choice on a particular model; we've ridden test K bikes with Michelin M and A 48s and M and A 49s, Metzeler ME33 and ME99s, Pirelli Phantoms, Pirelli MP7Rs and Continentals. This one came with the Michelin A48-and-M48 combo, and they are among the least confidence-inspiring tires we've ridden on recently.

The first problem is their behavior in freeway rain grooves; in the old days many tires wiggled slightly on grooves, but that's been rare in the last few years. These tires send the whole bike shaking and juking, up and down and side to side, as if possessed; even for our jaded test riders the feeling was unsettling. Even this would be a minor gripe; Los Angeles is the rain-groove capital of the world, and many cities have none. But the level of traction in cornering, especially at the front, is startlingly low for modern tires. Before the bike is leaned over to an even moderately sporting cornering angle, the front tire is beginning to turn in and push, leaving the rider with at least a shot of adrenaline and a resolution to stop at the nearest aftermarket tire dealer. We actually found ourselves avoiding corners in our daily commutes—and that's not in the usual repertoire of a *Motorcyclist* tester. We knew if we went around enough corners we'd grind something expensive off the bike, if not the rider. The last time we had a test bike with these tires was back in 1983. The bike was a Kawasaki 750 Turbo, and it went back to Kawasaki in pieces. If you have a choice, get a K bike with any other tires. Michelin's A49-M49 combo is a huge improvement over the ancient 48s.

The tires are the biggest impediment to sporting riding, but by no means the only one. The suspension is well out of its element at high cornering speeds or in quick transitions; it takes quite awhile for the chassis to respond to your last command, and it's usually not quite finished when time comes to make your next input. Rolling off the throttle and grabbing the brakes while leaned over is a special experience—to paraphrase Clint Eastwood, the chassis moves every which way *and* loose. Asking the K75 to carve through a set of esses is like forcing Jimmy Stewart to mouth a tongue twister against a stop watch. He'll get through it, but maybe not today. The basics are there: good

BMW K75

Suggested retail price:	$6750
Warranty:	36 months, unlimited miles
Engine type:	Liquid-cooled, longitudinal, in-line, 4-stroke triple
Valve arrangement:	DOHC, 2 valves, adjusting shims on top of buckets
Displacement:	740cc
Bore x stroke:	67.0 x 70.0mm
Compression ratio:	11.0:1
Carburetion:	Bosch LE Jetronic fuel injection
Transmission:	5-speed
Final drive:	Shaft
Front suspension:	41mm BMW, 7.3 in. travel
Rear suspension:	Single Boge damper, 4.3 in. wheel travel; adjustment for preload
Front tire:	100/90-18 Michelin A48
Rear tire:	120/90-18 Michelin M48
Wheelbase:	59.7 in. (1516mm)
Seat height, unladen:	29.7 in. (754mm)
Fuel capacity:	5.5 gal (21L)
Wet weight:	506 lb (230kg)
Instruments:	Speedometer, tachometer, odometer, gear-position indicator, clock; lights for fuel level, turn signals, high beam, neutral, low oil level, choke, battery, coolant-temperature
Color:	White
Average 200-yd. top-gear acceleration from 50 mph:	71.6 mph terminal speed
Best 1/4-mile acceleration:	13.86 sec., 95.2 mph
Projected best 1/4-mile acceleration*	13.54 sec., 97.8 mph

(*Projected performance with test-session weather conditions corrected to sea-level standard conditions (59 degrees F, 29.92 in. of mercury).

brakes, adequate power, a rigid frame and fork and felicitous steering. But when the suspension was handed out, the K75S was at the head of the line, and the garden-variety K75 came out on the slow end.

This is not a big problem. The K75 is a nice, friendly, classy-looking, reliable standard motorcycle, perfectly suited to the riding most people do most of the time. With the lower seat, the small fairing is more effective than before; it keeps the blast off your chest nicely, though it accelerates the wind enough to increase helmet noise. The seat works great for those of average height, and the smooth, miserly triple can pull lots of miles out of a tank of gas; K75s were getting better mileage than Suzuki's single-cylinder DR Big on Dexter's recent Russia tour. With the optional ($347.80) saddlebags the K is an excellent all-around machine, capable of effective commuting, light-duty sport-touring and even highly pleasurable continent crossing. Like all BMWs it suffers by price comparison with the Japanese offerings, but for many the finish, excellent utility, perceived quality and parts availability of a BMW are well worth the premium.

Now even short people can play.

20

BMW K1

TIM CARRITHERS
Photograhy by David Dewhurst
Motorcyclist, August 1989

Bavarian Flash in the Land of the Caesars

My friend Manzawa-san put it to me straight: "What kind of sport bike is this K1?" A good question. And after carving up kilometer after postcard-perfect kilometer of fast Italian tarmac through the lush green Alban Hills with motojournalism's assembled effete, I can match up the pieces of the puzzle that is BMW's newest single-track flagship to build an answer.

Up to this point, BMW AG has been a conscientious objector in motorcycling's horsepower wars. Unwilling or unable to join or beat the Japanese in such a high-stakes game, the Bayerische Moteren Werke engineers play the technological David to the Goliath across the Pacific. In such a scenario, the K1's different, even eccentric look makes perfect sense. The Germans needed a new spin on their latest fast ball to pitch to Europe and the U.S.

Back in the luxurious Hotel Helio Cabala, we are just a few clicks south of the eternal city of Rome and around the bend from the Pope's Castel Gandolfo summer compound. Though the K1 arrives in the States this fall, BMW brass saw fit to airlift press types from around the world for a whirlwind test session with preproduction examples of its first two-wheel supersport. Just a couple of days in the land of antipasto and autostradas on the fastest, best-handling street bikes ever to exit the Munich works— tough duty, to be sure.

We had seen the K1 before. But when the first photos arrived from its debut at the Cologne Motorcycle Show in September '88, it was hard to believe the visual and mechanical stunner came from the same drawing boards that brought us six decades of boxer twins.

If the liquid-cooled, longitudinal four in the K1 engine bay appears familiar, it should. Its 67mm bore and 70mm stroke are identical to the undersquare K100 power plant we first saw in 1983, but internal similarities dwindle from there. The 16-valve head is the single most notable change: four smaller, lighter valves are arrayed around a central spark plug in each cylinder. Each K1 intake valve measures 26.5mm across, compared to 34mm for the lone K100 intake poppet. Exhaust-valve diameter sits at 23mm in the K1 engine versus the K100's 30mm exhaust valve. Intake duration, however, remains the same at 284 degrees.

Since 16 valves could turn into a headache come adjustment time, BMW engineers streamlined the valve-lash adjustment process. Whereas the eight-valve engine used a shim and bucket system, the K1 simplifies matters by using revamped tappets and doing away with shims altogether. Considering its tighter tolerances and lighter reciprocating mass, the new valve train should require less frequent adjustment. And when adjustment is necessary, clearance is manipulated by swapping the tappets in precisely sized increments.

Combustion-chamber shape and valve angles differ as well, and compression jumps from K100-spec 10.2:1 to an even 11.0. The K1 pistons are slightly lighter, using the same Citroen-design labyrinth path through the rings to keep the vacuum formed in the cooling

engine from drawing crankcase oil downhill into the combustion chambers to cause smoky start-ups. In the technological trickle-down department, all 1989 K100s are fitted with smokeless pistons.

The K1 make-over mandated changes to the bottom end as well. Computer-aided Finite Element Method calculations shaved 2.87 pounds from the forged crankshaft. Connecting rods are lighter and stronger thanks to the same process.

A new integrated injection-ignition computer controls internal-combustion processes inside the K1 power plant. Where the K100 used discrete systems for both processes, the K1's Digital Motor Electronics (DME) system resembles the arrangements found in petrol-powered BMW automobiles. For starters, the newer, more sophisticated Motronic fuel injection replaces the K100's Jetronic system. With Motronic injection, the butterfly that measured air volume flowing through the old system is replaced by an electronic potentiometer on the throttle-butterfly shaft. The potentiometer feeds throttle-position data to the DME control computer to more quickly and accurately match injection volume with engine load, rpm, intake-air temperature, coolant temperature and altitude.

BMW claims a 4- to 5-horsepower gain from DME alone, but there are benefits on the service side as well. The computer has a built-in defect memory that lets mechanics

The K1 is the first K with the Paralever swingarm that beats shaft effect by floating the gear case on two U-joints and feeding drive torque back into the frame.

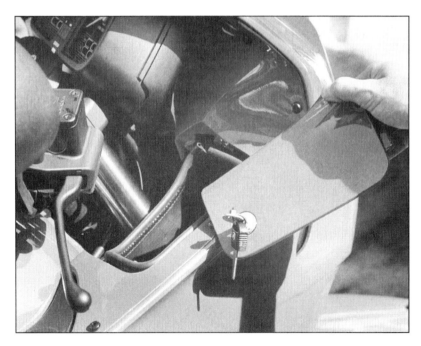

This small locking compartment in the front of the fairing carries the tool kit with room enough left over for extra little bits. All locks will use the same key.

equipped with BMW's latest diagnostic tester to retrieve error data in the event some chip should go haywire. And a fail-safe function built into the system keeps the engine running in the event some other subsystem should fail.

On the exhaust side, the tidy new stainless steel system disposes of spent gases through a compact cylindrical muffler rather than the K100's clunky bread box. The K1 gets the extra volume necessary for the new system from an expansion chamber tucked neatly out of sight beneath the gearbox.

The net effect of the mechanical make-over is an engine that BMW claims produces an even 100 horsepower, 10 horsepower more than the K100. Factory torque numbers jump from the eight-valve engine's 64 foot-pounds at 6000 rpm to 74 at 6750 rpm. And though further tuning changes could have extracted far more urge than that, BMW engineers took the conservative tack to maintain an even flow of power and to stay under the 100-horse ceiling for bikes sold within the fatherland.

Key bits and pieces throughout the driveline have been selectively strengthened to deal with the extra horsepower. And though the first four gears use ratios identical to those in the K100 box, both fifth-gear (1.61 versus 1.67) and final-drive (2.75 versus 2.91) ratios are slightly taller on the K1.

The new engine hangs as a stressed member in a familiar steel-tube frame, though the tubes are thicker and stronger through the center section where stresses are greatest. The new frame holds the nonadjustable 41.7mm Marzocchi fork at a more sporting 26-degree angle, dropping trail from K100-spec 4.0 to 3.6 inches. The K1's wheelbase stretches 2.1 inches beyond the K100's to 61.6, traceable mainly to the longer Paralever swingarm.

You'll remember the Paralever from the omnisurface R100GS boxer twin. BMW's unique single-sided swingarm neutralizes most of the dreaded shaft reaction, a vital concern considering the K1's extra power and more serious sporting intent.

The K1 rolls on wide, light, three-spoke, alloy wheels carrying modern 160/60VR18 (rear) and 120/70VR17 (front) radial rubber. The bikes we rode were fitted with Michelin radials, but production motorcycles will carry either Michelin, Dunlop or Metzeler rubber. The front wheel sports a pair of impressive-looking 12-inch (305mm) floating rotors and four-pot Brembo calipers fitted with asymmetrical pistons (32mm front, 34mm rear) for more even pad wear. The single rear disc is the same diameter as a K100 rotor but, at 5mm, is 1mm thicker than those of the original K.

The bad news is you can't fit saddlebags on the K1. The good news is these smallish locking compartments in the tail section will carry sport-touring essentials.

Though motorcycles destined for the European market will come with and without, all U.S.-spec K1s will arrive with BMW's FAG Kugelfischer antilock braking system. BMW completely recalibrated the ABS to accommodate the K1's new wheels, brakes, tires and chassis geometry. But since the entire system adds a hefty 26 pounds to the K1's weight, the engineers relocated the front-wheel pressure modulator, one of the system's heaviest bits, under the front of the fairing along with the tool kit and coolant-return tank.

One look tells you the K1 fairing is a radical departure for BMW, but like every other BMW translation, the German version of wraparound bodywork is decidedly different. Only the K100's 5.8-gallon fuel tank, radiator, headlight, taillight and instrument pod came along for the ride. Taking the form-follows-function design tack, BMW engineers faced a formidable task: optimize airflow and ergonomic concerns simultaneously. The wedge-shaped front fender they came up with cuts wheel lift and smooths airflow around the fork and wheel, making the transition to the rest of the fairing with minimum turbulence. An array of vents direct cool air to the brakes.

It's an undeniably slick package. BMW claims an impressive 0.34 drag coefficient (the coefficient of drag is multiplied by the frontal area to arrive at the total drag) with the rider tucked in. It's no surprise that the K1 doesn't accommodate standard-issue BMW hard luggage. Twin lockable compartments below the passenger's seat provide room enough (6 liters each) for sporting incidentals like a camera, spare gloves, maps and the like. A single key opens all K1 locks, including (please pause to applaud here) an integrated fork lock. BMW's accessory department has come up with an exceedingly well-engineered zip-together soft-luggage system that mounts easily to the passenger seat–tail section to add about 1.5 cubic feet (47 liters) of extra baggage-handling capacity.

Under the K1's slick front fender you find 12-inch floating discs and four-piston Brembo calipers that stop the K1 quickly. The Marzocchi fork gets a bolt-on brace.

With a firm grasp of the K1's vital statistics, we get a rundown of the following day's ride, route maps, phone tokens (regular money doesn't work), autostrada passes, along with admonitions to abide by local speed limits. Up until 18 months ago, limits on one's personal autostrada velocity were understood and summarily ignored. But lately, Italian traffic enforcement has become more than an oxymoron, and our hosts are careful to remind the American contingent in particular that Italian prison bears less than a passing resemblance to the Beverly Hills Hotel.

As the sun works at burning off an early morning haze, the bikes are readied, and we survey our route: a well-marked loop about 87 miles long winding past the Lago Albano through the green Alban Hills past the town of Marino and the Castel Gandolfo—the most famous of the 13 *castelli Romani* and summer home to popes since 1624. From cobblestones to autostradas and every road in between.

Swinging a leg over my assigned K1 informs me the seat is just over an inch lower than on a K100. The perfectly shaped bar proves a sporting grip can be comfortable. Putting about 26 inches between the soft, well-shaped grips, the handlebar feels much like a late '70s superbike bend. The levers are long, with plenty of room for a two-finger grip on the front brake. Switches are the same eccentric BMW bits you either love or hate, and the instrument pod comes directly from the K100. Bright yellow markings are the K1 tip-off, making the 280-kph speedo and 10,000-rpm tach easier to read.

Half choke and a poke at the starter has the powerhouse K four up and running cleanly; nary a puff of blue smoke or the characteristic high-pitched idle whine of previous BMW fours mars our first impression of the K1. Thirty seconds later, the Beemer is ready for Italian traffic before we are.

Only two true rules of the Italian road exist: There are no rules, and right of way goes to the brave. The meek shall inherit the curb. This is one of the few spots on earth where you'll see a 50cc Garelli moped flick it around a huge fuming garbage truck at the apex of a blind 90-degree bend. On a one-way street. Going the wrong way. Maybe you get used to seeing your life pass before your eyes more often than "M.A.S.H." reruns, but I wish the K1 had a real horn rather than something that sounds like a refugee from Pee Wee Herman's scooter.

Aside from the pegs that are too high and too far aft for my 35-inch inseam, the K1 is quite comfortable, so long as you stay in one spot. The riding position is strictly determinist; any other pose feels instantly unnatural. The only other comfort glitch surfaces while idling through Saturday-morning traffic; there's enough engine heat pouring from the rear of the fairing, especially on the left (exhaust) side, to slow-cook my calves, not exactly the ticket for late-August lane-splitting on the Ventura Freeway.

The suspension is surprisingly taut at low speeds, especially by BMW standards. Pick up the pace a bit, and the rear shock turns downright harsh, even dialed to the softest of four spring-preload positions. The fork does a better job over imperfect pavement. It doesn't dive much, even under heavy braking, and steering feels light and precise through bump-infested corners.

When the road and throttle open up, the 16-valve engine spins up with astonishing verve, though not nearly as quickly as a full-liter Japanese four. The Motronic injection provides seamless, stutter-free power delivery from idle on, but the K1 flexes its most impressive muscle beyond 5000 rpm. Keep the tach needle between 6000 and 8000, and it feels like a strong Japanese 750 but stirs up a good deal more vibration than I'd like in the process. Regardless, this is by far the best sporting power plant ever from Bavaria.

The Michelins begin to scuff in about the same time I've shaken the last clot of wheezing Fiat diesels clogging the road past Lago di Nemi. Hauling the bike down from a long 125-mph straight, I discover the new brakes are linear, powerful and nearly fade-free. There's leverage enough from the well-shaped lever for a confident two-finger grip. Feel is exemplary. But it's best to get all your braking done with the bike still vertical, because it stands up and goes straight if you touch the brakes while heeled over.

The K1's recalibrated ABS can still surprise an expert pilot by taking premature control of the brakes while stopping hard on clean, grippy pavement. When it takes over under such circumstances, the system cycles on and off abruptly enough to shoot me deeper into a corner than I expect in a series of heart-stopping staccato vaults. Even on the K1, ABS is biased more toward stretching the rider's life expectancy than lowering lap times, and on the street, that's just fine. It saves me from scuffing up my nice white leathers as I brake over an invisible patch of Mediterranean mystery ooze. After some acclimation time, I find myself using the brakes on the ABS bikes far harder than on the non-ABS models, especially on these unfamiliar roads. Working with a net is always easier, especially on a bike that stirs up this kind of speed.

This is the first BMW I can actually flick into a corner and come out hard enough to drift the rear tire. The Michelins are fine, but I'd order my K1 with Dunlops or Metzelers. And though the Paralever erases about 90 percent of the K100's annoying shaft reaction, it's

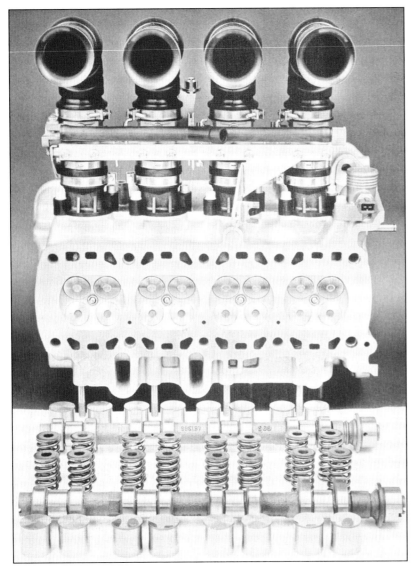

The heart of the K1: Twin cams act directly on the tappets in the 16-valve top end. New Motronic fuel injection is integrated with BMW's new Digital Motor Electronics.

still crucial to corner on the gas lest the side- and centerstand bite the pavement prematurely. Although the fairing and bodywork make hanging off difficult, ground clearance is more than adequate. Serious chicanery does take its toll on the undercarriage, while blatant motojournalistic geekery erodes the footpegs and fairing lowers. But that's licking the flap on the Michelins' traction envelope and inviting a painful relationship with some of the quaint Italian architecture lurking outside every other apex. Better to just say no.

The K1's steering is quite precise, and it flicks in *con brio* with no head shake on or off the gas. And though it's easily the best-handling K four by a margin, the K1 still disdains mid-corner corrections, demanding a much more premeditated riding style than an Asian supersport. It lives for those 100-mph corners, so long as they're reasonably smooth. The K1's suspension feels harsh over rough pavement taken at speed, especially out back. The bike never feels as assured cranked over through nasty bumps as Suzuki's 1100 Katana, for example. Running one quick, downhill chute on the gas, I fly for a bit as a truly memorable Italian whoop blows me straight out of the seat; the Beemer doesn't come close to bottoming its shock.

Facing a long, lonely straight with only sleepy cows as witnesses, I dial up 160 kph just in time to slash by an 80-kph speed-limit sign. Later that same second, a tiny blue and white spec in the sky grows into a blue and white police helicopter. But halfway through my third Hail Mary, the eye in the sky veers left 50 feet shy of citation altitude, settling harmlessly into the adjacent pasture, and the pilot waves as I drone by. I love this country.

All the police we blundered on displayed the same sporting attitude: Like the *carabiniere* who couldn't believe anyone on a bike like this could be dim enough to trail his tiny Fiat van through a 50-kph zone at 50 or the guy in the autostrada toll kiosk giving me a *molto buono* thumbs up at the sight of my 280-kph speedometer.

And while the K1 can't quite manage that velocity, it reels in the Italian superslab effortlessly at 160 kph (100 mph). A good deal of vibration sneaks past the rubber handlebar and footpeg mounts to tingle hands and feet at that speed, but it doesn't become bothersome for a couple of hours. The seat is great, and the fairing does an excellent job, leaving only my head in the wind, and without any nasty buffeting. Intermittently filling up with big 'Benz sedans and tapped-out Alfas testing their high beams on the back of my helmet, the bar-mounted mirrors provide a wide-angle rear view and stay crystal clear regardless of speed.

There's nobody ahead or behind at this point, so I invoke journalistic immunity, snick into fifth gear and lay on it. Air behind the fairing is calm, though the compound curves of the skinny smoked windscreen make it all but impossible to see through. I can stay under long enough to get 250 kph on the speedo—about 155 mph on the freeway. I *really* love this country.

Backing down to my usual 180-kph cruising speed, I encounter four more K1s and a ZX-10 in the midst of some high-speed stare down. We're about to see how fast the K1 really is. Seconds later the Kawasaki squares off with the lead K1, throttles mash against stops, and both bikes pull away. I stay close enough to watch them pull even for an instant, until the ZX-10 comes on the cams and disappears like the *Millennium Falcon* making the jump to light speed.

Returning to the sumptuous Helio Cabala Hotel, I'm beginning to see where the K1 fits in America. Upscale automobiles like BMW's own

BMW K1

Suggested retail price:	$13,500
Warranty:	36 months, unlimited miles
Engine type:	Liquid-cooled, longitudinal, in-line, four-stroke four
Valve arrangement:	DOHC, 4 valves, operated by followers
Displacement:	987cc
Bore x stroke:	67.0 x 70.0mm
Compression ratio:	11.0:1
Carburetion:	Bosch Motronic fuel injection
Final drive:	Shaft and bevel gear
Front suspension:	41.7mm Marzocchi, 5.3 in. travel
Rear suspension:	BMW Paralever, one BMW damper, 5.5 in. wheel travel; adjustment for spring preload
Front tire:	120/70VR17 Michelin A59 radial
Rear tire:	160/60VR18 Michelin M59 radial
Rake/trail:	26.0°/3.6 in. (91mm)
Wheelbase:	61.6 in. (1565mm)
Fuel capacity:	5.8 gal (22L)
Wet weight:	571 lb (259kg), claimed

M1, M3, M5 and as yet unobtainable Z1 roadster prove there is and should continue to be a market, albeit a small one, for Teutonic exotica with price tags to match. An American price hadn't been etched in granite by press time, but don't plan on paying less than $13,500 or so when K1s begin to trickle in this fall.

BMW plans to produce a total of 4000 K1s this year: 1400 for Germany, leaving 2600 for the rest of the world. At this point, the U.S.'s share of the K1 production is even more nebulous than the bike's sticker price. But figuring about 200 BMW motorcycle dealers in the U.S., a good estimate would be one each, with a few extra thrown in for California. In any case, there won't be many. But if you're rich and if you're lucky, you'll be on one of them.

21

Photograhy by Scott Killeen & Charlie Rathbun
Motorcyclist, December 1989

BMW R100GS PARIS-DAKAR

*From the Sahara Desert to the Streets of Santa Monica,
Think of BMW's R100GS Paris-Dakar Boxer as a
Round-Trip Ticket to Just About Anywhere*

Leave it to BMW. Who else would offer Americans a 550-pound boxer twin packing 9.3 gallons of gas and a $7860 price tag all dressed up for the African desert? Nobody else could. Slide your eyes once over this beast, and you wonder, "Have those legendary engineers of Germany been wandering around the Sahara too long without a pith helmet?" Not hardly.

The R100GS is its biggest seller on the Continent and beginning to catch on in America, launching a Paris-Dakar edition in the U.S. seemed inevitable, even if the logic behind such a move doesn't immediately jump out and grab you by the checkbook. This boxer is an acquired taste.

Who else but the Germans could pull this off, anyway? BMW knows more about the African desert than anybody outside the Afrika Corps. Though the Hondas are getting to Dakar first lately, BMWs have been there more often over the long haul, and that's what matters.

To European eyes, the Paris-Dakar GS is an alternative status cruiser, roughly equivalent to upscale all-wheel-drives like the Range Rover and Lamborghini LM002. Most of these off-road poseurs are after the look. They aren't about to take their expensive toys out in the dirt, though that's half the fun of owning one. On this side of the Atlantic the bike just looks big and weird. Paris-Dakar mystique doesn't work in American showrooms, and the trans-African boxer is left to trade on its functional merits and sheer eccentricity. Luckily for BMW, this one packs plenty of both.

In an age when motorcycle engines are becoming more technical and less accessible, the boxer hangs its opposed cylinders in the wind like aberrant thumbs in the eyes of conventional internal-combustion wisdom. Its brand of mechanical simplicity is a perfect match with the rest of the motorcycle.

Parked next to the BMW, the current crop of Asian Paris-Dakar poseurs look milquetoast-civilized, three-quarter-scale plastic-wrap copies of the real McCoy. Everything about the BMW feels solid, substantial, purpose-built to last.

BMW's desert uniform is built around the 9.3-gallon gas tank and its tubular bracket and headlight guard. Rotation-cast from PAG polyamide thermoplastic, the largest production fuel tank on any two-wheeler is light and remarkably tough. Surrounding the frame backbone and the top of the engine, it keeps a good deal of the boxer's rattle and hum from reaching the rider. The bad news is that without a charcoal canister to catch evaporating fuel, BMW's ship of the desert tank is stamped "off-road only" in California. Worse yet, the bike you see here won't be coming to California at all.

The rest of the Paris-Dakar look comes from a new fiberglass-reinforced, frame-mounted plastic fairing, including a swoopy new windscreen, contoured single seat, longer luggage rack, a sculpted engine fairing and expansive 4mm-thick aluminum skid plate. The P-D bike also gets wider mudguards with aluminum supports and a weird-looking front-fender extension to keep road filth off the rider. U.S. versions will arrive with electrically heated grips, and ours arrived with BMW's excellent optional saddlebags. If you already own a GS, the Paris-Dakar parts are available from your BMW dealer complete with paint and decals or unfinished for considerably less money.

Either way, underneath all that bodywork is the same R100GS we tested in our September dual-purpose duel. The most recent permutation of the perennial 980cc boxer is fundamentally unchanged, hanging in the same twin-downtube pipe-rack frame. Each 94.0-by-70.6mm cylinder breathes through its own 32mm Bing carb and two pushrod-operated valves arrayed in a hemispherical combustion chamber.

Power flows through a single-plate diaphragm-type dry clutch on the way to the five-speed transmission and ingenious single-sided Paralever drive shaft and swingarm system. First seen on the R100GS, the Paralever's floating shaft housing and torque arm keep the chassis from being torqued up and down by the shaft.

Up front, the nonadjustable 40mm Marzocchi fork carries a 21-inch wheel that laces straight-pull spokes through the outer edge of Akront alloy rims, allowing tubeless tires. A small, stamped fork brace keeps the legs in line. Out back, a single preload-adjustable, gas-charged shock controls the Paralever and similarly cross-spoked 17-inch rear wheel.

Throw a leg over the beast. You're sitting on the heaviest modern production two-wheeler ever intended to stray from the pavement. The whole package weighs 550 pounds with vital fluids. That's better than 100 pounds heavier than a Honda Transalp and 65 pounds porkier than a standard-issue R100GS. Adding the maximum 377 pounds of rider and cargo gives you a 926-pound gross-vehicle-weight rating. That's heavy.

And it's tall, too. Planting both feet on the ground is a stretch for sub-6-footers. Looking down, the vast expanse of red and refrigerator-white fuel tank between your knees is overwhelming at first. The tank is actually well shaped and unobtrusive, considering there's nearly enough fuel capacity to qualify for an OPEC membership. A lockable door behind the gas cap uncovers a nifty glove box with room enough for the obligatory pair of gloves, maps or a light lunch. But don't stow any water-soluble valuables; the lid leaks when it rains.

Just above, the frame-mount fairing's white dash panel carries a huge 120-mph speedo flanked by a silver-dollar-sized tachometer and quartz clock, with the usual complement of dummkopf lights in between. The speedo is an easy read, but the tach and clock are small enough to demand an occasional second look. A three-position rocker switch below the ignition switch meters heat to the grips. Bar switches are standard boxer issue.

Our Paris-Dakar was reluctant to wake up on cold mornings, more so than any BMW in recent memory. Cold starts took a minute of full choke and considerable fiddling with the throttle before the boxer settled into its signature agricultural idle. Once warm, it fired immediately. Out in morning traffic the BMW is the consummate urbane gorilla, er, guerrilla. A bulletproof clutch and smooth power from 2000 to 7000 rpm get you through maximum gridlock with minimal effort. The only glitch is a long-throw shifter that can take two or three tries to be coaxed into third gear.

Aside from feeling generally porkier, taking more muscle to maneuver at stall speed and displaying a tendency to tip into slow corners (especially with a full tank of gas), the Paris-Dakar behaves much like a standard GS on city streets. Sitting 33.9 inches over the pavement makes it easier to see and be seen in tight traffic.

Extra leverage from the wide bars makes low-speed steering easy if not quick, but they're a close fit for lane-splitting. And remember those cylinders and crash bars also require extra side clearance, or you'll make some special friends in tight traffic. The optional saddlebags widen the bike even more, but they add 44 pounds of watertight, lockable cargo capacity and along with the longer rack create an excellent solo commuter.

On the freeway, the Paris-Dakar is the best long-distance runner in the BMW line-up. Turning just under 4000 rpm in top gear into an indicated 70, the P-D blurs its rearview-mirror images and sends some tingles through the grips, but the boxer's steady, low-frequency rumble only gets objectionable beyond 80 mph. The ride is plush and a bit underdamped—like mom's old New Yorker floating over a sea of expansion joints.

The BMW's riding position feels as roomy as any American land yacht's. The big tank and new fairing make better wind and weather protectors than those on any other all-surface tourer. Our 6-foot-4-inch tester felt protected although the wind hit him at about eye level and buffeted his shoulders a bit; shorter riders experienced considerable buffeting around the head and shoulders. The same compound curves that redirect the wind create a hopelessly distorted world view if you try to tuck in and look through it. So don't.

A comfortable cockpit is essential on a bike with this kind of range. With the throttle mostly against its stop, the tank calls up reserve at 300-mile intervals, leaving a gallon in the tank. A judicious right wrist can coax 400 miles from a full tank with reasonable ease. And the mercifully comfortable saddle lets you sit through 300 to 400 miles at a time before terminal burn sets in. Aside from dim, uneven instrument lighting, the P-to-D is a pleasant enough place to be after sundown. The headlight's broad, even beam is the next best illuminant to daylight for picking your way down a desolate, high-desert road. The high beam burns a long, well-shaped hole in the night that's nearly strong enough to bubble paint on approaching traffic. The heated grips are great on a cold winter night, though the hottest position was uncomfortably so through thin gloves and the low position didn't do much of anything.

You'll ride through day or night alone on this one. Strangely enough, our bike came with passenger pegs, but the longer rack takes up space normally occupied by the passenger seat. The only way to carry two people in BMW's parts book is to buy an entire new dual seat. C'mon, guys, how hard would it be to throw in a bolt-on pillion pad and save us a few hundred bucks?

Though both use the same chassis and powertrain, the lighter GS is still our favorite BMW for cutting up a tasty piece of blacktop. Acceleration on the big guy is less than heart stopping (especially after a stop at the gas pump). It won't impress riders weaned on

No motorcycle has ever made me feel so ridiculous. This bike can make Arnold Schwarzenegger look like Peewee Herman (or Nick Ienatsch, for that matter). Its turn-signal switch is where the horn should be, the horn is where the headlight dimmer switch should be, and the dimmer switch is where the turn-signal switch belongs. For reasons unknown, there is no pillion for your favorite passenger, but the front of the bike is adorned with a gloss-red giraffe rammer to protect the headlight amidst a stampede. The gearbox has more floating neutrals than I could find use for, and the dash layout has all the slick ergonomics of a lawn tractor.

On the other hand, the engine has torque at nearly any rpm, and the bike handles quite well for being so tall and portly. The windscreen and fairing also do an excellent job of blocking the breeze at freeway speeds, although the asymmetrical screen looks strange and makes other objects look strangely distorted. Okay, so I guess it works well enough, but I'm holding my money for the Honda GL1500 motocrosser.

—Lance Holst

Four years ago on a hot summer night I rode the real Paris-Dakar racer, the very bike that Gaston Rahier kicked some booty on in Africa. The racer had an emergency-only electric starter that I used by jump-starting it from a friend's van, and the front of the Beemer had enough lighting to see through a brick wall. This bike was a mile high, and I remember wondering how Gaston (he's about 5 feet 4 inches) ever reached the ground as I balanced the roaring beast on the toes of one foot, warming the twin before slipping it into gear.

Gaston's bike was as wild as this replica is tame. Full-on sand knobbies, an exhaust system designed with only horsepower in mind and an eye toward light weight put the race bike sand dunes ahead of the replica in performance, and several tens of thousands of dollars ahead in R&D. BMW spent heavily to win P-to-D, and now we pavement guys get a look at what Gaston helped form.

The Paris-Dakar replica improves upon what I like about the standard GS, making it more crashproof, longer legged and better able to block the wind. Apart from the recalcitrant shifting and antiquated switches, I enjoy the GS as much as any bike I've ridden, especially in a sporting environment that requires a stable chassis and compliant suspension. A smooth, dirt fire road is also fun on the GS P-D, but anything rougher brings Gaston Rahier's accomplishments into perspective: how'd that little guy ride this BMW so fast through the Sahara desert?

—Nick Ienatsch

BMW's Paris-Dakar boxer is like a Club Med vacation without the girls: the perfect (almost) antidote for civilization. When I'm tired of choking behind Peterbuilts, dodging Ramblers packed with blue-hairs and just generally dicing it out with the balance of Southern California's Antidestination Society, it's time to top off the boxer and head for La Paz, Mexico. Sure it looks weird. But, hey, I *like* weird. It's simply bombproof and all but crashproof. Don't ask me how I know. Just toss another pile of shrimp on the hibachi, pop a Bohemia and pass the cocoa butter. My vacation starts today.

—Tim Carrithers

Japanese horsepower. The 11.2-inch front disc and Brembo caliper eat up more effort and real estate when stopping the heavier bike. Steering also takes more effort, but aside from that, the Dakar is surprisingly well behaved through a tricky set of corners—but only if you play by the rules.

The Paralever immunizes the chassis against driveline-induced rock and roll, but a smooth throttle hand is still the quickest way through a canyon chicane. Tires stick and there's plenty of ground clearance (watch the sidestand in left-handers), but the BMW prefers smooth cornering inputs as well. Flick it hard into a fast bend, and the under-damped fork and shock let the bike wallow like a huge wet dog. The wispy fork brace isn't enough to keep the tubes from flexing and twisting under the extra load. Cranking up maximum spring preload on the rear shock helps but turns the ride uncomfortably harsh. Packing bags with gear on the rack makes the situation worse.

BMW R100GS PARIS-DAKAR

Suggested retail price:	$7860	**Front wheel:**	1.85 x 21 in., spoked
Warranty:	36 months, unlimited miles	**Rear wheel:**	2.50 x 17 in., spoked
Engine type:	Air-cooled, longitudinal, horizontally	**Front tire:**	90/90-21T Metzeler Sahara tubeless
	opposed, 4-stroke twin	**Rear tire:**	130/80-17T Metzeler Sahara tubeless
Valve arrangement:	SOHC, 2 valves, operated by	**Rake/trail:**	28.0°/3.9 in. (99mm)
	pushrods and rockers; threaded	**Wheelbase:**	59.6 in. (1513mm)
	adjusters	**Seat height, unladen:**	33.9 in. (861mm)
Displacement:	980cc	**Seat height, laden with**	32.8 in. (813mm)
Bore x stroke:	94.0 x 70.6mm	**160-lb rider:**	
Compression ratio:	8.5:1	**Fuel capacity:**	9.3 gal (35L)
Ignition:	Battery-powered, electronically	**Wet weight:**	550 lb (249kg)
	triggered	**Color:**	White/red
Lubrication:	Wet sump, 2.5 qt	**Fuel consumption:**	38 to 45 mpg, 43.0 mpg avg.
Battery:	12V, 25AH	**Average touring range:**	397 miles
Primary transmission:	Direct to clutch	**Average 200-yd. top-gear**	78.3 mph terminal speed
Clutch:	Dry, single-plate	**acceleration from 50 mph:**	
Transmission:	5-speed	**Best ?-mile acceleration:**	13.94 sec., 93.9 mph
Final drive:	Shaft, 3.09:1	**Corrected best**	13.83 sec., 94.8 mph
Front suspension:	40mm Marzocchi, 8.8 in. travel	**?-mile acceleration*:**	
Rear suspension:	BMW Paralever, one BMW damper,		
	7.0 in. wheel travel; adjustment for	*Performance with test-session weather conditions corrected to sea-level standard	
	spring preload	conditions (59 degrees F, 29.92 in. of mercury).	
Front brake:	1, double-action caliper, 279mm disc		
Rear brake:	Single-leading-shoe drum,		
	cable-operated		

Past pavement's end, the Paris-Dakar will take you anywhere a 4x4 will and some places one won't. The bars are a bit low for stand-up riding, but steering is reasonably precise. Perfectly metered power, good traction and ample ground clearance get you through medium-to-nasty going, provided you take your time. The Paralever lets the rear suspension follow rough ground on or off the gas, and the shock rarely bottoms when set full stiff at a sane pace. But higher speeds or nastier terrain shreds the control envelope in a hurry as the bike shakes its head and bottoms both ends. Try high speed *and* nasty terrain and you'll likely get driven into the ground with a 550-pound mallet quicker than you can say intensive care.

This is one amazingly tough motorcycle. Running out of ground clearance on a rocky trail (just say no to speed), one editor hammered the undercarriage mercilessly with nothing more to show for it than a few battle scars on the skid plate. The fiberglass-reinforced plastic engine fairing is nearly as tough, surviving numerous direct hits from various forms of unfriendly terra on the same ride.

An impromptu 40-mph flying-W desert adventure that shaved years off one editor's life only managed to take a coat of paint off the BMW's crash bar and cylinder head. Needless to say, all essential (expensive) parts are well protected. Metzeler's Sahara tires work better than they wear. After 1200 miles of admittedly hard use on every imaginable surface, the front was going and the rear was about gone.

But the boxer is a shade-tree mechanic's dream compared to the current crop of complex mechanical nightmares from Japan. When was the last time your owner's manual told you how to adjust valve lash? And even if it did, you'd likely spend the first hour stripping away plastic before finding them. Valves, carbs, plugs, ignition and filters are all wonderfully accessible. Here's to simple machines, especially when they work this well.

But there's the same old litany of BMW nits to pick. Start with the fork lock hidden on the steering stern. Move on to the treacherous spring-loaded kickstand that's impossible for shorter riders to deploy from the saddle. Then consider that the cylinder heat that warms your feet in winter cooks your ankles in summer.

In the end, it's amazing that what is ostensibly a niche bike has such broad appeal. Though it nearly doubles some of their price tags, the Paris-Dakar is far more comfortable and better appointed than any bike in its class. It's like comparing a Range Rover to a Toyota Land Cruiser. The BMW devours state-sized chunks of freeway in a single sitting, going farther on a tank of gas than anything in anyone else's showroom.

And it's capable enough off-road to explore all those places street tires never tread. This one will take you as far away from it all as you care to go. So if your idea of touring is getting a few miles east of nowhere in particular, miles from bright lights, bars, surround sound and air-suspension anything, the R100GS Paris-Dakar is just about the perfect way to get there.

22

BMW K1

Photograhy by Scott Killeen & Mike Banks
Motorcyclist, March 1990

The Berlin Airlift: BMW's Aero Attack on the Powers of Japan

The ads in all the magazines say it quite clearly. A BMW K1, lurid fiberglass, wild graphics and all flash, posed in front of a space-shuttle launch. The ad's headline promises: "For $2,000,000,000 less you can have the same feeling."

And this, dear readers, represents a significant change in BMW's motorcycle marketing philosophy. After years of deliberately setting itself apart from the wild liter-class sport bikes and sport-tourers from Japan, BMW is now acting suspiciously as if it wants to be dealt into the game. And judging by the high-speed ergonomics, progressive technology and sporting look of the K1, it appears as if the Bavarian company has finally thrown its opening bid into the all-out performance pot.

In the high-stakes poker of spec sheets and press releases the new K seems to be holding a potent pat hand. The engine is derived from the K100 mill introduced in 1984, but almost everything except the cases and the cylinder block is new. Bore and stroke are still undersquare at 67mm by 70mm; with the four-cylinder engine running longitudinally, every measure had to be taken with the original K to keep the engine short. But the head is all new—and has a few wrinkles even the Japanese haven't come up with. Four valves beat the K100's pair, and the valve-adjustment system is a step beyond even the Yamaha FZR1000's slick shim-under-bucket setup. Each of the smaller, lighter valves has its own tappet, but the tappets have no provision for lash fine-tuning. Instead of swapping shims, the entire tappet is traded for a slightly shorter or longer one.

Compression ratio is up to 11.0:1. With the more efficient shape of the chambers, BMW decided it could go past the K100's 10.2:1 and still ward off detonation. Cam timing is purposely mild. In fact, intake duration is the same as the K100's. K100s have been known as very slow-revving beasts. The combination of massive flywheels, a large-diameter single-plate car-type clutch and a sluggish air-density flapper in the injection system combined to give the two-valvers all the immediacy of a big-rig diesel. The K1 is much improved in this respect.

First, computer-generated finite-element figuring allowed the engine guys to shave 2.87 pounds off the crankshaft and helped in creating lighter and stronger connecting rods as well. And the injection-system flapper is gone, replaced by a potentiometer linked to the throttle butterfly. The rest of the injection system is new to motorcycling; it's Bosch's automotive Digital Motor Electronics system, which combines fuel-delivery duties with ignition management. The setup is used on most gasoline-powered BMW autos, and it even has a built-in defect detector that can tell properly equipped BMW mechanics where any stray gremlins are hiding. If the system goes wacko en route—a highly unlikely occurrence—a default setting keeps the engine running to the nearest dealer.

The result of all this refinement and hot-rodding is a claimed 100 horsepower, a 10-Clydesdale boost over the K100. There's much more power available from the configuration, but BMW chose to build all K1s with the same cams and injection settings as the German domestic models, which are limited to 100 horsepower. Instead, the engineers concentrated on smooth power delivery and impressive midrange.

The allotted 100 horsepower can't hope to push the 613-pound Teuton through the quarter-mile with the impatience of Japan's best unrestricted liter bikes, of course. Our K1 got through the 440 in 11.87 seconds and 113.8 mph, a ways behind the best Japanese 600s and about 15 mph and a full second or more behind the best Asian open-classers. In our 200-yard, top-gear roll-on from 50 mph the K fared much better, as its midrange-tuned engine and precise fuel injection led us to expect. Its best run was an 80.2-mph effort, about even with the Honda CBR1000 in sixth gear. Top speed, even with its slickly

The front binders use 305mm floating discs and Brembo four-piston calipers with small leading pistons. The aero fender cuts drag, sending air over the fairing.

aerodynamic fairing, was 142 mph, again, about the same as the median Japanese 600s.

The new mill is quite a bit more responsive than its predecessor, and the new Citroen-designed labyrinth pistons help keep oil smoking on start-up to a minimum. You can still get a puff of blue, a puff that would signal serious ring-seating trouble on a Japanese bike, but compared to the down-in-flames cloud early K bikes poured out, the K1's whiff is next to unnoticeable. Now you can park your Beemer on the sidestand at a sidewalk café and be reasonably sure you'll be welcomed back the next day.

Speaking of the sidestand, the trick and sometimes annoying automatically retracting stand of the K100s is gone. A pull on the clutch used to pull the stand up, but now a simple sidestand switch keeps the ignition off if the stand is down. Unlike Japanese machines with similar systems, the K1 will not run at all with the stand down, even in neutral. At the San Antonio, Texas, press introduction more than one highly respected motorcycle journalist tried to grind the starter to meltdown before figuring this out.

The computer-controlled engine starts up cleanly and can be run soon with the fast-idle/enrichening lever pushed back home, even on cool mornings. With your feet on the ground, spread unnaturally wide to clear the flanks of the expansive fairing, the riding position seems very accommodating. The seat is an inch lower than the K100's ridetall saddle, and the tubular-steel handlebar is surprisingly wide, coming from the same company that brought us the stubby K100RS arrangement. Tall pilots, though, get their first shock when it's time to fold their landing gear onto the pegs. The distance lost in the seat came right out of the knee joints, so the ergonomics for the lower half of the body are right off an early GSXR750 while the upper half gets a much easier time of it.

The clutch is on the abrupt side, but at least the Paralever system controlling the torque reaction of the shaft keeps the One from bobbing up and down at the rear like the earlier Ks. Steering lock is limited; it's much harder to turn the K1 around in the width of a country road than it is on, say, the Honda 1500 Gold Wing. The final-drive ratio and fifth gear are taller, but first gear still runs out quickly. The tachometer, held over from the slower-revving K100s, lags as much as 2500 rpm behind the actual engine speed when accelerating in first gear. If you wait for redline to shift into second, the rev limiter shuts down the injection long before the tach needle reaches the red zone. With the still-high flywheel weight and long-travel, somewhat-balky gearbox adding to the effect, getting a good, clean shift to second under heavy acceleration becomes next to impossible. Sure, you can get second—if you don't need it in a hurry. If you need it to zap around a truck in slow going, you'll just have to ask nicely.

The new engine is much easier to manage than the old one, but its throttle response is still seconds behind any of the Japanese liter bikes. It's also smoother than the K100's, but at 5000 rpm there's still a distinct tingle that settles over the bars, tank and pegs and stays with you to the 9000-rpm redline. Just about the time the buzz begins, so does the power, steadily building to its slightly short-winded peak in the top quarter of the tach dial.

High-speed touring is the K bike's traditional niche of expertise, and while the K1, with no provision for the hard saddle boxes available on the rest of the BMW line, is aimed more toward the sport end of the sport-touring spectrum, we first wrung it out on its own kind of roads. We picked up our U.S.-spec K in San Antonio and spent the next two days blazing through the hill country northwest of the Alamo. We wondered why BMW chose San Antonio for the K1 launch—until we saw the roads.

The hill country is sparsely populated, with smooth, sweeping routes draped over the gently convoluted lumps and bulges of Texas. Serious sport riding here starts at 80 mph and goes straight up from there;

The rear disc and caliper are close to K100 units, but the disc is 1mm thicker for better heat dissipation. The huge Paralever housing reduces shaft effect substantially.

The Motometer instrument pod comes off the K bikes but with redline upped to the K1's higher figure. The fork lock is finally incorporated into the ignition switch.

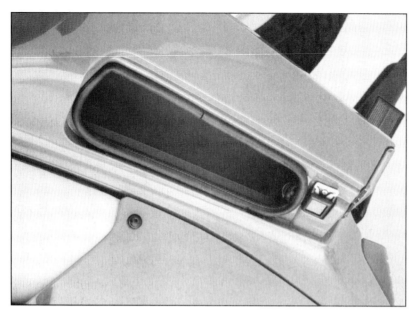

There are no hard bags, but these small glove pockets, opened with the ignition key, hold a few necessities. BMW System helmets click into the rear holders.

downshifting to fourth means the Texas equivalent of a hairpin is careening into view. The terrain was perfect to assess the One's high-speed aerodynamics and chassis behavior.

The slick K1 fairing does an admirable job of keeping air and water off the rider without adding turbulence to the mix. BMW claims a 0.34 coefficient of drag. We don't know about that, but we do know that a day spent behind the roomy yet highly protective shroud is no drag at all. The tiny molded windshield is too distorted to see through reliably at speed, but the upper lip is low enough to allow it to nearly disappear from the rider's consciousness.

With the K1, BMW has gone to industry-standard wheel and tire sizes for liter bikes. The front is a 3.50-by-17-inch rim with a 120/70ZR17 Michelin radial (Dunlops and Metzelers will also be used), the rear an 18-by-4.50 spinner with a 160/60ZR18 tire. Wheelbase grew 2 inches to 61.6 inches, mostly due to the longer Paralever system. The frame is basically the same as the K100's but with the highly stressed center tubes thicker than before. In adjusting for the longer wheelbase, higher-speed potential and wider wheels, BMW chose to reduce steering-head rake by a degree, to 26, and pare trail from 4.0 to 3.7 inches. The fork is a nonadjustable Marzocchi unit with 41.7mm tubes, 5.3 inches of travel and progressive damping that raises the compression- and rebound-damping rates when the fork is more than 50 percent compressed to give fluid action at low speeds and firmer response in more extreme situations.

The rear shock is a Bilstein unit, with only preload available for adjustment. Travel is 5.5 inches, and the shock uses an internal bottoming resister, much like that used on most forks, instead of the more traditional soft-urethane or rubber bump stop. Front brakes are upgraded from K100 specs, with 12-inch (305mm) floating discs, four-pot staggered-piston Brembo calipers and antilock braking standard on all U.S. K1s. The rear disc, also serviced by BMW's FAG Kugelfischer ABS system, is nearly the same as seen on K100s, but with its disc 1mm wider.

BMWs have traditionally been slow steerers, using 18- and even 19-inch front wheels for measured, predictable response at the expense of some ultimate flickability. With the K1's steep geometry and 17-inch front wheel, BMW is now firmly committed to flick-and-fly chassis design. At city speeds the One feels almost indecisive about its direction of travel. It'll go straight for now, it seems to say, but it could just as easily crank itself over into a hard turn with the merest of suggestions. At very high speeds the gyroscopic effect of even the small 17-inch Michelin takes over, keeping the K on course without much rider input. But tucked in at over the ton, the One never seems completely committed to any one line; the slightest push or tug on the wide handlebar alters its path immediately. And when the shock and the tubular steering damper get hot, the Bavarian Bomber sometimes feels right on the edge of a cyclic wallow in hard cornering.

On the smooth, fast corners of Texas the bike acquitted itself well. We rode hard all day and felt confident pushing the bike near the high limits imposed by the street-compound Michelins and the more-than-adequate cornering clearance. In tighter corners, though, with more hard transitions and less all-out high-speed running, the chassis shortcomings became more evident.

The rear suspension setup is problematic; none of our testers could come to terms with the spring and damping rates. The first impression is that of a very stiff spring combined with seriously inadequate rebound damping. The spring is

The flat, semisoft rear seat is exposed by removing two allen bolts. The passenger's pegs are high, but the K1 is not intended to be a long-distance two-up machine.

actually highly progressive, with soft initial travel and a very stiff final rate. But to keep the tail high enough with the soft initial rate, BMW was forced to jack even the first stage of preload sky high. This almost squashes the soft initial rate right out of the spring—the bike has lots of initial sag, followed by the very stiff final rate. And the rebound damping, presumably kept light to deal with the soft initial spring rate, can't control the high final rate and the massive unsprung mass of the Paralever final-drive housing. The rear end seemingly never stops bounding in enthusiastic riding, and in routine commuting we were never comfortable with the rear suspension action. And while the rear end is bobbing like Sugar Ray Leonard in the first round, the sensitive geometry is letting the front wheel wiggle side to side like a beach-comber with a metal detector.

After one hard run down a fast mountain road, two of our testers commeted that the bike needed a steering damper to help it feel more secure. Then, in the next day's studio photo session we discovered it already had one. We'd not be eager to ride the K1 hard without it. The bobbing and wallowing never got dangerously out of hand, but it did serve to dampen our enthusiasm when the time came to make time. Even our 210-pound tester found the first preload position on the shock excessive considering the limp rebound damping. We clicked the shock up to the middle setting and found the rebound damping even more over-powered, and the ride unacceptably harsh in routine city and freeway bumps and lips.

In more relaxed riding the suspension action is more reasonable, and while also short on rebound damping, the Marzocchi fork may be amenable to heavier oil as a remedy. But for anyone who intends to push a K1 or is at all discerning about handling even at a relaxed pace, we recommend swapping the shock for an aftermarket unit at the first opportunity. We are working with the White Brothers on developing a shock for the bike;

The accessory trunk slips on over the allen bolts that usually hold the seat fairing; two side panniers strap on around the trunk for added capacity on longer trips.

if you've already spent $12,990 for a K1, you probably won't flinch at another $400 to $500 to make it handle.

The brakes are powerful enough to arrest the One's newfound speed, but our bike let the lever come in too close to the bar for comfortable two-fingered braking. BMW says the ABS system has been recalibrated to suit the requirements of the K1, but for us it seemed to kick in too soon. Charging hard into a corner, a determined rider expects serious stopping when he rolls off the throttle and grabs for the brake. The K1's front ABS, though, seems to take control of the lever before the serious deceleration has occurred, leading to a moment of panic as the corner looms, the brake lever feeling welded to its pivot.

We suspect that the old 18-inch front wheel had enough extra rotating inertia to blunt the onset of the ABS robot but that the 17 is slowing with enough extra immediacy to kick in the computer. We know there brakes and these tires can stop much faster on clean pavement than they're being allowed to, and we strongly suggest BMW recalibrate the K1's ABS to give us more of the maximum braking the rest of the bike is capable of. The problem doesn't seem inherent in ABS, a feature we heartily endorse. But we feel BMW has perhaps played it a little too safe this time.

The extensive, uniquely styled bodywork sets off the visual pleasure centers of the general public like few other sport bikes. The wild yellow graphics turn what could have been an endless expanse of red or blue into something very bold and crisp. There will only be a few hundred K1s brought into the country for the 1990 model year, and we're confident the styling and the high-tech image of K1 will be more than sufficient to sell them all. The K100-based aluminum tank is back, but with large rubber guards keeping the often-hot tank from scorching the rider's inner thighs. A lot of heat is thrown off by the One's engine, especially on the left (exhaust) side; remember, the K1 was developed for Austria, not Arizona.

In daily riding BMW's new flagship works quite well, though. The headlight's Z-shaped low beam does a fine job of illuminating the road without scorching oncoming car hoods, and the high beam is strong enough to make it easy to stay within the range of your photon scouts. The seat is quite comfortable, though your position is not going to change much during a day's ride. The mirrors are attached, in conventional style, to the lever pivots instead of being integrated into the fairing. It's an effective arrangement: they're visually unobtrusive, andthe bar mounts place them wide enough apart to make rear vision superior to that of most other sport bikes. The two small rear fairing pockets are large enough to hold big gloves, a thin windbreaker or a modest lunch. The Captain

Suggested retail price:	$12,990
Warranty:	36 months, unlimited miles
Number of U.S. dealers:	Approx. 200
Recommended maintenance intervals:	16,000 miles

ENGINE

Type:	Water-cooled, longitudinal, in-line, 4-stroke four
Valve arrangement:	DOHC, 4 valves; adjustment by interchangeable tappets
Displacement:	987cc
Bore x stroke:	67.0 x 70.0mm
Compression ratio:	11.0:1
Carburetion:	Bosch DME Motronic fuel injection
Ignition:	Bosch DME Motronic
Lubrication:	Wet sump, 4.0 qt
Charging output:	460 watts
Battery:	12V, 25AH

Gear	Internal Ratio	mph per 1000 rpm	mph at redline (8300)
1	2.315	6.0	54
2	1.523	9.1	82
3	1.183	11.7	105
4	0.967	14.3	129
5	0.828	16.7	150

DRIVETRAIN

Primary transmission:	Helical-cut gears, 1.944:1
Clutch:	Dry, one-plate
Transmission:	5-speed
Final drive:	Shaft and bevel gear, 2.75:1

CHASSIS

Front suspension:	41.7mm Marzocchi, 5.3 in. travel
Rear suspension:	Bilstein damper, 5.5 in. wheel travel; adjustment for spring preload

Front brake:	2, double-action 4-piston Brembo calipers, 305mm discs
Rear brake:	Single-action Brembo caliper, 285mm disc
Front wheel:	3.50 x 17 in.; cast aluminum
Rear wheel:	4.50 x 18 in.; cast aluminum
Front tire:	120/70ZR17 Michelin radial
Rear tire:	160/60ZR18 Michelin radial
Rake/trail:	26.0°/3.7 in. (95mm)
Wheelbase:	61.6 in. (1565mm)
Seat height, unladen:	31.7 in. (805mm)
Seat height, laden with 160-lb rider:	31.0 in. (787mm)
Fuel capacity:	5.2 gal (20L)
Weight:	613 lb (279kg) wet; 582 lb (264kg) tank empty
Colors:	Red or blue
Instruments:	Speedometer, tachometer, odometer, tripmeter, LCD clock, LCD gear indicator; warning lights for battery charge, water temperature, brakes, choke on, neutral, high beam, low oil pressure, ABS malfunction, low fuel level, turn signals
Speedometer error:	30 mph, actual 27.6; 60 mph, actual 54.8

PERFORMANCE

Fuel consumption:	27 to 52 mpg, 38.5 mpg avg.
Average touring range:	200 miles
Average 200-yd. top-gear acceleration from 50 mph:	80.2 mph terminal speed
Best ?-mile acceleration:	12.13 sec., 111.2 mph
Corrected best ?-mile acceleration*:	11.87 sec., 113.8 mph

* Performance with test-session weather conditions corrected to sea-level standard conditions (59 degrees F, 29.92 in. of mercury).

	1990 BMW K1	1990 HONDA CBR1000	1989 KAWASAKI ZX-10	1989 YAMAHA FJ1200
PRICE	$12,990	$7598	$6599 (1990)	$6699 (1990)
CORRECTED 1/4-MILE, SEC. MPH*	11.87/113.8	10.74/128.0	10.97/128.7	11.05/122.9
WET WEIGHT	613 lb	595 lb	576 lb	583 lb
HIGH-SPEED PASS TERMINAL SPEED	80.2 mph (fifth gear)	82.1 mph	78.5 mph	87.4 mph (fifth gear)
AVG. FUEL CONSUMPTION	38.5 mpg	37.8 mpg	37.3 mpg	42.0 mpg
AVG. TOURINGRANGE	200 miles	233 miles	216 miles	235 miles

OFF THE RECORD

For me, the K1 is a great way to spend an Italian summer vacation, but it comes up short everywhere else. For $12,990 I expect sorted-out suspension, a cooperative transmission, livable ergonomics and something that goes around corners at least as well as a CBR1000. The visuals are stunning, but so is the price. As it stands, I'd rather look at a K1 than ride one. So for now the K1 poster on my office wall suits me just fine.

—Tim Carrithers

I'll ignore the K1's price tag here because retail prices are relative to annual income. If a bike retails for half your annual income, you'll probably look elsewhere, but if it's only a sixteenth of your yearly makings, it's undoubtedly within reach. With that economics-by-Ienatsch lesson done, let's talk bikes.

I look at the K1 and see the makings for a mechanical cross-country ticket with amazing capabilities. Because the stock performance is relatively low compared to current Japanese superbikes, ready and willing BMW aftermarket companies are just waiting for the K-bike owners to say, "Hmmm, I wonder if this could be any faster . . . lighter . . . better handling?" The answer is yes. K bikes can be all of those and more. I've seen and ridden K bikes from mild to wild, and they impressed me with their ability to withstand and benefit from modifications. One ride on any Luftmeister Turbo bike will convince you.

Some bikes impress me right off the showroom floor, but some, like the K1, capture my imagination with what they can become.

—Nick Ienatsch

Memo to those who must have a K1: Don't ride a Honda CBR1000. Don't ride a Yamaha FJ1200. Don't ride a Suzuki 1100 Katana. Don't ride a Kawasaki ZX-10. Just don't do it.

—Dexter Ford

The name BMW brings up images of reliability, refinement and precision German engineering. When BMW brings out its new state-of-the-art superbike, you expect a lot—or at least I do. I don't expect it to run with Japan's 1000cc sports bikes, but I do expect it to outperform the little CBR1000. It doesn't. I also expect that for nearly twice the price, it should offer the comfort and refinement of the new CBR1000. It isn't even close.

The K1's styling is bold and original and the fairing's protection exemplary, but the shifting and suspension are lacking. A suspension that's set up this poorly is embarrassing, but to make it nonadjustable, except for preload at the rear, is inexcusable. The cluttered, yellow on black instruments aren't terribly readable. Signaling a left turn necessitates a push on what would be the horn button on any other bike but isn't on this one; then to cancel, push up on the switch above the right turn-signal switch, where the starter button usually is. Reverse the order to signal right, and you end up honking the horn. I tried patting my head and rubbing my tummy simultaneously to get the shifter to work smoothly, but that didn't help; I'll have to look that one up in the owner's manual. With some work on the suspension, shifter and other small details, the K1 could work well, but for $12,990 I expect BMW to take care of those details.

—Lance Holst

The K1 suffered for arriving on the heels of the Honda CBR1000. The CBR costs less and performs better in almost every way (except braking on snotty roads) than the K1. The annoying part is that it wouldn't take much to improve the maximum Beemer; some suspension tuning, a slightly different handlebar and a trip to Young's or Corbin for a saddle are all changes I could easily make. If I were feeling ambitious, I'd also try to wire in a nice set of Japanese handlebar switches. Those changes, if they came standard, and the security of ABS would make what is essentially an enjoyable motorcycle just about worth its outrageous price.

—Art Friedman

Zoom tail section comes off with a twist of two allen screws, exposing the flat passenger seat. BMW's soft tail trunk and thin panniers then slip right on over the replaced allens, giving a solo rider enough space for efficient touring, especially if he also opts for the custom Multivario K1 tank bag.

BMW is trying to match the Japanese in building sport bikes. And in one way it has: the horn. Previous BMW honkers have been just that, comparatively lusty noisemakers.

—Art Friedman

Zoom tail section comes off with a twist of two allen screws, exposing the flat passenger seat. BMW's soft tail trunk and thin panniers then slip right on over the replaced allens, giving a solo rider enough space for efficient touring, especially if he also opts for the custom Multivario K1 tank bag.

BMW is trying to match the Japanese in building sport bikes. And in one way it has: the horn. Previous BMW honkers have been just that, comparatively lusty noisemakers.

But the K1 comes with a Japanese-style embarrassment instead of a real horn—it beeps, when it should be barking.

Is the K1 all BMW claims it is, a topnotch, hard-charging sporting liter bike? Objectively, we have to say no. Compared to such universally capable machines as the new Honda CBR1000, the Suzuki 1100 Katana, the Yamaha FJ1200 or the Kawasaki ZX-10, it's still years behind in all aspects of performance. And even in areas in which you'd expect such a high-dollar, high-prestige vehicle to shine, such as refinement and sophistication, the K1 still falls short of the best from Japan. Compared to a CBR1000 the K feels rough, unsorted, haphazardly developed—far from the mature, finely honed motorcycle we expect from such a well-respected manufacturer. As with the original K100, there's nothing inherently flawed with the K's basic design, but there's still a lot of work to be done if BMW hopes to produce the polished, pleasing motorcycle its ads, image and price tag promise.

The K1 is an impressive array of technology, and its advanced fuel-injection and ignition system, innovative Paralever rear end and standard ABS combined to make it our choice as the most significant motorcycle of 1989. For dedicated BMW aficionados, it is a substantial improvement over the K100. With a few choice improvements the K1 will be a breathtakingly unique and quite pleasing sport-tourer.

But in the liter-class sport-bike poker game, we'd have to say that with the cards all down on the table, it's clear that BMW is still bluffing.

23

BMW R1100RS

Motorcyclist, July 1994

Motorrad of the Jahr

So whose butt will we red-blooded-Amurricuns have to kick next to get a decent motor-cycle around here? Did somebody insert a clause somewhere after WWII that the defeated Axis nations—Japan, Germany, Italy—must reparate in the form of two-wheeled transport? *Motorcyclist*'s Bike of the Year has come from Japan for the last four years; this year the coveted award goes across the other pond, to BMW's sparkling R1100RS boxer.

Far be it from us to dredge up unpleasant memories, but war is really what put BMW into the bike business in the first place. When the Treaty of Versailles put a crimp in BMW's aircraft engine business following the first World War, it turned to motorcycles (and later, to cars as well). The first boxer—and in fact the first BMW motorcycle, the R32—debuted in 1923.

Over the next 70 years, the boxer underwent numerous upgrades in specification and displacement, but adhered Germanically to its original horizontally opposed, two-valve-per-cylinder root.

So what's new? For starters, the R1100 has been blessed with real power. If you'd grown accustomed to the old chuffer, twisting the new boxer's throttle is like making the leap from gas lamps to electricity. Mainly, that power increase was achieved with four-valve heads, oversquare bore and stroke dimensions, and computer-controlled fuel-injection. The horizontal twin's "heads-in-the-breeze" layout, along with clever internal oiling tricks, allowed BMW to get the power it wanted from the new cylinder heads (a full 50 percent more) without resorting to water jackets.

Fuel-injection, with its very precise delivery, made it possible to fit the new bike with a three-way catalytic converter, and to further appease environmentalists the world over, the boxer's six-gallon fuel tank is made from recyclable plastic. (Play along and pretend you didn't know we've been recycling steel for decades.)

Where the new boxer shines brightest, though, is in its chassis. Doing away with a conventional cradle frame, BMW made the engine itself the main frame component, to

174   CHAPTER TWENTY-THREE

which front and rear suspensions attach. Though Telelever-type front ends have been done before, none has come close to working as well as the boxer's. Rather than feeding front wheel forces up stiction-plagued fork tubes and then back down to the rear axle, the Telelever routes those forces through a ball-joint–mounted A-arm just above the front wheel, the other ends of which pivot directly in the engine case just above where each cylinder attaches. Telelever is really much simpler than the words needed to describe it; what's important is that it works. The boxer can be ridden through bumps, hard, with near-complete composure—harder than any other sport-tourer, hard enough to shame many all-out sport motorcycles. Brake and corner over bumps simultaneously—the bike doesn't mind.

The Paralever single-sided swingarm/suspension system has been standard operating procedure at BMW for a while now, and with good reason. As applied to the boxer, its single shock absorber has been moved from atop the middle of the arm to a more conventional location directly aft of the swingarm pivot for, according to BMW, greater rigidity.

When it's all bolted together, the new hardware results in a motorcycle so excruciatingly well-balanced that it just had to be our Bike of the Year. There's power there to push the bike up to 136 mph and spring a quarter-mile in 12.48 seconds at 108.9 mph. There's precise handling, sportbike steering quickness, excellent suspension—so anyone who can't get comfortable on the ergonomically adjustable boxer should stay home on the BarcaLounger. There is good fairing protection and hard saddlebags that lock with the same key as the ignition. Excellent ABS II is available for a few dollars more, too—all in a beautifully wrapped package weighing only 520 pounds.

As with any brand-new design, all was not perfect with the new boxer, but it was awfully dang close. Shifting gears quickly is still not the boxer's strong point. Start-up was a bit cranky on early models, too. But BMW believes in gradual refinement. Boxers produced after October of last year have updated Motronic computers that should make start-up easier, while O-rings have been added to quiet the transmission in neutral. One not-so-wonderful refinement, however, is the reworked rear-end ratio. BMW shortened the new-generation Boxer's final-drive gearing slightly, saying that the early production bikes were geared a bit too tall for American tastes. That may be true, especially considering the high-speed, long-haul demands that European riding situations place on the bike. But with the new final drive ratio of 2.8:1, the bike seems busier—and buzzier—at freeway speeds, as if it wants another gear. We like the old setup better.

Still, the beauty of the new, R1100RS boxer lies largely in the fact that, while BMW retained many of the sights and sounds that characterized all the boxers that came before, it has built a bike so super-contemporary that it's almost easy to picture it pottering down the Strasse, little changed, 70 years from now.

But then, a lot can happen in 70 years, can't it? As that unforgettable British statesman whatshisname once said, "In the absence of war, cast about for enemies." Especially if you like motorcycles.

BMW R1100GS

24

Photograhy by Wes Allison & Kevin Wing
Motorcyclist, September 1994

The Perfect Bike for an Imperfect World

In a perfect world, we wouldn't need BMW's omnivorous new-wave boxer. We'd be too busy blowing our tax-free paychecks on whippet-quick sportbikes, roosting triumphantly on endless stretches of perfectly smooth and totally deserted bits of serpentine blacktop, shredding miles of loamy trails on factory-tuned dirtbikes and cataloging indescribable sunsets from the helm of two-wheeled land yachts. Then we'd wash it all down afterward with 50-cent pints of Bass Ale.

More often than not, though, the world we live in comes up a few notches shy of perfection. But chin up, Bubba, because when it comes to staying sane while having a Good Time in a universe afflicted with potholes, radar traps, Roseanne Arnold (or is it Barr now?), two-hour commutes, expanding work weeks and contracting weekends, Fabio, love handles and just two weeks of vacation every year, BMW's new R1100GS may well be the ultimate weapon. And the ultimate revenge.

As the next logical step in the proliferation of BMW's reborn boxer that emerged as the R1100RS last year, the GS once again becomes motorcycling's answer to Bo Jackson. Strong, charismatic, possessed of broadband abilities and just a bit of weirdness, the all-purpose boxer is part sportbike, part standard, part sport-touring rig and part off-road explorer, all wrapped up in one large, powerful and stylish package.

Did we say large? Make that huge. Immense. Jumbo. Gigantic. Tipping the *Motorcyclist* scales at 572 pounds with a full 6.6 gallons of fuel, the more sophisticated R259-powered GS weighs 80 pounds more than the simpler R100GS. Technology has its price. And part of that price is paid in weight, starting with the GS skeleton.

Thanks to its large luggage rack, heavier cross-spoke–laced wheels, longer-travel suspension (7.5 inches up front and 7.9 in back) and other assorted bits, the new GS is also a tad heavier than the R1100RS. But aside from these and other strategic changes for all-surface duty, the basic R1100 platform is essentially the same.

A conventional tube steel lattice supports the seat and provides an upper mount for the Showa rear shock. And the pressure-cast neck bolted atop the crankcase supports the handlebar and BMW's elegantly simple Telelever front end. Beyond that, the boxer engine and driveline are still the major load-bearing members here.

And though the chassis concept is identical, vital GS chassis numbers have been stretched a bit from RS spec. Measuring 59 inches from axle to axle, the new GS plies the terra with an inch more wheelbase than the pavement-only RS. And up front, the Telelever gets 26 degrees of steering angle—slightly less rakish than the 25.1-degree RS. Both R1100s share the same 4.4 inches of trail.

Similarities outnumber differences in the engine bay as well. The 1085cc, air/oil-cooled engine marshals its eight valves via chain-driven cams pressed onto tough nitrided-steel shafts slung under each cylinder head to keep the mill relatively narrow. In fact, the new engine is 7mm narrower than the old R100 unit.

The remote shock preload adjuster inboard of the rider's footpeg makes roadside rear suspension adjustments a breeze; no tools necessary.

BMW's versatile Telelever is king of the rough road, but the frame-mounted headlight makes navigating tight roads after dark a bit sketchy.

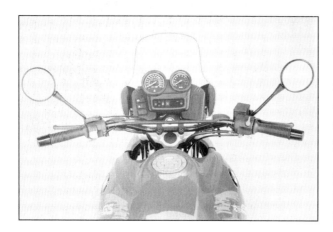

Welcome to the GS cockpit. The solid-mounted enduro-style bar turns heavy leverage into light steering, and a dashboard switch lets you deactivate the ABS for off-road work.

Since instant-on, low-rpm grunt is more important for all-surface duty than peak power, BMW basically flattened the RS torque curve by dropping compression from 10.7:1 to 10.3:1. GS camshafts were recontoured for more torque, and the Motronic engine-management system was recalibrated as well. The result is an engine that makes less peak horsepower than the RS version (80 claimed horsepower at 6750 rpm versus 90 ponies at 7250 rpm for the RS), but more torque with less engine speed (72 ft-lbs at 5250 rpm versus the RS's 70 ft-lbs at 5500 rpm).

A single-plate dry clutch modulates power as it flows to a five-speed gearbox that shares all internal ratios with the R1100RS. But a 3.00:1 final-drive ratio on the GS (versus 2.81:1 on the RS) drops overall gearing for all-surface work.

Once you file the parts manifest, the new GS adds up to surprisingly more than the sum of its parts. Surprise number one? This is clearly not a bike for the vertically challenged. With the seat in the lower of its two slots, a 5-foot-8-inch human can get a reasonable purchase on the terra. But in the upper position, it takes at least a 34-inch inseam to sit flat-footed. As you make the reach to the broad, flat, motocross-style handlebar, you're greeted by a spartan, effective cockpit free of peripheral distractions: instruments and love-'em-or-hate-'em switches pirated from the R1100Rs.

Through the magic of Motronic fuel-injection, the GS rarely needs more than a taste of the enricher lever before settling into its off-kilter idle. By the time exhaust gasses make it through the catalytic converter and upswept muffler, their flat, raspy whisper isn't enough to stir your soul or the neighbors.

So if you want soul, buy a James Brown album. The injected, catalyzed, computer-controlled boxer is a model of civility in the morning, adjusting so quickly to ambient conditions it's likely ready for the road before you can buckle your helmet and wave goodbye to your cat.

Just like your average Range Rover or Grand Cherokee, the GS will spend more time between places like home and work than Paris and Dakar. But even surrounded by the perpetual wasteland of L.A. traffic, our GS proved the perfect urbane guerrilla. Once beyond a walking pace, the GS is far more nimble than its imposing dimensional profile would suggest.

Forget profiling on a Harley. The BMW's post-apocalyptic elegance gets more looks than Rush Limbaugh at an ACLU picnic. And the tall seat provides the next best thing

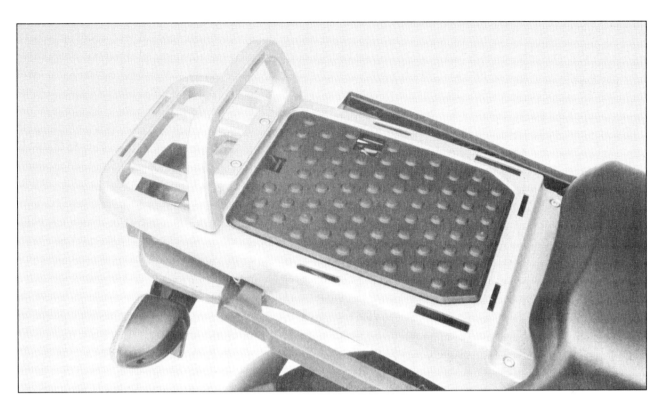

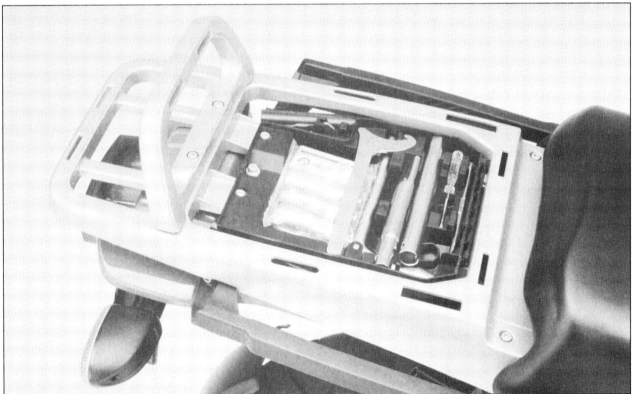

Pop off the pillion and there's room for a tent, backpack and sleeping bag. Pop the rack's lid and you have the best toolkit in all of motorcycling.

Elements like the fuel tank and two-piece saddle assume the third-generation GS's form in this clay mock-up.

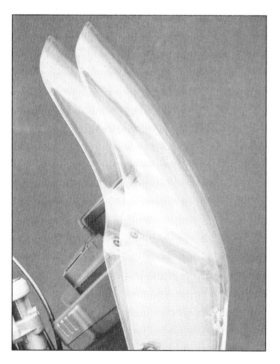

Small, yet nifty: The clear windscreen pivots fore and aft, matching the still air pocket to rider height. Euro models get a natty tinted screen.

to an aerial traffic report, getting you eye to eye with 4x4 drivers that tower over normal motorcycles. The broad bar delivers plenty of quick-flick leverage. The shorter overall gearing and flattened torque curve put an impressive spread of linear lunge-power at the GS rider's disposal from 2000 to 6500 rpm: linear, immediate acceleration right when and where you need it.

The only fly in the Teutonic ointment for around-town duty is perpetually clunky shifting. A running production change on R1100RS models carries over to the GS to smooth and tighten gear changes slightly, but our bike comes shy of perfection with audibly clunky progress through the gearbox, especially notching down from third through first.

Shifting smoothly to the interstate, the GS becomes an amazingly spacious, efficient mileage-disposal unit, double takes from Highway Patrol officers and little kids in the back of minivans notwithstanding. Shuffling along at an indicated 70 mph, the GS tach needle sits at 4000 rpm—and since that's right where the newly squashed power curve steepens, passing seldom involves more than a twist of the wrist.

Since the GS uses a solid handlebar mount rather than the RS's elastic set-up, hands and wrists pick up a taste more vibration through the grips—enough to fuzz mirror images at a steady 70 mph. The boxer never lets you forget there's an engine running down there. But even without the rubber vibe-buffers, the GS is quite smooth compared with all but the most fluent street-going fours.

Settling into the comfortably contoured two-piece saddle, the bolt-upright riding position allows a good bit more legroom than on the average sport-tourer. That adjustable frame-mounted fairing provides upper torso wind protection beyond its modest size, while the cavernous fuel tank and cylinders blunt the wind around the rider's lower half. But for extended stints in the saddle, especially in colder climes, we'd opt for BMW's optional hand guards and heated grips.

Even stock, the GS is a much more comfortable way to put a few hundred miles in the rearview mirrors than first impressions might lead you to believe. Good thing, too. At a steady 70 mph, that junior super-tanker–sized polyamide fuel cell goes 300-plus miles between refills. And though there's no reserve tap, a low-fuel light has you scanning for gas stations 250 miles or so after the last one.

OK, so excellent street manners and more sophisticated underpinnings make this version a more capable street machine than any of its predecessors. But GS roots still lie beyond the land of gas stations,

BMW's optional ($674.40) saddlebags go on and off in seconds, and lock with the ignition key. They also leak a bit in the rain and scratch too easily.

paved roads and freeway signs. Though there's no denying that hitting the dirt with something that outweighs a GSX-R1100 by a pound sounds like an invitation to the intensive care ward, the big GS acquits itself well…relatively speaking.

It's still armed with more power and weight than traction or suspension. So mix high speed with ruts, whoops, rocks, small mammals or other hairy bits of terrain and the GS will pound you into the ground like a tent peg in less time than it takes to say "Blue Cross."

But reined in to an exploring pace, accurate steering, smooth, linear power delivery and eight inches of ground clearance let Herr Boxer devour ground that would trash a normal streetbike. The street-biased Metzeler radials—though clearly out of their element in loose dirt or mud—work well enough on hardpack or fire-road duty. And the ABSII antilock computer is easily switched off at start-up to make skidding and sliding easier.

Skidding? Sliding? A little Paris to Capetown traveling music please. Pop off the rear seat and there's room on the rear rack to carry you and a week's worth of camping gear. Factor in BMW's excellent saddlebags (except for their easily scratched painted surfaces)

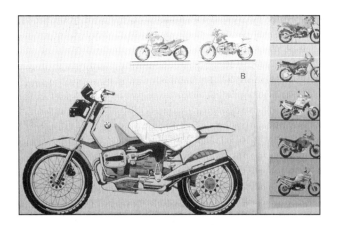

After the GS project began in 1991, Robb and his staff prepared stacks of concept drawings before settling on the look that would evoke the feelings they wanted.

and next thing we know we're squinting at squiggly little dotted lines between ghost towns and logging roads to take in a few hundred miles of indigenous outback.

But don't think you have to get dirty to get the most out of a new GS. To develop a true appreciation, point it down the choppiest, craggiest, nastiest, twistiest, most bump-riddled example of the road builder's art you can find. Flicking nearly 600 pounds of

They're doing some serious construction in the hills near where I live, with lots of fresh dirt roads and NO TRESPASSING signs—a clear invitation for the GS. I didn't get far in that fresh dirt, though, before coming to the conclusion that sliding around on this behemoth has much in common with rattlesnake ranching, hanging out with Jeffrey Dahmer or dating Lorena Bobbitt. Any pleasure you might derive is more than offset by the terrible consequences of what's likely to happen should the relationship become too familiar. The GS scores a 10 on the interesting machine scale, but I'd buy the RS boxer—unless I lived at the end of a long cow trail.

—John Burns

You'd never know to look at it, but BMW's newest GS is as close as I've come to the ultimate sportbike. Huh? What? Granted, your average fully faired, race-replica ego-massage unit carves up curvy pavement amazingly well. But so does the GS; up to 300 miles per sitting. And it's even more fun on bumpy pavement or broken pavement or no pavement at all.

So on the average weekend morning when your local Racer Road is clogged with brain donors trying to stick a knee puck through the grill of an oncoming squad car, I can aim the GS down some gnarly, deserted two-lane and roost till the cows come home. Only the GS is so quiet, neither the cows nor anybody else are likely to notice.

—Tim Carrithers

I expected to like the R1100GS, since I'm a fan of dual-sport/standard riding positions, anti-dive front ends and other practical touches like large gas tanks. But the bike didn't live up to my expectations—except for being ugly. The seat turned out to be less comfortable than it appears, and it feels even more boatlike than the old GS. And its utility on all but the smoothest dirt roads is gone, you can do as well off-road on an R1100RS.

This latest GS strikes me as an attempt to deliver the dual appeals of the new boxer engine and GS image, with little of the functional advantages that have previously accompanied the latter. In other words, if your eye falls on an R1100GS, decide between the engine or the GS concept, then go and get what you want elsewhere in the BMW line.

—Art Friedman

You may think it's ugly. And you may wince at the price. But if there's a more do-it-all streetbike on the planet, I haven't ridden it. Whether you're talking gnarly, rutted and twisty backroads, smooth, straight two-laners or the occasional Jeep trail, the new GS is completely happy (provided you don't forget you're on a 572-pound motorcycle while traversing that Jeep trail). Heck, I might even take the new GS on tour next month.

—Mitch Boehm

brutally effective Bavarian weirdness feels a bit strange at first. But the weirdness gives way to the clear realization that you're going like greased German stink, Hans, and those swoopy racer-boy poseurs aren't back there anymore.

No doubt—race-replica machines still own the fast, smooth blacktop. But over diabolically rough and tight roads where most pure-sports fear to tread, broadband horsepower, stellar suspension and potent brakes make the GS the ultimate weapon. Keep the tach needle between 3500 and 7000 rpm and the GS boots you out of corners with a seamless rush and very few trips to the shifter.

The Metzeler Enduro 4 radials on our test bike stick to the pavement better than any other all-surface rubber we've yet sampled. And with its preload adjuster on the second notch, BMW's flex-free Telelever layout soaked up the worst pavement we could find without unsettling the chassis, even while hard on the brakes. Out back, the Paralever driveline effectively isolates the chassis from torque-induced ups and downs. And with rear shock preload set six clicks stiffer than the "standard" setting on the no-tools-required remote adjuster and one-third turn out from max on the rebound damping screw, the

1995 BMW R1100GS

Suggested retail price as tested:	$11,890 ($10,690 w/o ABSII)	Front brake:	2, double-action calipers, 305mm discs with ABSII
Warranty:	36 months, unlimited miles	Rear brake:	Single-action caliper, 285mm disc with ABSII
Number of U.S. dealers:	Approx. 200	Front wheel:	2.50 x 19 in.; wire cross-spoke
Recommended valve-adjustment intervals:	6000 miles	Rear wheel:	4.00 x 17 in.; wire cross-spoke
		Front tire:	110/80ZR19 Metzeler Enduro 4 radial
		Rear tire:	150/70ZR17 Metzeler Enduro 4 radial
ENGINE		Rake/trail:	26 degrees/4.4 in. (111mm)
Type:	Air/oil-cooled, longitudinal, opposed, 4-stroke twin	Wheelbase:	59.0 in. (1499mm)
Valve arrangement:	SOHC, 4 valves, operated by pushrods and rocker arms; threaded adjusters	Seat height:	33.1/33.9 in. (840/861mm)
		Fuel capacity:	6.6 gal. (25L)
Displacement:	1085cc	Weight:	572 lbs (260kg) wet
Bore x stroke:	99.0mm x 70.5mm	Colors:	Red, white or black
Compression ratio:	10.3:1	Instruments:	Speedometer, tachometer, odometer, tripmeter; lights for neutral, high beam, turn signals, low fuel, alternator, ABS system fault
Carburetion:	Bosch Motronic MA 2.2 fuel injection		
Ignition:	Battery-powered, electronically triggered, digitally controlled		
Lubrication:	Wet sump, 4.0 qt	Speedometer error:	50 mph, actual 54.6
Battery:	12V, 19.5AH	Rpm at indicated 60 mph:	3400
DRIVETRAIN		**PERFORMANCE**	
Primary transmission:	Direct, 1.00:1	Fuel consumption:	35 to 48 mpg; 42 mpg avg.
Clutch:	Dry, single-plate	Average touring range:	300 miles
Transmission:	5-speed	Average 200-yd. acceleration from 50 mph, terminal speed:	5th gear, 82.4 mph; 4th gear, 73.8 mph
Final drive:	Shaft and bevel gear, 3.00:1		
		Best ?-mile acceleration:	12.89 sec. @ 99.3 mph
CHASSIS		Corrected best ?-mile acceleration*:	12.58 sec. @ 101.4 mph
Front suspension:	BMW Telelever, Showa damper, 7.5 in. travel; adjustment for spring preload		
		Measured top speed:	127 mph
Rear suspension:	BMW Paralever, one Showa damper, 7.9 in. wheel travel; adjustments for spring preload and rebound damping		

*Performance with test-session weather conditions corrected to sea-level standard conditions (59 degrees F, 29.92 in. of mercury).

GS's rear suspension delivered a ride every bit as composed, comfortable and compliant as the front.

Limited mostly by traction from its all-surface tires, the triple-disc Brembo brakes and BMW's excellent optional ABSII slow the boxer's pavement progress with a bit less authority than the best sporty bike brakes. Our only complaints were some fade under brutal use and spongy feel at the lever after 2000-odd rugged testing miles.

After covering that kind of distance over most every kind of surface California has to offer, this much is clear: From axle to axle, from skid plate to gas cap,

nothing about the R1100GS is normal or average or ordinary. For almost 15 years, BMW's GS has always been a different kind of motorcycle, one that creates its own genre rather than fitting neatly into somebody else's. It's a motorcycle built for riders who "don't fit the mold."

The point, then, is this: BMW's R1100GS ends up as sort of a 572-pound Swiss Army knife. It's motorcycling's once and future king of individuality, a two-wheeler dedicated to blazing its (and your) own trail. At $11,890 with ABSII (and $10,690 without), its brand of all-around capability and uniqueness isn't for everybody. But if your style of motorcycling doesn't end where the pavement does, scrape those nickels and dimes into a big pile, brothers and sisters. This is your motorcycle.

Sawtooth footpegs get vibe-killing rubber inserts. The weird plastic bit enveloping the rear Metzeler turns out to be an effective, aerodynamic rear fender.

25

Photography by Kevin Wing
Motorcyclist, March 1995

BMW R1100R

Stripped of All but the Bare Necessities, Bavaria's New Boxer Becomes the Standard by Which All Others Are Measured

Some things are not what they appear to be. Look at BMW's new R1100R, third in a series of machines powered by its new-generation R259 "boxer" engine. Does it appear a bit on the pedestrian side? Does the spinning propeller logo and the lack of paint-splashed plastic conjure up the "b" word? Boring? A bike for old guys?

Good. That's just the way us "old guys" like it, and when one of us riding an R-bike grows big in your mirrors on some twisty mountain road and leaves your neon-pink crotch rocket for dead, then you may begin the journey to enlightenment. You can begin by peeling off your "No Fear" stickers, grasshopper, and realizing that the left-off half of that epigram properly reads "No Brains."

BMW's revitalized boxers, on the other hand, are anything but brainless. The new R-model gets the same torque-laden, fuel-injected powerplant as the R1100GS. That motor, you'll recall from last September's road test, has a bit less cam timing than the RS version, and a smidgen less compression. While it produces about 10 fewer peak horsepower, it also puts out a few more foot-pounds of torque lower in the middle part of the powerband. In the GS, it's a highly capable engine. In the R, pushing 25 fewer pounds of motorcycle with less frontal area, it is very nearly a beast.

Then there's the GS's aspiration to be a quasi-dirtbike, a role it plays about as well as Sylvester Stallone might play Hamlet. To that dubious end, BMW endowed the GS with long-travel suspension that renders it relatively top-heavy and cumbersome in some situations. The R, however, rides low on the same suspenders the RS uses, with about five inches travel at either end. Though the R is longer in wheelbase and uses more shallow steering geometry than the RS, you'd never guess it when the road goes curvy. Much of that is due to riding position.

The R's wide handlebars reach up from the Telelever upper clamp like Roto-tiller handles. They're bolted on solidly instead of being rubber-mounted, as on the RS. The seat's well-shaped, supportive and three-way adjustable in height to satisfy a range of riders, and the footpegs are where they belong.

Honda was first to talk about mass centralization, but this particular BMW feels like maybe the best example of that concept at work. With Telelever in front and Paralever behind, the only large components north of the crank are half of the rider and the fuel tank. A firm nudge on either bar flings the R-bike into a corner right now, and once inserted, the R feels planted like few others; the stock Bridgestone Battlax tires let expert riders lean into corners until the cylinder heads begin to mill down on either side (don't worry, though; the easy-to-use-centerstand gives plenty of warning beforehand).

Telelever steering, as we've come to expect, is highly accurate and linear, with little brake dive. The R's front end shrugs off bumps both big and small. The rear spring feels softer, but slightly too much high-speed compression damping can hammer the rider over sharp bumps.

While the Paralever rear goes most of the way toward eliminating on/off throttle chassis jacking, the rear damper is soft enough that a bit of that endemic shaft-drive trait does show up on the R when the pace heats up enough to make the rider's hand less decisive. It never threatens disaster as on some older BMWs, but you can feel the rear rise and fall if you lose faith mid-corner.

Brakes are the same four-piston Brembo caliper/305mm rotors found on the RS and GS, and provide perfectly ample stopping power. Our test unit came equipped with ABS II, a system we've praised in the past but which now pales compared with Honda's (on the ST1100) and Yamaha's (on its GTS1000) ABS systems. On the two Japanese systems, ABS cycles in and out so smoothly as to be nearly unnoticeable. But on dry, grippy pavement, BMW's system seems

The R-bike's Telelever front end steers and suspends beautifully. A steering damper has been fitted below the horizontal A-arm should the R's light weight induce light-headedness.

Congrats, BMW. You've managed to build the "sleeper" of the year. Standard riding position, optional saddlebags, shaft drive—mile-mannered Mr. Rogers, out for a Sunday cruise, right? Wrong. Any unsuspecting sportbike rider will be wondering why they can't seem to get rid of that pesky Beemer once the road gets really twisty. And with its comfy ergos, gas-sipping motor and supple suspenders, you can play Dr. Jekyll and Mr. Hyde all day long. This bike is pure fun. Sign me up.

—*Kent Kunitsugu*

It might *say* BMW on the tank, but this thing sends different messages from the saddle. There's a little Ducati Monster involved, but the Beemer's much more practical and comfortable—and powerful, my pants tell me—and handles better. It feels a little Harley-ish with that bare headlight out front and various other chunks of hardware, but the H-D comparison ends there. In profile, the thing looks a little Guzzi-ish, and something about the rear end says Norton fastback. In short, this bike combines everything there is to like about motorcycles in a simple package capable of embarrassing most "sportbikes" on a curvy road. What're they slipping into the water at BMW these days?

—*John Burns*

I've watched Kent pirouette around 15-mph switchbacks on the rocker box covers. I've seen worse. Like Burns, complete with saddlebags, filling the mirrors of our CBR600F3 like some high-speed, leather-clad pullman porter. I've strafed apexes with it myself. But as well as it works, I cannot love the R1100R. Gimme a GS or an RS version of the R259 boxer. Better still, how 'bout a 100-hp edition of David Robb's steamy monoposto styling exercise unveiled at last year's Cologne show?

—*Tim Carrithers*

I've never gushed over a BMW before. But I'm going to this time, so don your bio-hazard suit before reading any further.

The R1100 Roadster caught me completely by surprise. I liked the RS well enough, but a few quirks—like the flexy handlebar setup—dampened my enthusiasm. The GS, for me, was a disappointment, and I expected to walk away from this modestly priced, plain-wrap version with a ho-hum reaction.

But I was dazzled. This is the best-handling BMW ever—by a significant margin. This "reduced-power" version of the new twin is that rare example of how reducing peak power *can* actually put more real power where you use it. I like standard-style ergonomics, and the Roadster's fit me perfectly.

A lot of the press seems hung up on the 1100R's looks. Who cares? It works fabulously. Everybody should have one.

—*Art Friedman*

The R-bike uses the GS-tuned R259 engine—the torquey one. Twin oil coolers, one per side, keep the 1085cc beast happy even when being flogged.

to suddenly just let go of the locking-up wheel; one moment you're stopping hard, the next you're freewheeling toward whatever you're trying to avoid. In the wet, the BMW system is less abrupt and might well save your hide, but in dry conditions it leaves you feeling you could stop better using your own software. You can deactivate the ABS with the touch of a rocker switch, but since the R is a minimalist motorcycle anyway, we'd save the weight and $1500 and do without ABS unless we planned to ride in the rain frequently.

And that wouldn't be much of a plan on the R, really, since there's no fairing to deflect rain and wind—though a windshield is available as an option (as well as heated grips, cross-spoke wheels, tachometer and clock, and hard saddlebags). Even without a fairing the R is easy to ride up to about 80 mph before you need to begin really holding on to the bars. The instrument panel and 5.5-gallon gas tank part the breeze somewhat, and the cylinders and neat

1995 BMW R1100R

Suggested retail price as tested:	$11,490 ($9,990 without ABS)	**Rear brake:**	One two-piston caliper, 276mm disc, ABS II
Warranty:	36 months, unlimited miles	**Front wheel:**	3.50 x 17 in.; cast alloy
Number of U.S. dealers:	Approx. 200	**Rear wheel:**	4.50 x 18 in.; cast alloy
Recommended valve-adjustment intervals:	6000 miles	**Front tire:**	120/70-ZR17 Bridgestone Battlax radial
		Rear tire:	160/60-ZR18 Bridgestone Battlax radial

ENGINE

Type:	Air/oil-cooled, longitudinal, opposed 4-stroke boxer twin	**Rake/trail:**	26 degrees/4.4 in. (111mm)
		Wheelbase:	59.0 in. (1499mm)
Valve arrangement:	SOHC, 4 valves per cylinder, operated by pushrods and rocker arms; threaded adjusters	**Seat height:**	29.9-32 in. (adjustable)
		Fuel capacity:	5.5 gal (21L)
Displacement:	1085cc	**Weight:**	547 lbs (246kg) wet; 514 lbs (231kg) tank empty
Bore x stroke:	99.0 x 70.5mm		
Compression ratio:	10.3:1	**Colors:**	Mystic red, Arctic gray
Carburetion:	Bosch Motronic MA 2.2 fuel injection	**Instruments:**	Speedometer, odometer, tripmeter; lights for neutral, high beam, turn signals, low fuel, alternator, ABS fault (tachometer and analog clock optional)
Ignition:	Battery-powered, electronically triggered, digital		
Lubrication:	Wet sump, 4 qt	**RPM at indicated 60 mph:**	3400
Battery:	12V, 19.5AH		

DRIVETRAIN

		PERFORMANCE	
Clutch:	Dry, single-plate	**Fuel consumption:**	34 to 45 mpg, 41 mpg avg.
Transmission:	5-speed	**Average touring range:**	235 miles
Final drive:	Shaft and palloid tooth gear, 3.00:1	**Average 200-yard acceleration from 50 mph, terminal speed:**	5th gear, 81.7 mph; 4th gear, 91.0 mph

CHASSIS

Front suspension:	BMW Telelever, Showa damper, 4.8 in. travel	**Best quarter-mile acceleration:**	12.65 sec. @ 104.3 mph
Rear suspension:	BMW Paralever, one Showa damper, 5.4 in. travel; adjustments for spring preload, rebound damping	**Corrected best quarter-mile acceleration:**	12.35 sec. @ 106.6 mph
		Measured top speed:	127 mph
Front brake:	2, four-piston calipers, 305mm discs, ABS II		

*Performance with test-session weather conditions corrected to sea-level standard conditions (59 degrees F, 29.92 in. of mercury).

twin oil coolers break wind for the lower body. The lip at the rear of the seat is comfy but firm, and helps buttress the rider.

Though it shares slightly lower final-drive gearing with the GS—4500 rpm nets 80 mph—the engine won't intrude on smooth sailing. Once in top gear, there's enough power from 40 mph on up to go-directly-to-jail to easily roost just about anything on the road. And in the twisties, the gearshift lever can go largely ignored—a good thing, since the improved five-speed gearbox remains a bit slow-shifting and the clutch a bit clunky until the rider learns to match rpm exactly.

Fourth gear seems capable of digesting faster roads easily, while third mops up tighter terrain. All the rider needs to do is roll the throttle on and off to access the R's thunderously smooth torque at as few as 2500 rpm, and the R's willing chassis makes it a simple matter to keep cornering speed high.

The single-sided Paralever controls 80 percent of shaft's torque reaction. The stainless exhaust contains a catalyst.

The R's headlight styling has set off a storm of controversy within the BMW ranks unparalleled since last year's goatee versus Van Dyck conundrum.

The steel fuel tank holds 5.5 gallons; seat height is adjustable (comfortable for all-day sittings) and offers a rear lip that holds the rider in place.

A little throttle hand smoothness helps, though: Slamming on the powerful brakes causes very little brake dive, but abruptly shutting the throttle does. Overall, the R is one of the easiest bikes out there to ride quickly. As a matter of fact, it accompanied the staff on our, uh, shall we say, invigorating 600 comparison street ride. We used it as a pack mule, really, but it thoroughly surprised several testers with its ability to easily keep up in the curvies.

For everyday use and around town, the R works superbly, though it rides rougher over bumpy roads and slabby freeways than either of its oilhead stablemates. Start-up on chilly California mornings is immediate, though we did notice this particular bike blowing oil smoke when cold. Over the course of 2500 miles, it used about a quart.

BMW's boxers have traditionally attracted buyers intent on maintaining their own machines, and there's no reason why they won't be happy with any of the current R259 line. Hoisting the R onto its centerstand is a doddle, and from there removing either cam cover is a simple matter of removing four bolts; valves adjust via screw-and-locknut adjusters, and the quality toolkit includes the proper feeler gauges. The spin-on oil filter is easy to get to, as is the underseat air filter.

What can we say? Everybody who rides this motorcycle loves it, including some dyed-in-the-wool sportbike types who didn't think BMW would ever produce anything particularly worthy. The hard part is deciding which oilhead we love best: RS, GS or R?

INDEX

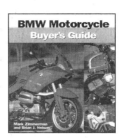
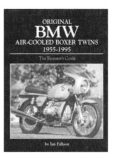